# Challenge . . . . . and Response

*A Protestant Perspective of the Vatican Council*

*Edited by*

Warren A. Quanbeck

*in consultation with*
Friedrich Wilhelm Kantzenbach
and
Vilmos Vajta

AUGSBURG PUBLISHING HOUSE

Minneapolis                    Minnesota

A German edition is being published simultaneously by Vandenhoeck & Ruprecht Verlag, Göttingen, under the title *Wir sind gefragt*. A French edition is also in preparation.

Scripture quotations are from the Revised Standard Version of the Bible, copyright 1946 and 1952 by the Division of Christian Education of the National Council of Churches.

# Foreword

The Second Vatican Council, from the moment of its announcement by Pope John XXIII, represented a challenge to the Protestant churches. Recognizing it as such, a group of Lutheran theologians prepared a volume, *The Papal Council and the Gospel*, describing Roman Catholicism on the eve of the Council and evaluating the theological issues involved in discussion between Roman Catholics and Protestants.

During the course of the Council it seemed desirable to the delegate-observers of the Lutheran World Federation to offer an account and assessment of conciliar developments. This account appeared in 1964 in the volume *Dialogue on the Way*.

The present volume, also the work of Protestant observers at the Council, deals with the proceedings of the Council's fourth and final session, September 14 to December 8, 1965. The authors of the individual articles are agreed that the Council is a formidable challenge to Protestant theology and Protestant churches. The Council left out of consideration some questions which are of importance to Protestant theologians; it also formulated some of its positions in ways which are not especially congenial to the theological tradition of the Reformation. But one cannot disregard the fact that the Council has raised questions which require answers. Not all of these questions are dealt with in this volume, nor can the answers be taken as conclusive. This volume too represents something of a dialogue on the way.

The Decree on Ecumenism sees the arm of dialogue as the preparation of the way in which "this brotherly rivalry will urge all

iii

men to a more profound understanding and a clearer demonstration of the unfathomable riches of Christ." We willingly accept this "brotherly rivalry" if it may lead both sides to a genuine struggle in the sense of Philippians 1:30, 1 Thessalonians 2:2, and 1 Timothy 6:12. In this brotherly rivalry we shall have to consider all our declarations as provisional (1 Cor. 13:8), but also seriously before the judgment seat of Christ (2 Cor. 5:10). In this community of sorrow, anxiety, listening, and waiting, the Holy Spirit gives a share in the unity of the church in Christ. This unity can manifest itself first of all in the unanimous testimony of brethren to Jesus Christ the Lord.

THE EDITORS

# CONTENTS

# Contents

## Part Three: Perspectives

*Translations from originals were prepared by Ernest H. Gordon, David J. S. Lee, Robert C. Schultz, and Walter G. Tillmanns*

# Part I
# Proceedings

Chapter I

# Chronicle of the Fourth Session of the Vatican Council

## SEPTEMBER 14 TO DECEMBER 8, 1965

In surveying the fourth and last period of the Council as a whole with its volume of extraordinary pronouncements and the great number of representative events which it brought with it we should not lose sight of the fact that this period, like the ones preceding it, was in the first instance characterized by the normal and intensive work of the plenary session and more especially of the commissions. This comparison shows a certain peculiarity insofar as the discussion of the schemata which had filled the weeks in the autumn of the past three years from the first to the last day had already been concluded about the middle of October 1965 and had involved comparatively few new arguments as all its themes had been dealt with at various lengths earlier. When we take into consideration that of a total of 544 votes required by the council, more than half were taken in the last period, then it should become clear that the weight had shifted to this particular aspect of the work. What was new was the interruption of the Council by three intervals from October 17 to 24, October 30 to November 6, and from November 20 to 29, for altogether more than 3 weeks, the general congregations were interrupted so as to make time for the commissions which prepared the texts on the basis of the emendations resp. "modi" submitted to them for the next working session. Intervals within

3

the several general congregations occurred after October 27 when the Council was required to do nothing but vote—intervals barely filled by reading out the texts or by choral singing or by notices of a technical kind spiced with humor or simply by private conversations. Although one awaited certain results with some kind of tension, soon a positive and constant line could be discerned. The opposition was mainly concentrated in a small group, the so-called "Coetus Internationalis Episcoporum" led by the active Italian bishop Carli, a group whose activity was devoted mainly to the problems of atheism, Judaism, and religious liberty, but which in the end was unsuccessful. Brilliant highlights were provided by the five public sessions (September 14, October 28, November 18, December 7 and 8), but as far as the ordinary business of the Council was concerned there were no dramatic incidents. All this should make it clear that the course of the fourth period was distinctly calm and steady and far less than in earlier sessions characterized by unexpected interventions and changes; rather this period was guided by the endeavor to bring in the harvest in a common effort and within the time permitted.

Among the eleven texts that were waiting to be passed there are five documents which may be grouped together: the decrees on the pastoral ministry of the bishops in the church, the renewal of the religious orders and the training for the priesthood in line with contemporary requirements, declarations on Christian education and on the relationship of the church to the non-Christian religions. The substance of these texts had already been approved by the Council in the previous year; what was lacking was the vote on the Modi (modifications) and their application to the texts. Beginning on the 29th of September the voting procedure was completed on the 15th of October with positive results throughout, so that in the public session on the 28th of October the texts were promulgated by the Pope.

The *Decree on the Pastoral Ministry of the Bishops* literally takes up the famous definition of the episcopate from the third chapter of the Constitution on the Church. The collegial authority of the whole episcopate is here confirmed and finds wider application in the future episcopal synod while fully safeguarding the papal primacy. The desire for a reform of the Curia as regards contemporary attitudes, methods, and composition is expressly stated. The ministry of the diocesan bishop is thoroughly analyzed as a three-fold munus (docendi, sanctificandi, regendi) and noticeably extended beyond the usual description of the traditional episcopal functions. The document values very highly the freedom of the church from the secular power both as regards the filling of a vacancy in an episcopal see and the exercise of the bishop's ministry.

Following a passage on the best way of fixing boundaries between the dioceses, a section deals with the bishop's collaborators. In the chapter on the cooperation of bishops for the common good of several churches the section on episcopal conferences deserves to be mentioned, for in the future these conferences will undoubtedly be of greater significance.

The evangelic reader of these texts is deeply impressed by the circumspection, responsibility, and experience with which one of the most essential ministries in the Roman Church is being re-shaped, and he discovers not a few points of contact with his own church. The parting of the ways begins with the thesis that fullness of the church's ministry exists only in the episcopate. While one gratefully assents to the practical unfolding of the episcopal office one cannot at the same time agree with the preceding exclusive transfer from the apostles to the Roman Catholic bishops as their successors—a pneumatological straitjacket!

The *Decree on the Renewal of the Religious Orders* is intended to help those who have undertaken to follow the three evangelical counsels not to be led into isolation but rather to be brought into a living relationship with the other members of God's people. The reform is brought about, first by going back to the sources of the monastic life, reading of Scriptures, liturgy, and eucharist, and also to the rule which records the intention of the respective founder. More effective than too many detailed regulations is a personal interior affirmation of the fundamental vows of chastity, poverty, and obedience. Regarding the leadership of the Institutes the attempt is being made to imbue the monarchical principle with the spirit of the family, and in practical questions as habit, procedure for dying monasteries, and regulations for enclosure, a beneficial rational attitude predominates.

Martin Luther from his own experience had warned against self-righteousness in religious orders. Perhaps the new decree may help consciously to banish this danger as far as possible.

Even if in the *Decree on the Training of Priests* the "century old proved laws" appear to stand out in greater relief than the renewal "corresponding to the changed conditions of the time," the demands of the present do find their place after all. What is required is the interior appropriation of seminar discipline, training in listening to others, and feeling one's way into a given situation in the pastoral ministry, further practical work already during the training with the purpose of being able to work in a team later on, and finally the particular supervision of those called to the ministry later in life. Spiritual education plays as great a role as scientific training. What is being said here on meditation, sharing in the life of the church, retreats, self-denial, training of character, and education toward community deserves to be considered in the evangelical church, although of course some specifically Catholic elements such as the veneration of Mary or the training for celibacy have their place in the scheme.

In regard to ecclesiastical academic studies the traditional step from philosophy to theology has been retained; yet the biblical-redemptive-historical aspect is clearly gaining more ground than had been the case in the past, and this applies to all disciplines. The alumni also are to get to know non-Catholic churches so as to be able to contribute "to the promotion of the restitution of unity."

The attempt in the evangelical church to counter the much-heard-of crisis in the study of theology and the decline, if not complete lack of spiritual life among the clergy might well attach a great weight to the utterances of the Catholic decree on the training of priests; perhaps we might even expect this decree to make a decisive contribution towards a solution of this problem.

The *Declaration on Christian Education* suffers from trying to give guidance which claims validity at least for the whole of the Catholic world although the pedagogic situation in different countries varies considerably. The maintenance of the principle of subsidiarity is twice demanded from the state: yet to North Americans this seems to be a too-far-reaching concession while bishops in France, where a kind of state monopoly for schools exists, demanded an even greater frankness of the declaration in relation to the state. Although the Roman Church does not in this text draw the same consequences from the existing social pluralism for herself which she demands from the state we should not simply accuse her of pedagogic monopolism; for in the first place she feels herself responsible for *Christian* education which, however, is not defined in any detail either in its relationship to any other education or as a larger concept in relation to "Catholic" education. The ecumenical dimension is totally lacking here; no differentiation is made between "Christian" and "Catholic." These deficiencies in the text were presumably the cause of the relatively large number of Noes at the final voting.

Until the last minute the threats of the Arab countries as well as a latent anti-Semitism on the part of certain council fathers threw a shadow on the Declaration on the Relationship of the Church to the Non-Christian Religions. The Secretariat for Unity had met the objections by a number of concessions: The Jews, who still constitute the chief theme of the declaration, are no longer mentioned in the title, the controversial section is preceded by statements on the other religions, and in the relevant section itself, contrary to former drafts, an express condemnation of anti-Semitism and a rejection of the accusation of deicide are lacking. Yet the opponents still numbered 260 Noes—or invalid votes—at the final voting and 91 at the public voting session.

Naturally the tactically reasoned observations on the other religions are not satisfactory, if alone because of their brevity; besides, they are too directly related to Christianity. Ultimately this context is bound to bring about a regrettable leveling down of the unique heritage of the Old Testament which binds Judaism and Christianity together. Taken by itself this fourth section, however, deserves genuine appreciation: In discussing the hotly debated questions of Jewish participation in the death of Christ, the concept of guilt was altogether avoided, perhaps in order not to conjure up the metaphysical background with its implication that all men would have to be declared guilty of the death of Christ. Rather, the distinction between the Jewish authorities and their abetters, on the one hand, and the present generation of Jews, on the other, appeals in a sound way to reason, and is based on a

purely juridical concept of guilt. It would be asking too much if
we demanded a fundamental discussion of the Jewish problem
from this shortest of all the documents of the Council; it is the
practical attitude that matters here. Under this aspect the section
seems to have succeeded, for its statements against anti-Semitism
as well as on the relationship with the Jews are brief, matter-of-fact,
and equally far removed from any Phariseeism as from an embar-
rassing self-accusation. By underlining the duty of the church to
proclaim Christ to the other religions the declaration makes it easier for the other churches to assent to its statements.

Two further texts, namely the Constitution on Revelation and
the Decree on the Lay Apostolate, had to be voted upon, first from
September 20 to September 27 regarding their substance and later,
on October 29 and on November 9 and 10, after evaluating the
modi that had been put forward in respect of this procedure, before
they could be promulgated on November 19. The initially very weak
opposition to both texts had in the end almost disappeared.

The *Dogmatic Constitution on Divine Revelation* contains in
the introduction a chapter on revelation itself and another on Scripture and tradition, followed by four chapters on the Bible. The
evangelical Christian is bound to express highest appreciation and
great joy in regard to the observations on Holy Scripture. He can
unreservedly acknowledge the continuous high estimation of the
Bible as the place where God speaks to his children, the principles
of exegesis moderately open to modern biblical scholarship, but
mainly the rich aspects of a practical handling of Scripture that includes the use of translations jointly produced with other Christians. Here is reason to hope that post-conciliar Catholic theology
may become predominantly biblical theology.

This hope, however, is considerably diminished by the way the
relationship between Scripture and tradition has been defined. It
is true that in the new Constitution the purely additive conception
of two blocs, which for centuries had dominated controversial
theology, has been overcome by strongly articulating the dynamics
and liveliness in their mutual relationship. But what one has done
is to confine oneself to describe in ever new formulations the relation, the connection, and the link between Scripture and tradition,
with the addition of a third entity in the shape of the church's

teaching ministry. At the same time we find that tradition has become a comprehensive term which embraces not only doctrine but also worship, practice, customs, virtually the whole life of the church, and which therefore has to be accepted not merely with the *ratio* (reason) but equally by meditation and feeling. If tradition is here simply identified with the being of the church, then the modus, included in the last minute at a papal suggestion, that this church "receives her certainty on all objects of revelation not only from holy scripture" merely expresses in a concentrated form what could already be inferred without it.

Most probably "Scripture and Tradition" will be among the most important subjects of the post-conciliar interconfessional dialogue; at any rate, it is in this field that the Roman Church will have to put the weightiest questions to the churches of the Reformation, and she will be justified in doing so. Unfortunately, in seeking for an answer the Constitution on Revelation does not help very much; for right from the start it excludes any thought of a regulative, critical function of Scripture over against the church.

The *Decree on the Lay Apostolate* sees in their participation in the sacraments, especially in baptism and confirmation, the specific mission of the laity. The purpose of this mission is the evangelization, the Christian ordering of earthly matters and the charitable activity in the spheres of the congregation, the family, social, national, and international operations. A special section is devoted to youth. Besides organized activity (*actio catholica*) the personal apostolate is not overlooked, an apostolate that is gaining greater importance in persecution and in the diaspora. Statements on the relationship between laity and hierarchy and on the training for the apostolate form the final chapters of the decree. Even if it is true that the pioneers of a "theology of the laity" are far more articulate in their observations and that they are nearer to the ethics of the reformers than this decree, it is still remarkable how here the people of God, described as such in the Constitution on the Church, is taken seriously as an autonomous entity with its own individual representatives over against the hierarchy. Noteworthy also is the determination in bringing the laity out of a Christian milieu and in sending them into the world.

The remaining four texts, namely the declaration on religious liberty, the pastoral constitution on the church in the contemporary world, the decrees on the missionary work of the church and on services and life of the priests may be taken together as a third group, inasmuch as, before their promulgation on December 7, they had to pass three stages: discussion, voting on substance, and voting on "modi."

The *Declaration on Religious Liberty* was under discussion from September 15 to September 22 and in the voting sessions (from October 26 to October 29 and on November 19) received both in the voting on substance and on "modi" approval of 88% on an average; there were still 78 Noes left in the last voting.

The declaration begins by stipulating that all men have the moral duty to accept the redemptive message of the Roman Catholic Church within which the true religion finds its concrete form of existence. But this duty is to be fulfilled in agreement with the conscience and responsibility of man and must not either be enforced or hindered through the use of external force, for this duty is a necessary concretization of an inward commitment to God. The state in particular must not put any obstacle in the way of individuals or groups to practice their religion unless the commonweal or public order be endangered. Civic preference may be given to a majority religion provided this is not done at the expense of citizens of other faiths. These notions cannot be directly derived from revelation but indirectly from the way in which Christ and the apostles paid due regard in their ministry of preaching to the liberty of the act of faith.

Opposition to this declaration was—as in previous years—mainly rooted in Latin countries. Their weightiest argument was to point to the objective truth which is to be found in the Roman Church only so that one must not concede any liberty to the propagation of error. This was also in line with the ecclesiastical tradition reaching into the last century. The church must guard against becoming an accessory to the destruction of Catholicism, the danger to a venerable spiritual heritage, to religious indifference, and to the undermining of public morals by allowing the rationalistic thoughts of the enlightenment any room in her doctrine. Other critical points were the statement on preferential treatment given to a particular religion and the observations on the limits of religious liberty.

These objections substantially influenced the finally published text either in deepening or weakening it. Thus in comparison with earlier drafts the biblical aspects are now standing out in stronger relief, but so does the notion that religious liberty represents, in the first place, the freedom of the Roman Catholic Church from constraint by state and civic authorities.

At this point we are led to ask the Roman Church that she should not only demand religious liberty herself but also grant it; for only if freedom reigns within the church can external freedom for the church be justifiably demanded.

The greatest amount of work went into the *Pastoral Constitution on the Church in the Contemporary World*. This bulkiest of all conciliar documents was first discussed from September 22 to October 8, then emended by numerous subcommissions in laborious sessions lasting many weeks when votes on the emendations were taken. The amended draft was then approved on principle in 33 ballots on matters of substance; at the same time something like ten thousands of "modi" were received and with admirable diligence evaluated so that the result obtained the *Placet* of the assembly on December 4 and 6.

This text was perhaps the only one that at times was seriously in danger. For nowhere else was there such an amount of justified and frequent criticism of the whole structure as here, and nowhere else was the desire voiced to postpone the whole complex of problems to some future date. Even the spiritual fathers of the document recognized that in the time at their disposal no substantial improvements of the unequal and immature text would be possible. The passing of the document was a courageous emergency solution, influenced through lack of time but at any rate preferable to a complete silence on these urgent problems.

During the discussion the arguments of the past year were largely repeated, at times even by the same speakers. With regard to particular problems comparatively many votes concentrated on the complex of atheism, marriage and family, war and peace. The section on atheism in its final shape was redacted by experts of the Secretariat for non-believers with the intention to lay bare the various roots of this phenomenon (including the joint guilt of Christians) and to offer means for dealing with it. The chapter "Marriage and Family" is the only case where regard is paid in an official document to particular papal wishes. In the question of birth control all that is said is to emphasize the authority of the teaching office of the church. Otherwise there is a compromise between the traditional concept of marriage, with its chief purposes of mutual support and procreation of offspring, and newer thoughts which stress love and personal fellowship of the partners. A similar pattern applies to war and peace where purely pacifist tendencies were eventually restrained by the distinction between aggressive and defensive wars, a distinction adapted to the atomic age.

Critical utterances in regard to the theological background could be heard and the question was justified if concepts like world, grace, redemption, and sin had received the necessary precision. This text deals in 93 sections "Of the Church and the Vocation of Man" and "Of some particularly urgent problems": It may well be that the mere fact of a discussion by the church is more important than the substance of the statements. In spite of all resistance, there is now awareness that the church must not leave the world to itself but that she must think, advise, care, and decide together with the world, even if she cannot offer ready-made solutions and because of it. The artist, scientist, and politician, the man who is socially and economically held down, the mother and the soldier, will in the future no longer feel left out by the church or even have their problems looked at with suspicion, but they will now be able to know that the church does her best to deal with them. All this has led at least to the awareness that contemporary ethics cannot be satisfied with casuistic particular counsels but will have to take into account fundamental personal decision and responsibility in the most differentiated situations.

The *Decree on the Missionary Activity of the Church* (discussion October 7-13, voting on substantial items November 10 and 11, voting on "modi" November 30) met with a fundamental difficulty over the statements on the theological necessity of missions inasmuch as the greater value now being attached to the non-Christian religions could lead to a relative position. At any rate, it became necessary to base missionary activity not so much on the salvation of the individual but rather on the expansion of the whole church. The ecumenical aspect of missions was much under discussion.

Doubts were voiced about statements, which in the end found satisfactory concrete expression, on collaboration with other Christians and churches, and even on a common witness to Christ's statements that are ultimately due to the written proposal of an observer. These doubts arose mainly because some of the bishops did not clearly distinguish between ecumenism and proselytism and because they had come to know non-Catholic Christians for the most part as members of sects. In the final result those voices prevailed which considered the divisions among the Christians as a hindrance to missions and therefore were ready to do all in their power to overcome them.

Argument about the reform of the central missionary authority, the so-called Congregatio De Propaganda Fidei, went on to the last. The Curia was afraid that the reorganization of the Propaganda as advocated by the Council might create a precedent and offered considerable resistance in the beginning. In the end, however, it was possible to secure greater opportunities for cooperation, and the right to vote, in the central missionary authority for individual missionary bishops and bishops' conferences.

One of the aims of the debate on the *Decree on the Ministry and Life of Priests* (discussion October 14-16 and 25-26, voting on substance November 12-3, voting in amendments December 2) was to define clearly the particular position of the priest as distinct from the laity, the religious, and the bishops. A solution was sought in combining the notions of the priestly mission and the participation in the priesthood of Christ. Further particular problems, however, as e.g. a fair distribution of priests in the several dioceses or that of the worker-priests, was soon overshadowed by the question of celibacy. Already on the 11th of October a letter from the Pope had been read in the aula which prohibited the public discussion of celibacy on the ground that nothing must weaken this ancient and very suitable law. The papal veto was thought to have originated in an intended vote, already submitted in writing to the secretariat of the Council, of a South American missionary bishop who demanded the institution of a kind of secondary married clergy for the remote villages in the Andes. In the ensuing discussion the papal veto was generally respected; Cardinal Bea, however, pointed out that the uniate-oriental churches had married priests, a fact which the decree must not disregard. This wish found fulfillment in that the text commends the married priests of the Eastern Church; yet the binding statements on the suitability of the celibate in the Latin church predominate. We shall have to wait for any future effect of these counter-forces that made themselves openly or covertly felt at the Council.

The Council completed its proper work with the promulgation of these 11 documents which will come into force with regard to any practical reforms they contain, on June 29, 1966. What remains to be considered is a number of extraordinary events.

Great excitement, hardly envisaged by those responsible, arose through the consideration of the problem of *indulgences* that lasted from November 9 to 12. Already at the beginning of October the Pope had made it known that he wished to issue new directives on some practical questions, especially penitential discipline and indulgences. The competent curial congregations had worked out drafts which during the first interval of the Council, from October 17 to 24, were to be studied by the national bishops' conferences and the result to be embodied in a memorandum. The presiding authority of the Council then decided to have these opinions, commonly arrived at by the bishops' conferences, reported in the aula between the voting sessions, and first those on the problem of indulgences.

The "votes" were preceded by an introduction into the "Positio" (Proposal) on the problem of indulgences submitted by the Curia: Its authors, it was said, had tried, with all due loyalty to tradition, to check certain abuses and human failings, in particular an inflation of indulgences, and in their stead to provide them with a quantitative enrichment. In the future, specific timings, which anyhow had been unintelligible, were to be omitted, privileges for particular altars to be abolished, and the number of complete indulgences limited. In this way piety would be strengthened, superstition done away with, and charity deepened.

In their utterances following the introduction the representatives of the bishops' conferences confined themselves mostly to small corrections and particular wishes. Among those who voiced more searching criticism Cardinal Doepfner's Votum deserves particular attention. He showed how, through the gradually arisen confusion of the distinction between divinely ordained temporal punishment and canonical penitence, dubious calculations had developed in this field. Here was the source of an arithmetical-quantitative misunderstanding as could best be seen in the customary material interpretation of the notion "Treasure of the Church" ("Thesaurus Ecclesiae"). Indulgences could become fruitful only if they were understood as the appropriation of the authoritative intercession of the whole church to the individual penitent.

Although there was no lack of fundamental consideration on the part of Doepfner and other theologians of the Council, hardly ever was a desire heard to abolish indulgences altogether. In spite of all the criticism, the pedagogic value of this practice was so highly thought of that one wanted to maintain it, even by using the boldest new interpretations. This meant that it was impossible even to make a beginning in overcoming the quantitative-synergistic mentality which through the centuries had developed in conjunction with the problem of indulgences, and this all the more so as a few days later many further expressions of opinion were categorically stopped by the leadership of the Council. That this affair came as a shock to many was quite obvious; evangelical observers were particularly dismayed in discovering that the discussion on indulgences and their background, which 450 years ago Martin Luther wanted to bring about, had until today not taken place in the Roman Church and that, in view of this latest experience, it will probably not be sought for in the near future.

A possibly even greater disappointment was felt that the Council came to an end without granting any relaxation in the practice of *mixed marriages*. There was a touch of irony in the situation when one remembered that in November 1964 the Council had already agreed not to postpone any longer a relevant proposition and that, because of its particular urgency, it had asked the Pope to promulgate it. Yet all the numerous rumors about an announcement to be made before and during the fourth period proved in the end without foundation. Certainly the doors have not been shut for new regulations in the future, either by papal *Motu proprio* or through the work of the Commission on the Codex. But the longer this is postponed the greater will be the loss of confidence on the part of all Christians. For the question is being put with particular urgency whether the Roman Church is willing to realize in practice the principles proclaimed by her on ecumenism and religious liberty.

The fourth period was further distinguished by the great activity on the part of the Pope which went far beyond the already mentioned influence on certain documents of the Council. Even before the work of the general congregations began, two remarkable pronouncements were published: the encyclical on the Eucharist and the *Motu proprio* on the institution of the Episcopal Synod.

The *encyclical "Mysterium Fidei,"* dated September 3, the feast of St. Pius X, is seen as the negative answer by Rome to certain attempts in Holland to develop a new interpretation of the Eucharist within the process of liturgical reform under the headings of "trans-signification" and "transfinalization." The great surprise which this encyclical caused not only among the observers but to a great extent also in Roman Catholic circles may be explained by the accents it is putting in a very unfavorable contrast to the intentions of the conciliar liturgical constitutions. Here we find extensive comments on the notion of sacrifice, an express revaluation of the private mass, a reaffirmation of the doctrine of transubstantiation in its most massive interpretation, and a clear call for the eucharistic cult outside the Mass. All this not only endangers the promising beginnings of a new understanding of worship which were noticeable in the Roman Church as a result of the liturgical constitution, but it means that the essential controversial issues over against the churches of the Reformation are being revived from the past in such a way that it calls in question an initial rapprochement because of the principles at stake. Quite apart from this the Pope generally attaches particular weight to the "regula loquendi" which had been practiced within the church for centuries, to the "formulae" by which it had been expressed and which was "adapted to all men at all times and in all places." This insistence, not only on the substance but also on the way tradition is to be expressed, together with a warning against new interpretations, is in contrast to that guiding call of John XXIII who had asked the Council at its start to seek for a new form of proclaiming the treasure of faith unchangeable in its substance.

On the 15th of September, even before the proper work of the Council had begun, the *Motu proprio "Apostolica Solicitudo"* was read to the Fathers assembled in the Aula in the presence of the Pope. This *Motu proprio* institutes the post-conciliar episcopal synod. In twelve paragraphs its task is described to inform and advise the Pope and to pass resolutions with his consent. To convene and preside over the synod, to prescribe its business, and to draw up an agenda is reserved for the Pope. Members of the synod, which may be convened as an extraordinary, special or general assembly, are the patriarchs, grand-archbishops and metropolitans of the uniat Eastern churches, bishops chosen by the national or regional episcopal conferences, ten members of religious orders, and the Cardinal prefects of the Roman curial congregations. Although the synod is described as "institutum perpetuum" the functions of the several members expire automatically at the end of every session.

An adequate judgment on this document and on the institution of the episcopal synod as such will be possible only when the synod will have been in session for the first time (in 1967). Meanwhile we may well raise the question whether, while fully safeguarding his primacy, the Pope might not have granted the members something more, perhaps a certain influence in determining topics and agenda, time and frequency of being summoned. The strict temporary limitation of its functions might well prove an obstacle to the continuity and growing autonomy of this institution. The clarification of the competences of the episcopal synod, on the one hand, and of Curia and College of Cardinals, on the other, will be of considerable importance. Because of the unconditional dependence of the episcopal synod on the Pope the answer to these still open questions will largely depend on how he will handle the convening of the synod and its mode of work. He could use the synod as a mere instrument of his own power, he could also assign to it, as the representative of the world-church, true responsibility and realize with this synod a collegial form of government.

The journey of the Pope to the Plenary Assembly of the United Nations in New York on October 4 was very closely interwoven with the events of the Council. Outwardly this became visible in the message of the Council the Pope took with him and in the fact that immediately on his return Paul VI was awaited in St. Peter's by the assembled Fathers. But the connection went much deeper; for in the numerous speeches held on this occasion by the Pope there could be recognized in ever new variations thoughts from the Pastoral Constitution on the Church in the World just then being debated. It was fascinating to observe the many layers of the role which Paul VI ascribed to himself. While personal modesty was the basic note throughout, he called himself, precisely in tune with his particular audience, head of a state, vicar of Christ, successor of Peter. On one hand, he understood himself as bearer of a message of peace to the politicians, on the other as the spokesman of any and every kind of human groupings, including the other Christian brethren. Yet on this journey, as well as later, especially during the last week of the council, the undoubtedly intended symbolic character of the events was at least as important as the contents of the papal speeches. What mattered was therefore not so much a logical analysis of what was said but rather the optical effect of impressive images intended to make their impact on as large a public as possible.

The *five papal speeches at the public sessions* were in general rather reticent. The only frequently recurring theme that may be noted was the fate of the oppressed church which was conspicuously oft remembered, obviously to make her aware that she was being drawn into the deliberations of the Council in spite of her physical absence. The opening speech made clear the intention to apply papal sympathy equally to all groups and to pacify all parties without letting any emerge from the struggle as victors or vanquished. The address on the 28th of October was a homily on the growth of the church and her efforts for peace. The speech of November 18 was devoted to desires for practical reforms, to the cautious fulfillment of which the Pope did not show himself averse, without, however, committing himself to any concrete measures. The directive he gave (in his speech) for initiating the process of beatification for Pius XII and John XXIII must be considered, in spite of considerable doubt regarding its substance, a diplomatic masterpiece. The address of the 7th of December tried to distil as the fruit of the Council its pastoral concern; with this was linked an appeal to the world to hear the new tone in the church and to receive positively her endeavors for modern man with his own distinctive character. Lastly, the speech at the final proceedings on

December 8 tried to express the universality conspicuously demonstrated by the external arrangement.

These events, however, belong to the last week of the Council which in a variety of ways clearly indicated that this time it was not merely a matter of bringing to a close a particular period of sessions but the Council as such.

Highly significant was the *ecumenical thanksgiving service* at St. Paul outside the walls on the afternoon of December 4. This service had been arranged for Pope, Council Fathers, and observers. Three of the latter shared actively in the scriptural lessons and the intercessions which, besides corporate singing of psalms and chorals and a papal address, formed the main part of the service. This service represented a maximum of what may be done together by Christians from different traditions and was undoubtedly intended to provide a pattern for similar occasions in the future. It was followed by a brief farewell audience in the same hall at the St. Paul's Monastery where nearly seven years ago John XXIII had made the announcement of the Council. The number of observers, including deputies and guests, had grown from 40 at the first period to 103 at the last one; the number of churches and corporate bodies represented had come to 30. The average number of those actually present at Council functions came, however, to only 50.

The *Apostolic Exhortation "Postrema Sessio"* of November 4 had declared the 7th of December to be the next to the last day of the Council. The publication of the *Motu proprio "Integrae servandae"* on this day represented a first cautious step toward a reform of the Curia by changing the name of what had until then been known as the Holy Office into Congregatio pro doctrina fidei. It has made little difference to the objects and structure of this Congregation which continues to guard the teaching of faith and morals throughout the whole world; we should, however, mention one of the twelve points of reform which demands that in future disciplinary action the person concerned and his bishop are to be heard.

On the same date there appeared the *Apostolic Constitution "Mirificus Eventus"* which proclaims an extraordinary jubilee for the first half of the year following the closing of the Council. What is conspicuous here is the firm connection between privileges and cathedral church and bishop. This represents a practical continuation of the revaluation of the episcopate which the Council had done doctrinally. What did cause great consternation was the fact that again partial and plenary indulgences were offered as if a discussion on this question had never taken place. The terminology in describing the special faculties of the confessors is rather disturbing: here non-Roman Catholic Christians are named heretics and schismatics (terms not used in a single document of the Council) and consequently grouped together with atheists, apostates, and Freemasons; their associations are called sects. This intolerable discrepancy might with the greatest possible forbearance be interpreted as a thoughtless application of former jubilee regulations, but at the same time it also goes to show how large the spheres are that are still closed to the ecumenical spirit.

But the most important event of the sessio publica of the 7th of December was the so-called *Reconciliation of Rome with Constantinople,* which was enacted simultaneously in both places. A delegation of the Patriarch, led by Metropolitan Meliton, had come to Rome. After the voting Bishop Willebrands read the common declaration of Pope and Patriarch. Then the guests were led from their seats of honor to the papal throne. Cardinal Bea read the papal Breve which Paul VI handed to the kneeling Metropolitan whom he then raised to exchange the fraternal kiss with him. The accompanying applause was immense.

Both the Breve and the "common declaration" show that the much used expression "Repeal of the Excommunication" is not quite exact. Rather there is a feeling here corresponding to the factual situation that a historical act cannot simply be undone. The declaration merely states that the events of 1054 had become an obstacle to mutual relations and adds an expression of regrets for the unfounded reproaches and despicable actions that had happened on both sides in those days and had eventually led to the breach of ecclesiastical communion. In order to pursue the way of brotherly love the regrettable events of the past should now be assigned to oblivion. The declaration is aware that this gesture is but a first beginning in bringing to an end the feud between Catholicism and Orthodoxy. It is precisely this soberness and reticence that lead us to judge that the form one has found for this reconciliation corresponds entirely to the facts of the situation and for that reason is indeed most fortunate.

The *Final Act* on St. Peter's Square on the 8th of December, aided by good weather, was an imposing demonstration of the splendor of the Roman Catholic Church. The act began with the procession of the bishops which lasted half an hour. The bishops, emerging from the basilica, made their way through the vast crowd —a passage had been reserved for them—and finally came to the semicircle before the main portal, with the Pope, borne on the Sedia Gestatoria, at the rear. Following the celebration of the mass, during which the aforementioned homily was read, Paul VI blessed the foundation stone of a future church of "Mater Ecclesiae." In order to remind mankind of its obligation towards its less well-off members the Pope then handed to five bishops each a check for a particular charitable project in their respective countries. This was followed by messages to the several estates, that is to rulers, scientists, artists, women, workers, the suffering, and the young. After the reading individual representatives of these groups each received from the Pope a copy of the message. The Final Decree read by the General Secretary officially brought the Council to a close; once more the 16 documents were formally confirmed. After the antiphonal chanting of the litany-like acclamations there followed the apostolic blessing and the dismissal of the Council Fathers with the words *"Ite in pace!"* the Second Vatican Council was at an end.

Already with the practical application of the Liturgical Constitution the post-conciliar epoch had begun, into which Roman Catholicism has now fully entered. We are eagerly awaiting the realization of all that has been decided in all the different spheres. The other churches will not be able, without harm to themselves, to keep out of the movement which has given such impetus to the Roman Catholic Church through the Council. Rather it should be the desire and hope of all that this movement will not be hampered or halted but that it will be spreading and constantly directed towards the goal which God has set for his church.

*Part II*
Evaluations

## Chapter II

# Scripture and Tradition

A PRELIMINARY STUDY OF THE DEVELOPMENT AND
CONTENT OF THE "DOGMATIC CONSTITUTION
ON DIVINE REVELATION (DEI VERBUM)"

## I. The History of the Document

On November 14, 1962, the fathers of the Vatican Council were presented with the schema of a dogmatic constitution on the sources of revelation, *De Fontibus Revelationis*. This document had been developed by the preparatory theological commission under the leadership of Cardinal Ottaviani, the chairman of the commission, and the Jesuit Father Tromp, the secretary of the commission.

From the very beginning it was expected that this schema would be intensively discussed. For this document represented the theological method of the older Roman theological school of the previous century, that is, it reflected an abstract, deductive, unhistorical theology which had not in any way been affected by the results of modern biblical exegesis and of the dialogue with non-Roman Catholic Christians. Even Roman Catholic theologians let it be known that this method of theologizing was the expression of a theological method that was actually typical of the Counter-Reformation.

This was particularly apparent at those places where the schema dealt with the relationship between Scripture and tradition. According to this document, Scripture and tradition represent two

25

independent and separated sources of revelation. Sacred Scriptures contain the truths of revelation which had been handed down in writing. Tradition, on the other hand, includes those truths which have been transmitted orally. This meant that there were truths in the Roman Catholic faith which did not have their source in Scripture. The content of tradition is thus greater than the content of Scripture. It was assumed that this was the position of the Council of Trent. The authors of this schema saw their task as the confirmation of this decisive truth. For this reason even the title of the schema speaks of sources in the plural, and the first chapter is explicitly titled "The Two Sources of Revelation (De duplici Fonte Revelationis)."

In addition, the character of this draft was thoroughly fundamentalistic. Had it been adopted it would have become completely impossible for Roman Catholic exegetes to follow the principles of modern historical criticism in their work. In a noteworthy way, this document exudes the antimodernistic atmosphere of 50 years ago. Furthermore, the role of the teaching office of the church was strongly emphasized. This means that had this document been accepted, innumerable Roman Catholic theologians and laymen would have labored in vain. The Roman Catholic Church might possibly have become strong, but it would also have become isolated, lonely, and alienated from the life of the world. Now that all this already belongs to past history, we can ask how such a document with its really fantastic narrowness—which has its own pathos—could ever have been possible.

For five days this document was intensively discussed, attacked, and defended. On November 19, 1962, the Council voted on a proposal to terminate the debate on this draft of the statement on the sources of revelation. The question thus was whether the document should be rejected or accepted as a basis for further discussion. The result was against the proposed document. There were 1,368 votes in favor of interrupting the debate, 822 votes favored continuing the debate, and 19 votes were invalid. A decisive majority of the Council fathers declared themselves in favor of a vital and specific theology formulated in terms of the history of salvation and rejected the domination of an older conceptualized and very conservative theology.

Afterwards the French Dominican Yves Congar, who was undoubtedly the most influential Roman theologian at the Second Vatican Council, asserted that this vote set the pattern of the Council. On that day the epoch of the Counter-Reformation came to an end in the theology of the Roman Catholic Church! The differences in the viewpoints of the bishops were often very deep, and were finally not differences on the answers to individual questions, but differences in approach.[1] This vote "was a shock for the victorious minority whom their opponents had considered to be halfway heretical. Their opponents had to accept the statistical evidence that almost two-thirds of the teaching church did not agree with their simple conservative attitude. Even eight days earlier, this result would have been impossible."[2]

At the same time, however, the situation on November 19 was also a catastrophe for the Progressives. For even though the majority had voted to reject the document, they still did not have the required two-thirds majority. The Progressives found themselves in a blind alley. It is understandable that the majority of the bishops were very discouraged. They were confronted by the prospect of a long series of wearisome debates in which the schema would be discussed chapter by chapter and revised; there was no reason to hope that this process would result in a satisfactory solution.

Then Pope John XXIII intervened to terminate the debate and directed a newly formed commission to prepare a new draft that would more fully reflect the views of the decisive majority of the fathers of the Council. There was a great sense of relief. On the next day a French newspaper characterized the result by saying that the Council breathed a new atmosphere. Another newspaper said explicitly: "The Pope intervened and brought the Council out of a blind alley."

Cardinal Ottaviani and Cardinal Bea were named co-chairmen of this new commission; Father Tromp, of the Holy Office, and Msgr. Willebrands of the Secretariat for Christian Unity, were appointed secretaries of the commission.

This commission met in Rome in February and March of 1963 and prepared a new draft. Their task was not an easy one, for two irreconcilable viewpoints confronted each other. They had to create a document which left the controversial question as to whether there are one or two sources of revelation open. This was an exceedingly difficult problem for the Conservatives, for they saw this question as a matter of faith, which the Council could not leave undecided.

The other side responded to this viewpoint by pointing out that a council cannot reach a decision on a question as long as there is no unity in the church on the answer. According to the viewpoint of the Conservatives, however, this was precisely the task of the Council: to establish a clear position on a question on which there was disunity in the church. In addition, they felt that the question about the sources of revelation had already been answered by the two councils immediately preceding this one.

On April 22, 1963, Cardinal Cicognani, the Secretary of State, distributed a new draft which, however, was never to be discussed in the Council chamber. The draft was sent directly to the bishops with the request that criticisms and suggestions for revision be submitted by January 31, 1964.

This new document was very different from the previous document. The title now read "On Divine Revelation." The question of the two sources was left completely open; and the rigid approach to questions concerning the Bible was abandoned; however, it still could not be denied that the document was now so short and colorless that it hardly paid to consider it any further. The two opponents had so counterbalanced each other that only statements that hardly said anything at all had been adopted. The dynamic of the doctrine had been lost.

During the second session, in the autumn of 1963, everyone was in the dark about the schema on revelation. Many assumed that the entire question had been dropped and that it would not be taken up again. And some felt that this was the best solution, for it was obvious that the situation was not yet ripe for a discussion of this doctrine by the Council. These men felt it would be better to leave the question to the theologians and hope that they would clarify the matter.

However, events were to take a different course. In his address at the close of the second session of the Council, Pope Paul VI named the schemata that were to be considered in the next session.[3] The schema on revelation was listed among these. The bishops continued to submit their evaluations until January 31, 1964. Most of these, of the Conservatives as well as of the Liberals, were very critical. The Conservatives had to reject unconditionally the new basic approach to the problem of the relationship between Scripture and tradition. The Progressives did not agree with the cautious and compromising approach of the document. Both parties desired a deeper discussion of the controversial points and particularly of the concept of tradition.

These critical commentaries made high demands on the members of the commission. They were, however, tireless, and in the autumn of 1964, they began work on a new schema. The way was now cleared for the preparation of the final document. In a meeting of the entire commission at the beginning of June 1964 the two chapters on the relationship between Scripture and tradition, which had been prepared by a sub-commission, were the object of difficult discussions. Seventeen members of the commission voted to accept the draft, seven voted to reject it. Those who voted negatively objected to the fact that the prepared text did not explicitly say that the content of the truths revealed in tradition is greater than the content of those revealed in Scripture. They were thus asserting that there are two sources of revelation. This was, they felt, the genuine Catholic tradition which had the support of the First Vatican Council as well as the papal encyclicals, to say nothing of pre- and post-Tridentine theology. In their opinion, the schema in its present form could have disastrous effects both for the people and for the teaching office of the church.

This new schema, the work of a commission that was not only mixed but divided, was discussed during the third session of the Council from September 30 to October 6, 1964. There was spirited discussion of the basic principles. The entire question of Scripture and tradition was raised once again, but it was still not possible to reach an agreement. This discussion, however, made it possible to treat the problems in depth. One must wonder how it was possible for the Council to carry on an often impassioned discussion of so difficult a complex of problems in a disciplined and peaceful manner. During this discussion it was evident that the Roman Church is not a monolithic structure, but rather a spiritual and changeable entity which is able to tolerate sharp contradictions within itself.

As a result of this discussion it is certain that the number of those who would vote in favor of the new viewpoints increased. However, a powerful and energetic minority, represented by the vivacious Bishop Carli of Segni, tried until the last moment to make principal changes in the document. We shall later see that their efforts were not in vain.

After this discussion, the schema was sent back to the commission so that it could once again be revised on the basis of the addresses given in the Council and of the written opinions that had been submitted. The commission began this work immediately so that the fathers of the Council received the revised schema before they left Rome. This was important, for it enabled the bishops to clarify their own positions by the fourth and final session in September 1965.

The outline of the revised schema became the outline of the final document under the title "On Divine Revelation." This is followed by an introduction and six chapters: Chapter I "Revelation Itself," Chapter II "The Transmission of Divine Revelation," Chapter III "The Divine Inspiration and the Interpretation of Sacred Scripture," Chapter IV "The Old Testament," Chapter V "The New Testament," Chapter VI "Sacred Scripture in the Life of the Church."

The schema on revelation was presented for the last time during the fourth session of the Council from September 20 to 22, 1965. There was no further discussion and only a vote was taken. The great majority of the bishops voted in favor of the present form of the document. Some of the bishops, however, accepted it only with reservations (iuxta modum) and for the last time submitted suggested revisions. The number of votes can be gaged from the vote on the much-discussed second chapter taken on September 21. A total of 2,246 fathers were present at this session of the Council; 1,874 voted yes, 9 voted no, and 354 voted yes with reservations. This meant that 354 suggestions for revision were submitted.

Three of the many suggestions for change which were considered in the following days were of special significance. These came directly from the Pope. They were, however, not papal revisions which were to be introduced into the document without change, like the revisions in the schema on ecumenism which had been submitted by the Pope in the previous year; rather these were proposals for change which had been sent to the Pope personally by others. The Pope then referred them to the commission so that they could be considered according to the usual procedure. "In the case of all three changes, the Pope had not taken the initiative himself, but rather had functioned as a mediator between the overwhelming majority of the Council and a small minority which, especially after the first votes, wished to determine the relationship between Scripture and tradition on the basis of the material insufficiency of scripture."[4]

Even though these changes do not substantially alter the document, it is still unfortunate that they were inserted. They clearly reveal the tendency to underline the constitutive significance of tradition. We shall consider these changes later.

This conciliar document had finally reached the end of its long and eventful road. On October 29, 1965, the final vote was taken. Only 27 votes were cast in opposition.

On November 18, 1965, the Constitution on Divine Revelation was then formally promulgated. There was great joy among the Catholic theologians who were fighting for freedom in the Roman Church. I met the French Father de Lubac in the assembly hall. He expressed his feelings thus: "This is the finest and most important document of the Council. Now Catholic theologians, the dogmaticians as well as the exegetes, can continue to work in freedom. The church has indicated the direction it intends to go. It has shown that it recognizes a new theology, has abandoned the attitudes of the Counter-Reformation and is now prepared to enter into dialogue with other Christians. The problem of the relationship between Scripture and tradition remains an open question. The theologians have complete freedom to discuss this problem further with the Protestants." Naturally, other theologians and churchmen were less excited; many of them were even disappointed. They could not join in the general atmosphere of rejoicing, but rather had to recognize that the Council had moved in another direction than they had expected and hoped for. The difference between the document "On the Sources of Revelation" prepared by Cardinal Ottaviani and the finally accepted "Constitution on Divine Revelation" is great. However, it is not so great that the Roman Catholic Church cannot tolerate this difference within itself.

Following this historical discussion we now turn our attention to the content of the document itself.

## II. The Theological Content of the Dogmatic Constitution on Divine Revelation

### The Preface

An important change in the short preface was made at the very last moment. As a result of this change, the first two words of this document are now *Dei Verbum* (Word of God); these two words will become the future title of this Constitution. This change is symptomatic of a movement which has left its impression on the entire Council. The Roman Catholic Church desired to place the Word of God in the foreground. The church exists to hear the Word of God for itself and to communicate it to others. Everything depends, however, on what is understood as "Word of God."

The preface consists of two very brief sections. The first section reminds us of the introductory words of the First Letter of John (1:2-3): "We announce to you the eternal life which was with the Father, and has appeared to us. What we have seen and have heard we announce to you, in order that you also may have fellowship with us, and that our fellowship may be with the Father, and with his son, Jesus Christ" (1).[5] This is an excellent biblical and Christological prelude to the following discussion.

The second section, which was added later, says that the Council intends to follow in the footsteps of the Council of Trent, as well as of the First Vatican Council. Listening to the Word of God and aligning itself with these two Councils, it now proposes to speak about revelation in such a way that the whole world may hear and believe the message of salvation. A reference to Augustine expresses the intention that "by believing it may hope; and by hoping it may love" (1).[5] Thereby, a clear biblical orientation is combined with a conscious connection to the later tradition of the Roman Catholic Church. Already here, Scripture and tradition are united.

## Chapter I. Revelation Itself

The document begins with a discussion of the essence and content of revelation. It is especially surprising that revelation is described in concrete, historical, and personal terms rather than in the abstract and conceptual understanding of revelation which dominated Roman Catholic theology in and after the period of Modernism. Thus, in one definitive presentation of the doctrine of revelation, revelation is described as follows: "Revelation is that free and essential supernatural act by which God—in order to bring the human race to its supernatural goal, which consists of the vision of the divine nature *[essentiae]*—speaks to us through the prophets and finally through Christ and thus clarifies the supernatural mysteries as well as the natural truths of religion, although he does so with a certain obscurity."[6] Here revelation is understood as essentially the transmission of supernatural truths.

There is a great difference between such a statement and the document adopted by the Council. To begin with, the language itself is different. The abstract and pedagogical style has been replaced by a more charismatic, pastoral, and concrete style. However, it is even more important that the means of revelation is no longer a series of didactic statements; rather revelation occurs through actions and words in reciprocal interaction. Christianity is more than a doctrine communicated to us by God; it is a divine act which manifests itself in the incarnation.[7] Revelation takes place fully in Christ himself, in his person, in his historical presence among men, in his miracles, acts, and words, through his death and his resurrection and in the sending of his Holy Spirit. The content of this revelation is explicitly described as the witness to the God who "is with us to free us from the darkness of sin and death and to raise us up to life eternal"(4). Revelation has occurred once and for all. Before the return of Christ, we may not expect any new revelation.

At this point the Council has actually broken out of an intellectualistic concept of revelation and stated its understanding of revelation in terms of persons and of the history of salvation. Whether the somewhat forced parallelism between the revealing word and the revealing act is valid, is of course, another question;

however, we cannot deny that a new tone and a new kind of thinking has been expressed in the official document of the Council. A Catholic exegete from the U.S.A. expressed the opinion that the decisive breakthrough already occurred in this second chapter.

For this reason, the traditional character of the immediately following description of faith as man's response to God's revelation is all the more noticeable. One would expect that a personal and biblical mode of expression would also be used here. However, almost without exception, faith is described in the old conceptual framework as an act of the intellect moved by the will, through which man offers an act of obedience to God. Since some fathers of the Council suggested a more biblical and more personal description of faith, similar to that which has been used in the discussion of revelation, the following sentence was inserted in response to their request: Faith is an act of obedience "by which man entrusts his whole self freely to God" (5). That insertion does not, however, adequately take the biblical understanding of faith into account.

The very brief presentation of the natural knowledge of God does not at any point go beyond the statement of the First Vatican Council and basically consists only of quotations from that Council.

## Chapter II. The Transmission of Divine Revelation

This second chapter brings us to the center of very difficult controversies, not only between Roman Catholics and Protestants, but also among Roman Catholics themselves. We must therefore first attempt to form a general impression of this important section which unfortunately is not always clearly formulated.

It is a great advantage that the Constitution begins with the discussion of revelation itself. This one revelation, which reached its earthly fulfillment in Christ, may be compared to a spring which flows out in two streams. This one revelation was committed to the apostles by Christ and the Holy Spirit. They in turn have transmitted it partially through *oral* proclamation, through their own examples, and through ordinances. They have partially communicated it *in writing*. The *apostolic Scriptures,* which were gradually gathered together in the New Testament, thus constitute one of the two streams in which the one revelation confronts us. The *apostolic tradition* forms the other stream in which we encounter this one revelation. It comes to us through the oral proclamation, the apostolic teaching, the divine worship, and the entire life of the congregation. Probably this description of the position taken by this Constitution already goes a step too far, especially when it implies that the content of these two streams is identical. This is precisely what dare not be expressed in the Constitution. This question was made an open question and must also remain such.

It is interesting to compare the various drafts of this document beginning with the first draft formulated under the leadership of Cardinal Ottaviani in the schema of 1962 until the final formulation of November 1965. The various stages in the struggle to arrive at proper and precise expressions can be clearly delineated.

(a) As we have already pointed out, the original schema spoke quite clearly of two sources of revelation. There were truths of revelations which could not be found in the sacred Scriptures, but had to be based on tradition alone. And even though the two sources were distinguished in principle, they were still coordinated with each other.

(b) The first schema of the mixed commission (April 1963) uses as few words as possible to say that Scripture and tradition are so related to each other that one cannot exist without the other (*ut altera alteri extranea non sit*). Later versions omit this formulation, because it could be understood polemically as a rejection of the conservative "two-sources theory," that is, as though it said that these two sources were ultimately one and the same. The second version of this schema says that Scripture and tradition are closely and integrally related. They flow from one and the same divine source.

(c) In the third version of this schema (July 1964) this relationship is explained. "Sacred Scripture is the word of God inasmuch as it is consigned to writing under the inspiration of the Holy Spirit" (9). Tradition conveys the opinion, the teaching, the example, and the commandments of Christ which have, with the assistance of the Holy Spirit, been accurately transmitted through the proclamation of the apostles and their successors. In this, the commission was attempting to make it clear that tradition is not only a tradition of words and of teaching, but also a tradition of "realities."

(d) The revision of this document after the discussions during the third session in the fall of 1964 actually resulted in a new text which attempts to arrive at a final and clear formulation. The characterization of Scripture remains unchanged, but tradition is now described in these terms: "To the successors of the apostles, sacred tradition hands on in its full purity God's word, which was entrusted to the apostles by Christ the Lord and the Holy Spirit. Thus, led by the light of the Spirit of truth, these successors can in their preaching preserve this word of God faithfully, and make it more widely known" (9).

(e) Almost immediately before the promulgation of the Constitution, a very important change was made, in the form of an insertion after the sentence quoted at the close of the preceding paragraph. This insertion came directly from the Pope and had the following content: Tradition is understood as the transmission of the word of God from the apostles to their successors and on down through the ages, so that these successors, that is, the bishops may, under the leadership of the Spirit of truth, serve Christ by explaining and interpreting it. This now implies "that it is not from sacred Scripture alone that the Church draws her certainty about everything which has been revealed" (9). There are, therefore, truths of revelation which can with certainty be derived from Scripture. There are, however, also truths of revelation which cannot with certainty be derived from the sacred Scriptures alone.

The *formulation* of this insertion, which, as we have said, came from the conservative minority and was transmitted through the mediation of the Pope, shows that the commission itself did not want to bow to the conservatives' desire, that the "two-source theory" should still be worked into the document at the last moment. The commission actually went quite far in responding to this desire by admitting that there are revealed truths whose certainty cannot be known to the church through Scripture alone. The obvious but unspoken assumption is that in such cases certainty must be based on tradition. One thinks of infant baptism, the seven sacraments, the proper understanding of the words of institution of the Lord's Supper, and so forth. Conversations in which I participated gave the impression that some of the Progressives, although certainly not all of them, accepted this statement with satisfaction. They were concerned that they might, because of their ecumenical concerns and premises, have indeed gone too far. The meaning of the inserted statement is certainly not entirely clear, and actually permits more than one interpretation. The expression "Certainty about everything which has been revealed *(certitudinem suam de omnibus revelatis)*" is very carefully formulated.

The unclarity about the question as to whether there are one or two sources of revelation seems almost intentional; but this unclarity was paid for at its own price.

A stumbling-block has been placed in the way of accurate understanding of the present text. At some places Scripture and tradition are described as two separate elements. At other places, however, the impression is created that tradition is the superior factor within which Scripture, which has its own particular value, is contained. It is possible that the Council actually wishes to say both: the apostles have transmitted a single revelation to us in two forms. First, they used the oral *tradition* which, viewed in purely historical terms, came first and has a certain kind of primacy. Within this tradition, *Scripture* has also developed as the inspired Word of God. In Scripture we encounter the certain and closed Word of God. Tradition, which also contains the Word of God, however, goes beyond this and within itself also contains Scripture, which has its own particular value.

Now, however, something extremely important is said about this ongoing tradition. Tradition which has its source in the apostles unfolds itself under the assistance of the Holy Spirit; it progresses, it grows. What constitutes this progression or growth? The schema is careful not to interpret this as growth in an objective sense. Had that been said the "two-sources" theory would have been recognized. The schema explicitly describes this as a "growth in understanding" (8). This growth of knowledge is effected by three forces: The first is the work of the theologians. Through their studies they arrive at an increasingly deeper understanding of the "words," that is, of the doctrines and certainly also the Scriptures, and of the "realities," that is, of the various "ordinances" (4) and of the service of worship with its various forms and the "mysteries." Secondly, growth of understanding results from direct *experience* and the mystical understanding of the words and realities which arises within the believer himself. We can briefly characterize these means of growth as human study and direct inner insight. Third, this growth also takes place "through the preaching of those who have received through episcopal succession the sure gift of truth" (8).[8] The bishops, naturally, are not in any way inspired; through their ordination, however, they have received a "sheer gift of truth *(charisma veritatis)*" (8) which helps them not only to faithfully preserve the deposit of faith, but also to explain it. It is through this living explanation that tradition makes progress, that is, the church grows into an increasingly fuller knowledge of the truth.

In this threefold way a constant growth and perfection in the understanding of revelation takes place. Tradition is thus a living presence in the church, through which the church grows into a better and deeper understanding of the divine truth until it becomes the glorified church which fully understands all that God has said and done.

Tradition can be understood as though God were engaged in constant conversation with the bride of his beloved Son. In the words of the Constitution, "the Holy Spirit, through whom the living voice of the gospel resounds in the Church and through her, in the world, leads unto all truth those who believe and makes the word of Christ dwell abundantly in them" (8).

Cardinal Meyer, in an address made in the Council hall in the autumn of 1964, drew attention to the very optimistic tone of this section. He pointed out that this was an unjustified assertion of an ecclesiastical triumph. Since the tradition of the church has often been subject to the limitations and defects of the church of sinners, the Cardinal wished to make the following addition to these paragraphs: "However, this living tradition does not always and everywhere grow into perfection. For since the church considers these divine matters here upon earth, where it is the church of the pilgrims, it can be unfaithful in some of its members. This actually takes place. For this reason, the church always carries the norm of the sacred Scriptures within itself and by measuring her life on these sacred Scriptures is constantly corrected and perfected." Unfortunately, this fine address had no effect on the document—much to its disadvantage. It would have made the discussion of the growth of tradition more believable. Now, however, the theory of harmony continues to pervade ecclesiology.

A final section discusses the relationship between Scripture and tradition on the one side and between the whole church and its teaching office on the other side. Scripture and tradition together constitute the sacred deposit of faith. Together they are the Word of God. This statement is extraordinarily significant because it clearly states that God's Word is to be understood not only as Scripture but as Scripture *and* the entire constantly growing tradition. This is the basis on which the church rests; and this is the source of the life of us all from the Pope and the bishops to the youngest and poorest members of the church. In this respect, all are equal without exception. However, the authentic *interpretation* of the Word of God as it confronts us in Scripture and tradition is exclusively committed to the teaching office of the church. The teaching office of the church is exercised in the name of Jesus and that means by his authority. It has actually been instituted by Christ.

The first brief schema of the mixed commission in 1962 already asserted that the teaching office is not above the Word of God. This was certainly inserted at the request of Cardinal Bea. This insertion was intended as a response to the concern of the churches of the Reformation who feared that the word would be imprisoned by the teaching office of the church. To avoid misunderstanding, it must, however, be said that this statement is not an answer to the concern of the Reformers for the simple reason that God's Word as used here does not refer to the sacred Scriptures, but to Scripture *and* the tradition of the church. In the thinking of the Reformers there was a distinction and contrast between the Scripture and the tradition of the church; nothing similar to this is found in the Roman Catholic Church. The document says that the teaching office does not function as a master but only as a servant. It carefully listens to that which is said in the Scriptures and what is transmitted in tradition, preserves it, and explains it faithfully (9).

Without this understanding of the inner relationship between the sacred Scriptures, tradition, and the teaching office of the church, there would be no Roman Catholic theology. These three belong inseparably together; one does not exist without the others. The art of theologizing consists in the ability to respect this three-foldness on the one hand and on the other hand carefully to distinguish these three components, for each exists and functions in its own way. This brief phrase "in its own way," conceals a whole complex of problems which repeatedly make themselves felt (9).

Within this "trinity" of Scripture, tradition, and the teaching office, the Scriptures occupy a prominent and very special place. In the following section we will now turn our attention to a more precise description of this position of the Scriptures.

### Chapters III-V. The Divine Inspiration and the Interpretation of Sacred Scripture; the Old Testament; the New Testament

The first chapters of the Constitution speak primarily of the tradition of the church. Now, in the last chapters, the Constitution deals especially with the sacred Scriptures. This means that by far the largest part of the Constitution on Divine Revelation is devoted to the problem of Scripture. The discussion begins with the inspiration of the Scripture, but later deals with both parts of the Bible, the Old and the New Testaments, separately. Our commentary will restrict itself to some of the main thoughts.

The Constitution clearly asserts the fact of inspiration. However, it leaves the question of the "how" open. It states that the Bible was written under the inspiration of the Holy Spirit—God is its author. The inspired authors, the so-called sacred writers, wrote down those things which God wished to communicate. As we have said, a theory of inspiration is not proposed, but is left in the hands of the theologians. The question is a delicate and difficult one; the theologians are, however, given the freedom to present it in more and more precise form.

Earlier drafts of the Constitution contain the expression "inerrancy." However, to the amazement and anger of a number of conservative theologians and bishops, this expression was omitted from the final draft of the text: "The books of Scripture must be acknowledged as teaching firmly, faithfully, and without error that truth which God wanted to put into the sacred writings for the sake of our salvation" (11). The last wording of this section to be rejected contained the expression "saving truth *(veritas salutaris).*" Many of the fathers of the Council objected to this formula because the Bible is without error, not only in relationship to the truths of salvation, but also in other respects. That is, Scripture is absolutely and completely without error. However, the commission did not permit this objection to influence its decision, and the Constitution does not assert that Scripture is inerrant in its scientific and historical statements. The expression "saving truth" was replaced by the circumlocution quoted above; it is admittedly difficult to recognize a distinction between these two. The understanding of Scripture expressed in this Constitution is thus formulated in such a way that there is room for the liberal as well as the conservative viewpoint. As a result, neither of the parties was absolutely satisfied, although the Conservatives probably had the most objections.

The inspiration of Scripture does not prevent it from being a completely human book. The Constitution's understanding of Scripture is not monophysitic. In the sacred Scriptures God speaks through men and in a completely human way. Therefore the exegete must carefully investigate what the sacred writers intended to say and what God intended to reveal through their, that is, through human words.

In order to understand exactly the expressions used by the biblical writers, it is necessary, among other things, to discover and carefully observe the "literary forms" that are used. Here the Constitution adopts a decisive thought of the important encyclical on the Bible of 1943, *"Divino afflante Spiritu."* This principle could have far-reaching effects in exegesis. These "literary forms" can be of the kind used in history, in prophecy, in poetry, but there are also others. Through these various literary styles, the one truth is expressed in various ways, none of which is more perfect than the others. The interpreter of Scripture must thus use very exact methods and utilize all the scientific aids at his command to determine the meaning intended by the individual authors. The fact that the writer was bound to the limitations of his own historical period is not something which is only an external matter of secondary importance; rather, this is precisely the form in which the divine word comes to us. The more deeply one penetrates the specific character of this form, the better one understands what God is saying to us through it.

The task of the exegete is thereby not yet complete, for one cannot be satisfied with the literal sense of Scripture. If it is true that the author (or perhaps tradition as a member of which the author wrote) worked under the inspiration of the Holy Spirit, this factor may not be ignored in interpreting Scripture. The exegete must take into account the rest of the content of Scripture and its unity, the living tradition of the church, and the analogy of faith. At this point the hermeneutical question really becomes difficult—both within the Roman Catholic Church and in conversation with non-Roman-Catholic exegetes.

The exegetes dare not forget that the interpretation of Scripture is ultimately the business of the teaching office of the church. Therefore the teaching office has the right to intervene when it feels that the exegetes are going too far. One can, however, also imagine that the opposite might sometime be the case and that the teaching office might have to take steps against an uncritical fundamentalism. This was the case immediately before the encyclical on the Bible was issued in 1943. We may not overlook the fact that the Pope personally intervened in the controversy about the Papal Biblical Institute, which according to the view of the papal Lateran University engaged in a too liberal form of exegesis, and defended the Biblical Institute.

The relationship between the teaching office of the church and the exegetes is a twofold one. The teaching office is responsible for the true understanding of the Bible. Its judgment is final. However, to arrive at this final decision, the teaching office needs the help of the exegetes, who are to carry out their work conscientiously, and that means also scientifically. Ultimately, however, the teaching office has the last word. Without this final authority of the teaching office, the understanding of Scripture would disintegrate into individual subjective opinions.

In the section on the New Testament an important thought was added to the section on biblical hermeneutics. It is concerned with the exegesis of the Gospels, which constitute the most important part of the New Testament, because they speak of the life and teaching of our Savior, the incarnate Word. It is formally emphasized that the Holy Mother Church has always asserted the "historical character" of these writings. The expression "historical character" is one of the revisions which the Pope suggested at the last moment. As we have said, it came not from the Pope himself, but from the conservative minority. The full significance of this term is not completely clear. When used by a conservative Roman Catholic theologian, it certainly asserts that the factual character of the story of the childhood of Jesus is to be assumed. The first schema prepared under the direction of Cardinal Ottaviani explicitly spoke of this. The word can, however, also express the conviction that the Gospels speak of a historical person whose life, words, death, and resurrection are truly and faithfully recorded. This would not necessarily imply that the question of the "historical character" —understood in the narrower sense—of many individual accounts in the Gospels had been decided. This question is very closely related to the question of literary forms, which we discussed above.

The following statement is very significant for the hermeneutical principle to be followed in interpreting the Gospels: "The sacred authors wrote the four Gospels, selecting some things from the many which had been handed on by word of mouth or in writing, reducing some of them to a synthesis, explicating some things in view of the situation in their churches, and preserving the form of proclamation but always in such fashion that they told us the honest truth about Jesus" (20).

As I understand this statement, the Council thereby recognized the basic concerns of the form-critical method. Compared with earlier forms of the document—to say nothing at all of the first schema prepared under the direction of Cardinal Ottaviani—this represents amazing progress. Many of the conservatives saw and still see the form-critical method as a very serious danger for the historical character of the Gospels. In the thinking of these men, the form-critical understanding of the Gospels as the testimony of faith given by the apostles in the early church is not very far removed from a modernistic understanding of the supposedly more or less legendary character of the reports contained in the Gospels.

An earlier draft of the Constitution explicitly rejected this danger of modernism. It pointed out that the Gospels may not be considered to be "made-up stories which have their source in the creative imagination of the early church." The commission omitted this anti-modernistic statement as referring to an antiquated form of thought on which it no longer needed to express itself.

The Council thus decided in favor of a formulation which preserves the historical character of the Gospels without committing itself to an unscientific fundamentalism but, on the contrary, respects and encourages the ongoing attempts of exegetes to delineate more clearly the individual character in each of the Gospels. And it does so by indicating the patterns for such exegesis.

This is the result of the great inner struggle during the Council. Even though a number of exegetes cannot subscribe to everything that is stated in this Constitution, yet Roman Catholic exegetes, by and large, have good reason to be thankful. Protestant exegetes, on the other hand, will carefully read this text and observe the development of Roman Catholic exegesis with intense interest.

### Chapter VI. Sacred Scripture in the Life of the Church

In this last chapter the written word is presented in its exclusive preeminence, which exceeds the greatness of tradition as well as of the teaching office of the church. The question must be raised whether the relationship between chapters II and VI is clear and consistent. In Chapter II the assertion was made that both forms of the word of God, Scripture and tradition, were—according to the principles established by the Council of Trent—to be recognized and reverenced in the same way. This Constitution, however, makes a significant advance. For the decrees of the Council of Trent refer only to Scripture and apostolic tradition. In the present document, however, tradition refers not only to apostolic, but also to postapostolic tradition. Oscar Cullmann properly draws attention to the fact that this Constitution has overlooked a theologically significant difference between these two. In Chapter II tradition is almost always referred to before the Scriptures. Both together constitute the Word of God, the deposit of faith, and both are given equal rank. Here, in Chapter VI, however, Scripture is clearly placed before tradition and, in terms of its content, even given a superior position, although here too Scripture and tradition are joined together. Is this a consistent viewpoint, or do the two chapters look at the problem from a shifting perspective? If so, this document is in the final analysis almost unnoticeably composed of two strata.

Chapter VI begins: "The Church has always venerated the divine Scriptures just as she venerates the body of the Lord, since from the table of both the word of God and of the body of Christ she unceasingly receives and offers to the faithful the bread of life, especially in the sacred liturgy" (21). Here the Scriptures are placed on a level with the body of Christ in the Lord's Supper. The words of this Constitution may be compared with the words of the Constitution on Sacred Liturgy: "He is present in His word, since it is He Himself who speaks when the holy Scriptures are read in the church."[9] It appears to me that the term "Scripture and tradition," used here in Chapter VI cannot simply be identified with its mirror image "tradition and Scripture" used in Chapter II. In Chapter II the two elements of this term are equal, but in the chapter now under discussion Scripture is without any doubt primary. Tradition here is to be understood only as interpretative tradition. In Chapter II one does not know (and *may* not know) whether tradition is only interpretative or also has constitutive significance.

We may use another example. "All the preaching of the Church must be nourished and ruled by sacred Scripture" (21).[10] In this sentence, too, Scripture is elevated above tradition, for this preaching of the church is actually the same as the preaching of the bishops which is a dynamic factor in the growth of tradition (cf. Chapter II, 8.9). Thus, Scripture ultimately does not stand on the same level as tradition. Chapter II, however, gives the impression that they do stand on the same level.

A third example: "In the sacred books, the Father who is in heaven meets His children with great love and speaks with them" (21). This can mean only that Scripture is an effective means of grace with the power of a sacrament. For this reason Scripture is to be translated and is to be translated on the basis of texts in the original languages. Wherever circumstances permit, it is recommended that such translations be made in cooperation with exegetes of non-Roman Catholic churches.[11] In addition Roman Catholic exegetes are, under the supervision of the teaching office, to study the divine texts jointly with theologians representing other disciplines, so that the people of God will be nourished by the sacred Scriptures through the servants of the divine Word. Thereby the people's spirits will be enlightened, their wills strengthened, and their hearts set on fire with love to God (23). Priests and deacons to whom the service of the divine word has been committed must without exception have time to read and study the Scriptures thoroughly so that they do not become lazy preachers of the Word. A quotation from Saint Jerome emphatically draws attention to the fact that "ignorance of the Scriptures is ignorance of Christ" (25).

The concluding paragraph once again draws attention to the relationship and connection between the Word of God and the Eucharist. "Just as the life of the Church grows through persistent participation in the Eucharistic mystery, so we may hope for a new surge of spiritual vitality from intensified veneration for God's word, which 'lasts forever'" (26). Just as at the beginning of this Constitution, so at the end we are confronted by the term "the word of God." This is the concept which was also the dominant center of the Reformation. How did this happen and what does this mean? This question is posed by the text of this Constitution but has not yet been answered.

## III. A Brief Commentary

In the Constitution on Divine Revelation a new way of thinking which decades ago began to take root in the Roman Catholic Church is confirmed by highest authority. We may not forget that this cannot simply be taken for granted and that it happened only as a result of a struggle. When we consider that a document of a Council almost of necessity must stand on a lower level than that reached by the best part of Roman Catholic theology, that it was often necessary to act with regrettable consideration for other viewpoints, and that therefore compromises of the kind that, viewed objectively in terms of their content, ought not be allowed, were often unavoidable: then we must be astonished that so much was achieved. This is particularly true with reference to the concept of revelation and the position of Scripture in the church. We must recognize the fact that doors which might have been closed remained open or were even opened wider. Questions which were asked by Protestant theologians were taken into account. The Council did not neglect its ecumenical concern.

Therefore Protestant theologians should carefully consider this document. It invites us to enter into a genuine conversation, a responsible and critical dialogue, and not a talking-back-and-forth at one another. Protestant theology may not entrench itself in old positions which can no longer be defended, but must move out into the open country which perhaps has not even been plowed or harrowed. In the last years Protestant theology has in fact done much work with these problems. Hermeneutical questions are the order of the day and the problem of tradition has been raised in new ways. Attention has often—and quite properly—been drawn to the relationship between this statement of the Council and the report of the Fourth World Conference on Faith and Order in Montreal in 1963.

This Constitution on Divine Revelation is a contribution to this discussion and it demands an answer. A simple rejection or an uncritical acceptance of the Constitution would not contribute to a considered and helpful treatment of this text. In what follows I will briefly discuss some of the more important points.

### 1. The Bible and the Church

There is a Protestant conception of the Bible which forgets that the Bible does not exist in a world in which things have meaning out of context but rather exists within the specific context of the church. "For some hundred and fifty years or for one and a half century, the church lived, preached, baptised, and celebrated the Lord's Supper, before it was given a canon of the New Testament writings as an instrument to be used in exercising its apostolic authority."[12] In this church the Bible developed; and in this church the Bible has its place. The church was not built upon a book, but rather on the living oral proclamation of the apostles and the early church. At the beginning there was not a scripture, but a confession to the living Lord.

Even though the assertion of the Danish churchman and theologian N. F. S. Grundtvig that Christ himself gave the Apostles' Creed to the apostles cannot be true, it is in any case correct to say that the church was constituted through the confession to God's saving act in Christ and not through a book. The congregation is not a reading circle and Christianity is not a book religion, but rather a historical and living entity; it is a people that have been brought into existence through the living word of the apostles and through baptism. When Luther said, "The church is the creature of the word of God,"[13] he understood "word" not primarily as the word of Scripture, but rather as the living spoken word, the living voice of the Gospel (*viva vox Evangelii*). "The gospel is nothing else than the preaching and proclamation of the grace and mercy of God, purchased and won by our Lord Jesus Christ through his death. It really is not to be found in books and can not be put down in words, but is rather a spoken sermon, a living word and a voice which sounds forth in all the world and is publicly proclaimed so that people may hear it everywhere."[14] "Therefore the church is a place where the mouth speaks and not where the pen writes (*ein Mundhaus und nicht ein Federhaus*). It is characteristic of the gospel and of the New Testament that it is preached and taught by the spoken word and the living voice. Christ himself neither wrote nor commanded us to write. Rather he commanded us to preach."[15] Such passages clearly indicate that the Reformation's conception of Scripture was not a faith in the dead letter or a stubborn biblicism.

The Bible is heard, explained, and preached in the church. The church was there before Scripture, just as the risen Lord was the Lord of the church before Scripture existed. The Gospels and the Epistles were written out of the faith and within the context of the church; and Scripture is to be understood within the context of the apostolic faith in Christ.

All of this does not deny the fact that the Bible became the ultimate authority in the church. The fact that the New Testament was gathered in and by the church does not support the conclusion that the tradition current in the church is the basic principle for our interpretation of Scripture; rather the church must constantly continue to listen to Scripture so that it may have a valid criterion for distinguishing between true and false tradition in the church.

As the witness of the apostolic faith and apostolic proclamation, Scripture remains the apostolic voice in the church for all time; this distinguishes it from all other official authorities in the church. The words of the Constitution on Divine Revelation should have been preserved as they were formulated after the discussion in the fall of 1964, that is, that "like the Christian religion itself, all the preaching of the Church ought to look to Scripture both as a norm and an authority by which it is ruled and judged."[16] For all time the Scriptures have the function of controlling and judging all the official ecclesiastical authorities that have arisen in the history of the Christian church. The Bible is not an isolated book, but is the book of the church. It was written in the church and for the church. Within this church, however, it will continue to raise its independent voice as the lord of tradition. The Bible presents the witness of the apostolic faith within the church and, by virtue of this, stands above that tradition which lives and grows within the church. Herewith we have already formulated our position on the difficult question of relationship between Scripture and tradition. There are statements in the Constitution on Divine Revelation which do not necessarily contradict the position here outlined.

## 2. Scripture and Tradition

We shall approach this same problem again, but this time we shall speak not only of Scripture and the church, but directly of Scripture and *tradition*. The church and tradition may not simply be identified with each other. The church is the people of God. Tradition is that material which is active within God's people. It includes the Word of God as well as the many "ordinances" of ancient and modern times. Tradition thus cannot simply be identified with the church, rather the church has its tradition. What then is the relationship between Scripture and tradition in the people of God, that is, in the church?

There is no "purely objective" Bible. Rather, the Bible always exists as the interpreted, heard, and preached word. The Bible is present for us because we constantly hear and interpret it. Is this situation not the point at which the problem of the relationship between Scripture and tradition lies? This problem thus exists for all Christians and it is true of all of us that we live in tradition. As Gerhard Ebeling has said, "Tradition is a structural element of historical existence."[17] History, freedom, and tradition belong together. Tradition does not automatically extend the past into the future, but tradition is created in freedom and responsibility. The fact of receiving, working through, and passing on tradition is a process in which we are personally involved and in itself has nothing in common with a lazy traditionalism.

The church lives as a "paradosis" or tradition; this means that the church is involved in the process of receiving a tradition which has a definite content appropriating it by listening in faith, and then transmitting it to others. Christian tradition is the constantly proclaimed message of salvation in Christ which is received in faith. Or to use other words, tradition is the process of "transmitting" the proclaimed event of salvation which took place in a particular time and in a particular place (*illic et tunc*) to men who live in another place and at another time (*hic et nunc*).

The particular historical place at which this hearing and receiving, this understanding and this proclamation occurs is not insignificant. For transmission of the Gospel is never the monotonous repetition of certain words, but a living proclamation which itself is a historic event that takes place at a particular time, in a particular place, and under particular conditions. The men involved never participate as though they had no experience apart from this; and the Gospel is never a finished manifesto, the text of which has been determined once and for all, but a living proclamation whose text and language are influenced by the particular conditions in the time and at the place it is proclaimed. Because Christ is the living Lord, the Gospel always "incorporates" itself in various forms. At some later time and some later place the men involved will possibly understand aspects of the proclamation which men of earlier times did not see in the same way. Christianity was not interpreted in the same way among the Jews as it was among the Greeks and the Gospel was not proclaimed in the same "language" in Samaria as it was in Colossae. What is involved, however, is always the same living Christ and the same message of salvation that was first (*illic et tunc*) made known. That which we call tradition is this process of moving from the first and basic place and from the very particular time in which the revelation first occurred to all other particular historical places and times. There is therefore a problem in the relationship between Scripture and tradition.

The living Word of God is Christ himself. The New Testament reliably transmits the apostolic witness of this Word of God in various forms and therefore is itself also called the Word of God. This process of receiving, of hearing, and of interpreting, which constantly happens and must happen over and over again, takes place through word and sacrament, through the ministry and the witness of the church. This process is a living movement because Christ is the living Lord. This process which we call tradition is *in and of itself* nothing else than the ongoing hearing and proclamation of the Word, the administration of baptism and of the Lord's Supper, the functions of instructing, admonishing, and encouraging in the name of Jesus, the doxology of faith, hope, and love—all to be performed until he returns. Naturally, tradition creates forms, customs, "ordinances," new ways of confessing faith, and so forth; all of this, however, is not something "new" or independent, but only an expression, instrument, and sign of the one original message of salvation in Jesus Christ which because it is made a living force through the Holy Spirit, creates faith, hope, and love. Tradition in all its elements serves the saving Word of God which is made known to us in the Bible, and which lives among us in the living Christ.

Therefore the Bible, because it is the message which always makes itself effective and witnesses to the original act of God which is present in every age, occupies a unique position in tradition.

Scripture also has a critical function. God himself has given the Scriptures to the church as the criterion of its preaching and of its teaching. Scripture is the norm and judge. It is the criterion by which false and genuine traditions may be distinguished in the church. This tradition is, in the strictest sense of the word, an interpretative tradition. This interpretative tradition, which forms the tradition to be judged by Scripture, is the work of the people of God who are gathered together within the structure of the church, who give their praise to God and are gathered around baptism and The Lord's Supper. Their interpretation of the Word of God is, however, not a restricted and anxious interpretation, but occurs in openness to the scientific and "secular"; and it actually never occurs without the prayer for the assistance of the Holy Spirit. This tradition is of some significance for the interpretation of Scripture. However, it is never a "constitutive" principle but is only the particular and not insignificant historical context in which the hearing and interpretation of the word occurs. At this point, however, we must draw attention to a particular condition which leads our discussion a step farther.

### 3. Scripture, Tradition, and the Traditions

Every church has its own tradition as this has been developed through the centuries. The tradition of a church is a very complex phenomenon. It has come into existence over a period of years, indeed of centuries. Cultural, psychological, and sociological factors, diverse non-theological considerations such as history, race, or the nation, have worked together with religious and theological motives to produce it. Every church-tradition represents a particular system of knowledge and conviction which makes sense to its supporters and very often establishes itself after a relatively short period of time.

This church-tradition naturally plays a great and important role in the question of the interpretation of the Bible. For the method and approach with which we interpret the Bible is "bound to the tradition through which we have received the Scripture as authority" (Albert Outler). When we read and hear the Bible we confront it through the medium of our own knowledge and understanding. It is true that we always have the Bible as a heard and interpreted Bible, but there is another side to this. For we are always threatened with the possibility that we might hear only half the Bible and thereby falsely interpret it, because we—perhaps without even knowing it—hear our own voice and not the actual voice of the Bible. We thus become the captives of that tradition in which we of necessity live. In other words, the tradition can shut its ears to the sovereign voice of the Scripture and then becomes a factor that restricts and dominates the Scripture. Tradition is then not open and free to receive, understand, and transmit but has become "constitutive," an independent element which stands alongside the message of Scripture. In this case, the problem of Scripture and tradition actually arises because these have in some way or other become two independent elements. Perhaps people are clearly aware that this is the case. Perhaps they are not aware of it; indeed it is even possible that they always speak about "Scripture alone." And it is always more difficult to set one's self free from something when one does not know that it exists.

It is in this way that tradition becomes a hermeneutical principle. Thus at the time of Lutheran orthodoxy the Bible stood under the threat of a "constitutive" church-tradition with its theory of the Bible and its previously determined understanding of the Scripture. In spite of the emphasis on "Scripture alone" Lutherans can imprison Scripture. And the Roman Catholic Church is in very special danger of not hearing the voice of Scripture itself, insofar as it openly declares that its infallible teaching office makes it alone competent to explain and proclaim Scripture authoritatively.

Tradition is therefore not only the necessary movement of the good news of the church through the ages, but also something which "must be overcome." This does not mean that tradition must be done away with, for one cannot do away with tradition any more than one can jump over his own shadow. Tradition must be overcome in the sense of overcoming the always powerful temptation to make it a "constitutive" factor. How is tradition overcome? Ultimately the word of Scripture itself must overcome it. The mystery of the word of Scripture consists in its power to overcome the independent authority which tradition asserts for itself. This is as true of those "traditions" which consciously live as a tradition as it is true of the very anti-traditional traditions which always speak disparingly of tradition.

Scripture itself contains that which criticizes and overcomes tradition. What is really the content of Christian tradition? Ultimately, it is Jesus Christ himself who, in his words, his life, death, and resurrection, completely destroys and overcomes the usual "tradition of humanity." That is how it was then and that is how it is now too. The Jesus-tradition is therefore a power which overcomes the church-tradition, a power which always fulfills the tradition of *God* by shattering the tradition of *men.*

The "tradition" of the history of salvation is full of the overcoming of tradition, indeed of the shattering of tradition, for the sake of God's tradition. In the midst of this overcoming of traditions stands Jesus himself who fell victim to the strong and all-powerful religious tradition of his own time.

The Greek verb *paradidonai* unites two meanings within itself in a peculiar and terrifying way. At one and the same time it means to transmit, to hand on, to deliver, to put under the power of someone, and to betray. The same is true of the Latin word *tradere;* "*tradere Jesum*" can also have a twofold meaning. It can mean to transmit the message of Jesus or specifically to hand over Jesus himself, and it can also mean to deliver Jesus to his enemies, to give him up and betray him. Every ecclesiology must carefully pay attention to this; for here we are speaking of the great adversary, the Antichrist, who always follows close on the heels of the church. There can be no ecclesiology and that means also no doctrine of tradition apart from the knowledge of the constant threat of the Antichrist.

### 4. Scripture, Tradition, and the Teaching Office of the Church

We come now to the last point of our commentary. We have already said that it is an essential characteristic of Roman Catholic theology to think always of these three, Scripture, tradition, and the teaching office of the church, as closely related to each other. This close relationship is an extremely fine fabric which is spun out of three threads. None of these three can do without the others. If the thread of the specific teaching office of the church is missing, the web breaks in two. This means that Scripture also cannot function or hold together without the tradition and the teaching office.

In a brief essay published in 1951, "*Schrift, Tradition, und Kirche,*" Hanns Rückert says that these three constitute a "magic circle" which cannot be broken. He points out, "the statement that the church alone, that is, naturally its teaching office, can decide on the true meaning and the proper interpretation of the Scripture

. . . is that which closes the magic circle." This statement guarantees
that the Scripture can never be used as a critical argument against
the church but must always serve to justify the position of the
church. Oscar Cullmann says the same in his chapter, "The Bible in
the Council." In the Roman Catholic Church the Bible is not understood as something which is separate and distinct from the church.
"The church itself can never be judged by the Bible as though the
Bible were an authority which confronted the church, for the Scripture can be interpreted only through the church as such."[18]

Both of these Lutheran theologians are right. We must, however,
carefully investigate whether it might not be possible, even within
and in spite of this magic circle, that Scripture is in fact superior
to both of the other authorities. It cannot be denied that the new
Roman Catholic theology and also this Constitution reveal an
intention which clearly points in this direction. Earlier we en-
countered the statement, "Like the Christian religion itself, all the
preaching of the Church must be nourished and ruled by sacred
Scripture" (21). The statement is intended to be taken seriously.
It would mean that every ecclesiastical decision of the teaching
office from the most formal definition of a dogma to the smallest
decision of the Commission on the Bible must be ruled by sacred
Scripture. Karl Rahner, in an article on biblical theology, has given
a very fine and deep expression to this intention. He knows that
the rule of faith in Roman Catholic dogmatics is the teaching
office of the church and its proclamation of the faith. In spite of this
he says that Scripture has its special place and that it is subjected
to nothing else. For this ongoing proclamation of the Word by
the teaching office of the church occurs only in an "ongoing,
constantly new, and necessary reference to that which God himself
has guaranteed as 'pure.' This specific origin and source of this
proclamation can be distinguished from the later teaching of the
church; and this specific origin and source can be found in Scripture and only in Scripture."[19] Here Rahner comes to terms with
Scripture as the ruling factor described in this Constitution. At this
point we most certainly have a clear assertion that Scripture exists
independently in relationship to both other parts of the triad.
Does this not break through the "magic circle"?

In answering that question we have to take into account such factors as Karl Rahner's assertion that all Roman Catholic dogmas —for example, the dogma of the Assumption of Mary into heaven— are implicitly contained in the Bible. Can one really say that the teaching office of the church in defining this dogma referred back to the stable origin and source of the proclamation which is guaranteed by God himself and which is specifically present *only* in Scripture? This is the question which must be asked in view of Karl Rahner's compelling statements on Scripture.

If the position of Scripture in the Roman Catholic Church really is what Rahner describes it to be, then we must ask not whether too much, but whether all too little apostolic authority is exercised in the Roman Catholic Church. If the teaching office of the church carried out its work as Rahner describes it, would the growth of the living tradition in the Roman Catholic Church not be different in many ways? Thinking of Scripture, tradition, and the teaching office of the church as so closely interrelated brings with it the danger that one may close his eyes to reality. The living subject is really the teaching office. How can it exercise this fantastic authority without the constant, active, and real cooperation of the other authorities, which possibly are not always "agreeable" partners, for example, those engaged in the historical research on the Bible, where methods most certainly cannot be limited by the teaching office.

In spite of these questions, I feel that Roman Catholic theology frequently intends to rank Scripture ahead of the other authorities— without breaking the "magic circle"; and Protestant theologians are usually moved by these intentions, for they also intend to do this. They know the burden of tradition, even though in another way, and they too know that they can easily become so involved in the preliminaries of biblical interpretation that the meaning of the word escapes them. Protestant theologians, however, cannot believe that a genuine, authentic understanding of the Bible can be dictated by the teaching office of the Roman Catholic Church or by any other ecclesiastical authority whatsoever. This does not mean that Scripture is not to be understood within the church. However, the expression "in the church" needs to be carefully explained so that it is not misunderstood and does not seem to be unbelievable.

Among other things, we must ask whether it is possible in our day and age to understand the Bible if we do not read and hear it in the midst of the *world*. In brief, will it be possible for Catholic theology to give Scripture the ruling position in the final sense of that term? On the other hand, the Roman Catholic Church has a right to keep on asking whether Scripture really rules in the Protestant churches today. Answering this question will be no simple and easy task.

Ultimately, the question about the proper understanding of Scripture is the question about the Holy Spirit himself. The Roman Catholic Church believes that the Holy Spirit works through the teaching office of the church. The divine promise of the Spirit has been given to the teaching office. At this point we are confronted by the most difficult question and problem in the ecumenical dialogue. The circle seems to be closed; and it seems impossible to break through it.

Once again: we have not yet come to the end of our task. For in spite of the certainty and harmony which seem to characterize this Constitution there is still tension in the discussion of this problem. A hidden dissatisfaction remains which can never be done away with and which repeatedly breaks through, especially among the best Roman Catholic theologians; here, as among their Protestant counterparts, we constantly find the tension between the Word of God and the ministry of the church, between sacred Scripture and the teaching office of the church, between the Holy Spirit and ecclesiastical authority. And this tension can *never* cease, precisely because God is God.

To summarize: The Constitution on Divine Revelation remains within the traditional framework of thought. It moves within that "magic circle" of which Rückert speaks and apparently has no intention at all of stepping outside this circle. This means that we as Protestant theologians are required to express serious criticism. However, in doing this we must precisely observe how this Constitution and many Roman Catholic theologians today understand the process of living within the circle. Here it seems to me that the Constitution strikes new tones and that the tension and unrest can be felt, which we know exists among Roman Catholic theologians —and which is also a vital force among us, even though we know that it comes to us in another form. Therefore this Constitution on Divine Revelation in its own way points forward and requires us to move beyond itself. I hope that theologians on both sides who experience this unrest which has its source in the situation itself will meet one another in thorough conversations and join with one another in studying the matter in depth.

# Notes

1. *Informations catholiques internationales*, December, 1965, p. 5.
2. von Galli, *Das Konzil. Chronik der ersten Session* (1963), p. 93.
3. December 4, 1963.
4. *Herderkorrespondenz*, December 1965, page 734.
5. Numbers in parentheses refer to the sections of the text of the "Constitution on Divine Revelation, in *The Documents of Vatican II* (Published by Guild Press, America Press, and Association Press and copyrighted 1966 by the America Press. Used by permission).
6. Reg. Garrigou—Lagrange, O.P., *De Revelatione* (1929) I, 139.
7. On this entire subject, cf. *Die Offenbarung und ihre Weitergabe, Herderkorrespondenz*, December, 1964, pp. 130 ff.
8. This statement was added at the last moment. It must be understood as a concession to some of the conservative fathers of the Council who desired that the infallible teaching office of the church should be explicitly referred to. From this we can see the reservation and understanding with which the commission dealt with this matter. However, we can also see how much influence the minority was able to exert because of their energy and perseverance—even though they

were not able to change the basic character of the document.
9. Chapter 1, 7. *The Documents of Vatican II*, p. 141.
10. In an earlier draft, this passage was much more strongly formulated. It read: "Like the Christian religion itself, all the preaching of the church ought to look to Scripture both as a norm and an authority by which it is ruled and judged."
11. At the moment, this is taking place in England and also in France; plans have been made for this to occur in Germany. In Denmark, Roman Catholics have for a long time used the translation of the Bible authorized by the Danish Ev. Lutheran Church.
12. Peter Brunner, *Schrift und Tradition* (1951), reprinted in *Pro Ecclesia* (Berlin: Lutherisches Verlagshaus, 1962) I, 33.
13. *WA* 6, 560; cf. *LW* 36, 107.
14. *WA* 12, 259.
15. *WA* 10, I, 2, 48.
16. See above, Note 10.
17. *Die Geschichtlichkeit der Kirche und ihrer Verkündigung als theologisches Problem* (1954), p. 34.
18. *Dialogue on the Way*. Edited by George Lindbeck (Minneapolis: Augsburg, 1965).
19. "Biblische Theologie," in *Lexikon für Theologie und Kirche*, Vol. II (1958), pp. 449 f.

*Chapter III*

# The Decree on the Pastoral Office of Bishops

## A. The Discussion at the Council

The decree "The Pastoral Office of Bishops" first came before the Council during the second session (1963) under the title "The Administration of Dioceses." It followed upon a prolonged discussion of the schema on the church, during which much excitement had been generated over the questions of the collegiality of bishops, the reestablishment of the permanent office of deacon, and whether the role of Mary in the church should be treated in a separate schema or as a chapter in the schema of the church. Since these questions touched upon the most sensitive issues before the council, papal primacy, celibacy, and Marian devotion, interest was intense and the debate sharp. In this atmosphere the new schema became the occasion for a contest of strength between the bishops of the Council and those of the Roman Curia.

The debate on the new schema produced sharp reactions at once, when members of the commission responsible for the schema rose in the aula to charge that the document as presented had not been approved by the commission, and had in fact been subjected to extensive tampering. In the course of the discussion it was revealed that the chairman of the commission, Cardinal Marella of the Curia, had undertaken revision of the document with the assistance of members of the commission who lived near Rome. Although this

procedure perhaps meant a saving of time and money for the
members of the commission more remote from Rome, they spent
little time at the Council expressing their appreciation of it. Several of them objected to the procedure as a bypassing of diocesan
bishops on the commission, and protested also the character of the
revision as being concerned only with the rights and privileges
of the Roman Curia. The heat thus generated in the aula was also
ventilated at press conferences, to the delight of the journalists
and the dismay of curial officials. This was but one of a series of
collisions between diocesan bishops and curial officials which en-
livened the second session. At issue, of course, was the procedural
question whether the majority of the Council could make decisions
or whether they would be overruled by curial officials who controlled
key positions in the conciliar commissions.

Discussion of the schema was not, however, limited to questions
of procedure. The substance of the schema was subjected to sharp
criticism, chiefly because it took little or no account of the theology of the schema on the church, which had occupied the attention
of the bishops in the opening weeks of the session. This theology
represented a major change in thinking about the church and put
all of the problems of church life and administration in a new light.
In place of the theology of the Counter-Reformation period with
its emphasis upon the church as hierarchical institution, its juridical mode of speech and its triumphalist tone, the schema on the
church used the language and thought of the biblical and patristic
periods of the church's life. This program involved profound
changes in the church's way of thinking of her life and function, and
the bishops insisted that it should be taken seriously in the rethinking of the problems of diocesan life and administration. Several of the emphases developed during the debate on the schema
on the church were significant for rethinking the schema on administration of dioceses.

1. During the period following the Reformation Roman Catholic
theology had identified the church with the hierarchical institution.
Even the encyclical of Pope Pius XII *Mystici Corporis* of 1943,
which otherwise represents a major advance in ecclesiological
thinking, continues the identification of the church as mystical body

with the church as institution. But the growing influence of biblical theology and increasing openness to the thought of the church fathers and of the Orthodox churches of the East were apparent in the discussions of the Council. It was pointed out that the historical church and the church as mystical body are identical only eschatologically, that is, in the final accomplishment of God's redemptive purpose for his world. At the present stage of historical existence it is necessary to distinguish them and to recognize that the church represents the mystery of God's work in the world. It is at once a human institution composed of frail and sinful persons, and yet has within it the active, dynamic presence of God at work in the world for his own purposes. It may be questioned whether the schema on the church expresses adequately the tension between the human and sinful aspect of the church and the mystery of God's redemptive action in it, but the presence of this biblical and eschatological dimension was certainly of great importance at the Council and may well be even more influential in the future.

2. Roman Catholic thought on the church has usually begun with the hierarchy, the Pope, the bishops, and their representatives, the priests. The emphasis lay upon the hierarchy and their administration of the sacraments, and not much was said of the role of the laity. This approach was challenged at the Council by bishops from churches of the eastern rites as well as by those influenced by newer biblical theology. It was pointed out that in the Scriptures and in the early fathers the approach is rather to begin with baptism and the divine establishment of the people of God and to discuss the ministry in terms of God's gifts to his people. Ministry is then seen as a service of God's people, and the "higher" the office in the church, the greater the responsibility for service. This leads to the recognition of the fact that the work of a bishop is not merely that of administering a diocese, but that he is a pastor of the people of God. As a result of this discussion, the schema was completely recast, and its new title, "The Pastoral Office of Bishops," accurately reflects the changes in its contents.

3. When the church is defined as the people of God, the biblical emphasis upon the priesthood of all God's people returns to the center of ecclesiological thinking. Priesthood of all believers is then

no longer a strange and dangerous teaching, cultivated chiefly by heretics and sectarians, but an essential point of view for grasping the relationship of the people of God to Christ the Lord and of understanding the function of the church in the world. Baptism is understood as the sacrament of initiation by which individuals are incorporated into Christ and made members of his body, the church. The individual's participation in the priesthood of Christ is the way his worship and his life in the world are consecrated by God and given redemptive meaning. Holiness, moreover, is seen not as solitary spiritual athleticism, but as the individual's sharing of the holiness of Christ, his consecration to God in the world, and the specific shape which holiness takes in his life is appropriate to his situation in the world. With this reshaping of ecclesiological thought, a new understanding of the episcopal office necessarily follows.

4. Another important aspect of the work of the Second Vatican Council was the definition of the collegiality of the bishops. Pope John XXIII had indicated early in his pontificate his hope of completing the unfinished work of Vatican I, which defined papal primacy but dispersed before finishing its agenda. He also showed in various ways that he regarded himself as a bishop among bishops, and not only as ecumenical bishop. Yet when the collegiality of bishops was first proposed in the Council's discussions, many bishops reacted strongly against it as an idea too novel to be taken seriously, and one, moreover, which threatened the primacy and infallibility of the Pope. In the course of the discussion most of these objections were answered. It became clear that the scriptural basis for collegiality was at least as impressive as the evidence for papal primacy and infallibility. The charge of novelty was disposed of, and it was shown that collegiality has a venerable history in the ancient church, and was not unknown in the latter history of the western church.

In the course of the discussion the bishops were persuaded that collegiality was a proper expression of their common responsibility for the welfare of the whole church, and that it provided a possible corrective to the unbalanced working out of the 1870 decree in the direction of curial centralization and domination. Bishops from the eastern rites heralded collegiality as a necessary step toward recovering the riches of unity in diversity, riches frequently overlooked in recent centuries because of the dominance of Latin rite discipline and ways of thinking. Unity, they insisted, was not to be seen as uniformity, but as a broad, rich, and complex mystery accompanying the Spirit's gifts to the church.

This view of unity had special attractiveness to those who were aware of the different problems confronting the church in various parts of the world. The problems of the church in Africa differ from those of the church in Latin America, Canada, India, or Poland. Many bishops were convinced that these problems could not be solved by decrees handed down by the Roman Curia, which was not informed on the concrete realities of local situations, and in some cases was suspected of being unsympathetic to the procedure of confronting problems, but required for their solution knowledge of the local situation and the special gifts or insights of the regional church. Collegiality was also viewed with favor by those who harbored the suspicion that papal infallibility, although carefully qualified by the decisions of Vatican I to apply only to decisions of the Pope speaking *ex cathedra,* had been extended by curial officials to mean in practice curial infallibility, and this with virtually no qualification.

Although the discussion of collegiality attracted greatest attention during the debate at the Council, at least four other areas of concern caught the interest of the bishops.

In his address to the Curia on Sept. 21, 1963, Pope Paul suggested that "Should the ecumenical council evince a desire of seeing some representatives of the episcopacy . . . associated . . . with the supreme head of the church in the study and responsibility of ecclesiastical government, the Curia will surely not oppose it." The suggestion was not lost on the bishops. Beginning with the discussion of the schema on Administration of Dioceses and continuing to the end of the session, they expressed their approval of the plan frequently, gave numerous reasons for its adoption, and were eager to speed its formation. The traditionalists opposed it, chiefly on the ground that it threatened the authority of the Pope, but being fewer in number and less persuasive in argument, they had to rely on maneuver in committee to make their point. The discussion of the

Senate of bishops became so important a part of the expectation of the progressive majority that the delay of papal action in this matter led to widespread fear that the Pope was either unable to make up his mind or was the captive of the immobilists in the Curia. When the announcement of the Episcopal Synod was made at the opening general convention of the fourth session in 1965, it came as a kind of anticlimax and was greeted with much less enthusiasm than might have been expected. It was only later in the session, when the Pope had shown that he could act decisively, that the bishops began to realize how important the new agency might be.

National or regional conferences of bishops also came in for much discussion. These conferences are comparatively recent in origin and provide a forum in which bishops of a country or region can discuss common problems. Theologians at the Council pointed out that the definition of collegiality probably required some stress upon episcopal conferences, for otherwise the swing from overcentralized administration might lead to excessive decentralization. They suggested that power should not be concentrated either in Rome or in the diocese, but the principle of subsidiarity should be followed, permitting the local administrative unit to do whatever it can do well, and reserving for the regional or central administration only the elements that require the coordination or cooperation of larger groups. Three points of view quickly became apparent. There were those, like Cardinal McIntyre of Los Angeles, who opposed giving any real power to episcopal conferences, preferring to divide authority between Rome and the diocesan bishop. Others, like Cardinal Meyer of Chicago, favored an arrangement in which the decisions of the conference should be morally but not juridically binding on the bishops. This was probably the largest group at the Council. Cardinal Ritter of St. Louis became the spokesman of those who were convinced that regional conferences needed real authority and should make decisions binding on the member bishops.

A third topic, and one which generated some heat, was the question of a retirement age for bishops. Cardinal Suenens of Brussels urged that a mandatory retirement age of 65 for bishops be established and argued that its necessity was obvious. You have only to look at dioceses headed by aged bishops, he pointed out, to see how much damage the church suffers. Some thought that 75 was a better age for retirement. Others argued that ancient tradition requires election for life, and that a bishop could always resign if ill health prevented him from doing his work. And some pointed to the advanced age of Pope John XXIII and Cardinal Bea, suggesting that the blessings of their work in the Council and church would have been lost had a retirement rule been in force. In the end the bishops were to do nothing about setting a retirement age, and thereby deprived Pope Paul of a useful tool to aid him in the reorganization of the Roman Curia for which so many were asking.

Criticism of the Curia and proposals for curial reorganization were also heard frequently in the aula during these days. At first there were only mildly irritated questions about the appropriateness of language granting faculties to bishops. If collegiality were ancient Catholic practice, as the Council fathers were hearing at this time, then the faculties belonged to them by right, and did not come as concessions from a generous Curia. Criticism became more tart when Eastern rite bishops complained of discrimination, of the dominance of Latin discipline and Roman managerial techniques. But it became sharp and specific when Cardinal Frings on November 8, 1963, singled out the supreme curial congregation, the Holy Office, for criticism for confusing administrative roles with legislative ones, for the secrecy and arbitrariness of its procedures, and for methods and behavior which "do not at all conform to the modern era and are a cause of scandal to the world." The burst of applause which greeted his words made it plain that he was not alone in holding these opinions. The angry reply of Cardinal Ottaviani, the secretary of the Holy Office, twenty minutes later heightened the drama, but did nothing to diminish the effect of Cardinal Frings's statement. From this point to the end of the second session bishops were quite frank in discussing the need for reorganization of the Curia, for bringing diocesan bishops from all over the world into positions within it, for reducing its function as a policy-making body, and for making use of the special training and skills of laymen. The report that Cardinal Frings had received assurances of Pope Paul's approval of his speech did nothing to discourage such discussion.

The preliminary discussion on the schema came to an end on November 15, 1963. The document was approved in principle and sent back to the commission for redrafting it in the light of the nine days' discussion. The revised document was discussed for four days during the third session, September 18-23, 1964, and received general approval. It was expected that the commission would submit the amended text during the same session, especially as the third was expected to be the closing session of the Council. Its failure to appear caused some anxiety, and gave rise to rumors that the document was being tampered with again, that the curial contingent on the commission had altered the definition of collegiality and the relation of the bishops to the Pope. As these rumors coincided with an unwelcome explanatory note to chapter 3 of the schema on the Church, alterations to the text of the decree on Ecumenism, and the postponement of even a preliminary vote on the Declaration on Religious Liberty, they added to the sense of disappointment and frustration with which the third session ended. Many of the bishops returned home anxious about the intentions of the Pope and deeply concerned about the Curia's repeated frustration of the will of the conciliar majority.

The fourth session of the Council began on the same note of uncertainty. The promise of the last session had been kept, and the Declaration on Religious Liberty was the first item on the agenda. But many bishops, knowing how the traditionalists detested and feared the declaration, wondered whether it would actually come to a vote. The papal encyclical *Mysterium Fidei*, which had appeared three days before the opening of the session, contained a number of disturbing statements and raised questions about the Pope's understanding of the theology of the Council. Pope Paul's opening address, which seemed an attempt at the style of Pope John XXIII, did little to dispel doubts or relieve anxieties. It was therefore a surprise when the Pope attended the opening congregation of the session, coming in on foot through the north transept with only two attendants, taking his place among the presidents of the Council and remaining for the reading of his *motu proprio* announcing the establishment of the synod of bishops. The bishops had another surprise when the schema on the Pastoral Office of Bishops was distributed. It showed no traces of tampering or of the kind of conspiratorial activity so widely rumored during the previous session of the Council.

## B. The Text of the Decree

The decree is comparatively brief, consisting of a preface and three chapters, dealing respectively with the relationship of bishops to the universal church, the bishop in his diocese, and the cooperation of bishops for the good of many churches. The preface asserts the primacy of the Pope and the collegiality of the bishops, who are united in a body together with the Pope and under his authority. In this relationship they carry out their work as teachers, rulers, and pastors of the church through the Holy Spirit.

The opening chapter summarizes the teaching of chapter 3 of the Constitution on the Church, and touches briefly upon two manifestations of collegiality, the Synod of Bishops, through which selected bishops from all over the world serve in a deliberative body to assist the Pope in governing the church, and the expression of mutual love and responsibility in the work of missions, in mutual assistance in understaffed areas of the church, and in concern for poor, imprisoned, or persecuted bishops. The chapter also proposes the reorganization of the Roman Curia to adapt it better to the needs of the times. It urges especially the internationalization of the curial offices in order to express the truly universal character of the church, and the desirability of drawing in diocesan bishops to take advantage of their experience and insight. It also suggests that ways be found to utilize the knowledge and experience of laymen, so that they too may have their proper share in church affairs.

The second chapter is notable for two things: its stress upon the pastoral and servant character of the episcopal office, and its emphasis upon adaptation. The bishop is above all a pastor, responsible to all men, including those who do not belong to the church. He must be concerned with persons, especially the priests of his diocese, including those who have lapsed; he is to foster ecumenism by dealing graciously with separated brethren; and he is to give special attention to those who are not easily reached by the parish organization, such as travelers, migrants, gypsies, and exiles. In his pastoral and catechetical work he must be sensitive to the need for adaptation to the times, being willing to learn from the social and psychological sciences, and being open to new methods and experimentation.

The third chapter establishes the rules for Episcopal Conferences. It threads a careful way through this difficult ground, encouraging national and regional conferences, providing for a good deal of local authority in drawing up regulations, allowing the conference to have as much authority as the majority of its members desires to give it, and at the same time safeguarding the special responsibilities of bishops in charge of dioceses and the rights of the Holy See. It makes a cautious gesture toward the Eastern rite Catholic churches, urging them to remember the common good of territories where many rites coexist and encouraging interchange of views among the Eastern rite churches themselves.

Compared to the draft of 1963 with its dominantly administrative concern, its juridical tone, and its preoccupation with curial control, the present decree is obviously a great improvement. It has a much better understanding of what the church is, for it has learned much from the discussions of the Constitution on the Church. It has a more consistently pastoral tone, showing that the many lectures on pastoral theology by bishops at the Council were not offered in vain. It breathes concern for persons, and has a positive, ecumenical mood in sharp contrast to preconciliar attitudes of aloofness and suspicion. It provides the structures to make collegiality a reality and not only a theological vision. Its emphasis upon adaptation, experimentation, and receptivity to the work of modern science encourages openness and flexibility on the part of bishops, many of whom heard of these things for the first time during the Council. To the extent that it reinforces the experience of the Council in the work of bishops it will be of real assistance in the renewal of the Roman Catholic Church.

A Lutheran who has observed the remarkable developments within the Roman Catholic Church is of course impressed by many things and grateful for them. He is even moved to reflect on ways of developing the same kind of self-criticism and inner renewal in the churches of the Reformation. The new atmosphere of openness and friendship means that topics formerly handled in a polemical way can now be discussed in sympathy and candor. It is clear gain that the antipathies and resentments between the churches can give way to friendliness, for it offers the hope that some of the barriers between the churches can be removed. For example, the emotional barriers of fear, suspicion, resentment, and hostility may in the course of a generation largely disappear, permitting the cultural and theological differences to be discussed in a dispassionate atmosphere. But it is perhaps of some importance to note that even if the emotional and cultural factors have been properly discounted, the theological issues separating Roman Catholics and the tradition of the Reformation are still formidable. Some of the issues have become less divisive in the last century, largely through the contribution of biblical and historical studies in the churches. The doctrine of the Lord's Supper, for example, appears in a somewhat different light today because of light shed by theological studies. But the difficulties concerning the papacy and episcopacy have increased rather than lessened in modern times, and the contribution of the Second Vatican Council has been ambivalent in this respect.

## C. Some Questions Addressed to the Decree

1. The papacy remains a point of sharp difference between Roman Catholics and Lutherans, a difference aggravated by the definition of papal infallibility at the first Vatican Council. When the Roman Catholic states that the Pope has "supreme, full, immediate and universal authority by divine institution" and therefore "a primacy of ordinary power over all the churches," the Lutheran is perplexed. Even when he has been instructed as to what the words say and do not say, he cannot comprehend this assertion as the testimony of the Scriptures or any inference validly drawn from them. The use of Matt. 16:16-19, Luke 22:32, John 21:15-19 and other passages does not seem a convincing exegetical foundation for so far-reaching a doctrine of papal authority. For even if the Roman Catholic interpretation of the passages concerning the person and office of Peter were to be granted, a point that exegetes of the tradition of the Reformation find less than persuasive, it would still remain to demonstrate the succession from Peter to the bishop of Rome, a point not obvious from the Scriptures and not without historical difficulties as well.

Many who stand in the Reformation heritage would be willing

to grant that the bishop of Rome has historical credentials to serve as an ecumenical bishop, as a symbol of the unity of the church. They are ready to acknowledge the services of the papacy to the church through the centuries and to grant the Pope the "superiority over the bishops which he possesses by human right, making this concession for the sake of peace and general unity among Christians," as Melanchthon added in his subscription to the Schmalkald Articles. But to claim this as of divine right, as the clear teaching of the Scriptures, and as necessary to the faith of the Christian seems an overstatement of the position which is in danger of turning historical relativities into divine absolutes.

The problem of infallibility can also be recognized as a valid theological concern. The people of God ought to be alert to the problem of continuity in the Gospel. It is essential that the authentic Gospel be proclaimed, that the same Lord Jesus Christ who was crucified and raised from the dead be present as the Lord of the church. Protestants realize from their own history how the yearning for authority and assurance leads churchmen to reach out for absolutes: an infallible Bible, a perfectly integrated system of doctrine, a correct church discipline, an authentic personal experience, or the charismatic gifts of the Spirit. All of them are worthy aspirations, but the assurance of the church and of the individual Christian is ultimately trust and confidence in the God who raises the dead, and no other source of confidence can or ought to replace this faith. The only absolute is God, and he is known and possessed only in faith; the other assurances have their proper relative value but must not be confused with the ultimate assurance who is God himself.

2. Episcopacy is a second persisting problem. As a form of church government episcopacy holds few terrors for Lutherans. Many Lutheran churches have episcopal polity, in the case of the Church of Sweden an episcopal government going back to the first missionaries to the north countries. They respect and value bishops as a sign of the continuity of the church with its apostolic origins, and should not have to swallow hard to accept episcopacy, properly defined, as a condition of a future reunion of the churches. But they have serious difficulties with the statement that bishops

are successors of the apostles and that the authority given by Jesus Christ to the apostles is now exercised by them. This statement needs qualification to be acceptable as a scriptural and evangelical position.

To say that the apostles have successors is indeed true, but not without qualification.

a. The apostles exercised a ministry which was in one respect unique: they had been with Jesus from his baptism by John through his ministry up to the cross and were witnesses of the resurrection (Acts 1:21, 22). As such they laid the foundation of the church through their witness to Jesus the Messiah and by baptizing believers into a new relationship to him. This ministry of laying the foundations of the church belongs to the apostles alone and was not handed on to successors.

b. The authority given by Jesus Christ to the apostles was a delegated authority with conditions. They were responsible for handing on the sound doctrine concerning Jesus Christ, to correct those who went astray in their preaching and teaching, and to oppose all false teaching that obscured the glory of Jesus Christ, the Son of God. They possessed authority from Christ himself so that he who received the apostle received his Lord and he who opposed the apostle opposed Christ. But this authority is not without limits; it is authority under Jesus Christ and subject to the terms given by him. The apostle has no message of his own; his message is that of Christ himself. And therefore the one called to be an apostle is an apostle only so long as he responds to God's invitation. If he develops projects of his own unrelated to his commission from God, he does so as a private individual and not as an apostle. And if he changes his message and announces something other than the good news of God, he has ceased to act as an apostle. The same conditions apply to those commissioned by apostles to preach the Gospel, whether they are designated bishops, presbyters, evangelists, or catechists. Their authority depends upon their proclamation of the apostolic Gospel as transmitted in the apostolic tradition, a tradition codified in the course of time in the church as the Scriptures. Those commissioned by the apostles are faithful to their calling only as they stand in the apostolic tradition, and this faithfulness is measured in the post-apostolic times by the canon of the Scriptures. The Gospel of Jesus Christ as preserved and witnessed to in the Scriptures is the standard, guide, and judge of those entrusted with the apostolic message.

c. Those who, qualified in this way, are appointed to carry on apostolic functions in the church include, according to the New Testament, not only bishops but presbyters as well. In the New Testament the terms bishop and presbyter are applied interchangeably to the same group of church leaders. If we are to speak in this qualified way of the successors of the apostles, there is no theological reason for limiting them to those today designated bishops. The selection of certain "metropolitans" from among the presbyters and the custom of reserving the title of bishop for them are later developments resulting from a variety of factors in the life of the early church. The custom is a venerable one and can be respected as such, but to claim divine authority for it seems to go beyond the evidence. If we are to speak of collegiality in the leadership of the church, it would seem more appropriate from a biblical standpoint to speak of the collegiality of presbyters. It would seem to be especially appropriate in our day when the office of bishop has become a dominantly administrative task and the preaching, teaching, and pastoral tasks are actually carried out by presbyters. It is the whole body of ministers, called to the proclamation of the Gospel and the administration of the sacraments, who are the successors of the apostles under obedience to the apostolic Gospel.

Limiting the authority to teach, govern, and sanctify to the bishops not only deprives the presbyter of his proper responsibility and authority and his proper share in the collegial ministry, it also reduces the role of the laity to insignificant dimensions. The New Testament knows a varied ministry ranging through apostles, prophets, evangelists, teachers, workers of miracles, healers, administrators, speakers and interpreters of tongues (Eph. 4:11, 1 Cor. 12:28), not all of them clergymen in the modern sense of the term. The historical development in church life has concentrated all the ministries in the hierarchical priesthood, with a resultant loss of diversity, the growth of clericalism, and widespread apathy among laymen. The decisions of Vatican II hold out some hopes of improving this situation, but the ailment is sufficiently serious to require both strong medicine and a prolonged course of treatment.

Another consequence of the narrowing of the ministries to the hierarchical priesthood is the loss of effective communication between bishop and priests and clergy and laity. This communication is not only desirable for the effective functioning of the community of believers, it is essential as a check upon the ministry of the hierarchy. Since even bishops are sinners and therefore capable of moral insensitivity, theological misunderstanding, and even disobedience, it is necessary that bishops too be subject to checks and judgments. It is not enough to speak of prophetic charisms in the church. Unless there are structures through which the voice of prophecy can be heard in the church, there is great danger that bishops may lose contact with the vivifying and judging power of the Word of God. The jest that a bishop never has a bad meal, reads a good book, or hears the truth has at least this much substance: authorities may easily be surrounded by underlings who tell them only what they want to hear.

d. It seems strange that, given this complex set of relationships between apostles and present-day bishops, the latter should be so confidently defined as possessing by divine institution apostolic authority to teach, govern, and sanctify the church. The assertion does not find support in the Scriptures or in any conclusion properly drawn from them. If it is to be supported by observations drawn from the history of the early church, it can only be on the basis of a doctrine of development which does not appear to be at hand even in the Roman Catholic Church. The churches of the Reformation can grant that there is development, that the Holy Spirit may guide the church to the adoption of practices which were not known in the church of the first century, as, for example, infant baptism. But they would insist that such developments be continuous and natural developments out of the apostolic Gospel, and not contrary to the Gospel. Nor should such developments be designated as being of divine institution. Useful, yes, and venerable, advantageous and edifying, but still not qualifying for the designation "by divine institution."

Two further considerations occur to the Lutheran pondering this subject. The first is pragmatic and sociological. The study of power structures in contemporary society has shown that a variety of forms of administration can be used to get things done. There is no form of government which is best or most effective *a priori* or in the abstract. A certain form of government may be best in a given historical situation and a different form prove more adaptable in another situation. The early Christian community used the administrative resources which were available, adapting Palestinian forms in the Palestinian setting and Hellenistic forms in Hellenistic culture. Since the Reformation, episcopal, presbyterian, and congregational forms, with variations of each, have been used in the church of Christ. Under all of them men have heard the Gospel, come to living faith, experienced the work of the Holy Spirit, and responded to the will of God in worship and the service of the neighbor. Inasmuch as the church has in its history used different forms of government and has done its work effectively through all of the different forms, it seems unrealistic to insist that only one of them permits the effective communication of the Gospel.

Another question, a historical one, is raised by the history of the Reformation. It is now acknowledged by Roman Catholic exegetes, to say nothing of dogmatic theologians, that Luther interpreted Paul's message correctly. Since there seems to be little doubt that Paul's position is catholic, it should follow that Luther's interpretation of him could be accepted as catholic too. Yet when a loyal son of the church, out of concern for the welfare of his parishioners, objected to manifest abuses in the discipline of the church, and appealed to Paul in support of his position, he was threatened, rebuked, and finally excommunicated. It is of course obvious that the situation was a very complicated one, involving national, social, political, and economic as well as disciplinary and theological factors ranging all the way from the emperor's political problems to the mortgage on St. Peter's. But if an office is of divine institution, it should work under difficult conditions. There was no shortage of bishops in the sixteenth century, and the controversies were protracted enough to allow time to examine the questions carefully, but no bishops spoke up for what is now acknowledged to be in accord with the Gospel, and the result was the painful and offensive divisions of the church. One can only conclude that if episcopacy is the divinely given office for the preservation of the unity, truth, and holiness of the church, something was seriously wrong with it in the sixteenth century. In the circumstances one may understand why the reformers examined not only the structure of episcopacy but raised questions about its theological foundations as well.

The ecumenical movement has made Lutheran theologians aware of the fact that church order involves both practical and theological problems, and that they are far from being solved within the Lutheran tradition. The study of the history of Lutheran theology and church order has shown how many complicating factors there are, and also how many different situations exist even within the Lutheran family. The basic approach to the problem, however, remains that of Article 7 of the Augsburg Confession which affirms that for the unity of the church it is sufficient to agree on the teaching of the Gospel and the administration of the sacraments. What is essential to the church is the presence of God in Christ. Through word and sacrament he grants ever anew his preserving, redeeming, regal presence to call the church into being, to renew its life, and to equip it to carry out his work in the world. Within this understanding of the bases of the church's life, episcopacy can be recognized as a useful structure for giving expression to the continuity of the contemporary church with the church of apostolic times. As a historical development within the church, the bishop can also be seen as a ministry or service of teaching, administration, and pastoral concern and also as an expression of the ecumenical solidarity of God's people in the world. To say more than this is to formulate a definition which in the light of the present condition of historical studies seems at least premature, if not also a confusion of the divine institution of the church with some of the historically developed structures which have served it in the course of its history.

Chapter IV

# Priests and Laymen

The discussion of ecclesiology occupied the center of attention at the Second Vatican Council. Thus it is not surprising that the question of the hierarchy was thoroughly discussed. In this discussion the Council tried not only to arrive at a clear definition of the relationship between pope and bishops and to come to a new evaluation of the true essence of the office of the bishop, but it also published a decree on the ministry and life of the presbyters (De Presbyterorum Ministerio et Vita).

Father Yves Congar has correctly called our attention to the fact that the question of the priestly office presents a great, if not decisive, hindrance in the dialogue between Catholics and Protestants and often makes it difficult to arrive at a mutually satisfactory understanding. He voiced his own personal opinion when he said that this chasm could be overcome even though it was a deep chasm.[1]

As we begin to study the ecclesiological decisions of the Council, we will soon be confronted by this question. Indeed, most of what has been criticized in Catholic ecclesiology during the era of the Reformation is connected in one way or another with the problem of the hierarchy. What used to be identified as "church" in medieval theology was all too often the same as "hierarchy" and its official function. This state of affairs remained in effect also after the Reformation and has become more pronounced to such an extent that even Catholic theologians have been disturbed by the one-sided emphasis on the hierarchy.[2]

Therefore, we shall ask how the Council has overcome this problem. We shall ask especially whether these new developments may lead eventually to a diminishing of the differences. In order to be able to give an answer to this question and to see more clearly the profile of the Catholic concept of the ministry, we shall discuss the decree on the priesthood together with the decree on the apostolate of the laity *(De Apostolatu Laicorum)*, for by relating the priesthood to the laity and by showing the boundaries between the two in regard to their essence and their special mission we shall arrive at the clarification of the problem of the "hierarchy."

A comparative study of the priesthood and the laity is not only of importance for the clarification of the position of the reformers. The very fact that for the first time in the history of the Roman Catholic Church a council has tried to define the essence of "the lay apostolate" is quite important. In both decrees there are a great number of references to each other. Our investigation of necessity will examine the theological relevance of the relationship between the priesthood and the laity.

May I be permitted to make one more preliminary remark. Although primarily we will occupy ourselves with the above-named two decrees, we will have to make reference in the theological evaluation of these decrees also to other decisions of the Council. This holds true especially of the constitution, Light of the Nations *(Lumen Gentium)*. In this basic ecclesiological document the Council has retained the dogmatic bases for the hierarchy and the laity (Chapters III and IV). In the decrees concerning the priesthood and the lay apostolate we have merely a further elaboration of this position. In this connection it is not unimportant to ask in which sense the new beginnings on the basis of the concept of the people of God (Chapter II) means also a new beginning concerning the definition of priests and laymen. It may be helpful to note here that the word "lay" is originally derived from the word "*laos*" which means people and thus essentially is based on the concept of the church as the people of God. If we want to understand the concept "priesthood" correctly, we cannot pass by this fact.

## The Mission of the Church and of the Hierarchy

The salvation of the world has been accomplished and has been given through the sending of the incarnate Son of God, Jesus Christ, into the world. A traditional school of Catholic theology sees in the sending of Jesus Christ the origin of the hierarchy. "As thou didst send me into the world, so I have sent them into the world" (John 17:18). This passage from the high priestly prayer of our Lord represents, according to Catholic interpretation, the basis for the doctrine of the chain of succession which preserves the hierarchy throughout the ages. God the Father sent his Son who in turn chose the apostles to whom he entrusted the passing on of his divine mission. "This divine mission, entrusted to the apostles by Christ, is going to last until the end of the world (cf. Mt. 28.20), since the gospel which they have to transmit is the principle of all life for the Church for all time. This is the reason that in this society with its hierarchical arrangement, the apostles took care to arrange the appointment of successors."[3] The succession in the apostolic office is thus the responsible agency which brings salvation to the whole world.

Thus the words "this society with its hierarchical arrangement" mean the college of the apostles with Peter as its head and his successor the Roman pope. The apostles made provision for the fact that bishops should be appointed, who acting as their successors would take care of the appointment of priests. This chain of succession exists only on the episcopal level of authority, for priests are not in a position to pass on the mission of Christ to others. All priestly authority is centered in the bishops. The parish priests are merely delegated by the bishops to take care of their ministry in their absence in the congregation.[4] Only by way of the bishops, that is through the mediation of the chain of succession which is nearest to him, can a priest be considered as a person who "in his own way assumes the person of Christ himself."[5]

The distinction between the episcopal office and the office of the priest has played an important part in the discussions of the Second Vatican Council. The fact that the episcopal office increased in stature during the Council can be seen in the fact that it was recognized as a sacrament, although no attempt was made to distinguish it from the sacrament of ordination. Both bishop and priest are still under the one sacrament, but here exists the possibility that the episcopal office in a further development may finally be recognized by a special sacrament.[6]

It is in keeping with this hierarchical structure of the church when the bishops of the world form a college under the direction of the pope. To this college corresponds on the diocesan level the presbytery of the priests under the direction of their bishop.[7] In asking about the relationship between pope and bishop the problem of authority has been recognized and there is a tendency to consider the bishops not merely as delegates of the pope. But this problem has not been discussed in defining the relationship between the bishops and the priests. The priests do not have "the high dignity of the pontificate; they are dependent on Bishops for the exercise of their power," although they are united with their bishops "in priestly honour." However, in the local parishes they are merely "prudent co-operators of the episcopal order."[8]

The regular parish priest, you might say, is merely the representative of the bishop. We must ask in this connection whether this interpretation preserves a remnant of the understanding of the episcopacy in the ancient church. If this is the case, who then are the "priests" who are carrying on the ministry in a specified place, in a specified parish? The question must be asked whether this new stature given to the office of the bishop during the Second Vatican Council has not led to a concentration of the ecclesiastical office in the person of the bishop notwithstanding all assurances of the priestly dignity of the parish priest. This can, of course, be the fault of the doctrine of apostolic succession in the office of the bishop, for it is the bishops who are under succession and not the priests. They are merely caretakers of an office which is included in the episcopal office, and it is delegated by the bishops to the priests.

This definition of the hierarchy in the frame of reference of apostolic succession has led to a separation of the office from the people of God. Such a hierarchy is quite independent. It continues to develop in isolation and forms the counterpart to the people.[9] On the basis of this view, the priestly office has been identified with the authority of Christ in the church.[10] In this definition is, of course, included the idea that the office is concerned with the people of

God, for the mission of the hierarchy to the world includes also its mission to the people of God. But this definition means the loss of the ecclesiological basic structure of the office of the priesthood. This change from a church-centered concept of the office to a hierarchical has led to the result that "ecclesia" is identified simply with "hierarchy." This change which we know from the history of dogma and which is opposed to the emphasis of the ancient church upon the office has been accepted without criticism by the Council as part and parcel of the theological tradition of the Catholic Church.

In recent Catholic ecclesiology there has been for some time a certain uneasiness about this one-sided emphasis on the office of the priesthood, although this concept retains in fullest measure the doctrine of the church as an "institution of salvation" (Heilsanstalt). It is recognized that the church is also a "communion of salvation" (Heilsgemeinschaft). The institutional aspect of the church has been preserved completely in the hierarchical structure of the church, but the communion aspect must also be emphasized because the church finds its fulfillment only when the Holy Spirit edifies people to become the temple of God.[11] In that event the church is no longer identical merely with the hierarchy, but with the people of God called from among the nations by the Word of God and by living the sacramental life.

During the discussions of the Council a new understanding could be felt when the dogmatic constitution *Lumen Gentium* was being considered. In the description of the concept of the people of God (Ch. II) there is a reference to the basic passage from Holy Scriptures concerning the "chosen race, a royal priesthood" (1 Peter 2:9-10). In this connection we must consider the specific New Testament emphasis which does not equate priesthood with hierarchy, but with the believers as the chosen people of God.[12] This messianic race which proclaims the wonderful deeds of God and brings spiritual sacrifices acceptable to God is recognized as "the instrument of salvation" *(instrumentum redemptionis)*. Thus we read in *Lumen Gentium:* "Although this messianic People does not in fact embrace all men, and more than one has had the appearance of a tiny flock, for all that, it has the toughness of the rising shoot of unity, hope and salvation for the whole human race. It is founded by Christ for a fellowship of life, charity and truth. It is taken up by him as the instrument of salvation for all men. It is sent on mission to the world at large as the light of the world and the salt of the earth (Cf. Mt. 5, 13-16)."[13] Here we have a clear recognition of the people of God as primary instruments of the mission of salvation in contrast to the mission of the hierarchy which we have discussed above. This passage has an important influence upon the definition of the role of the laymen in the church and also upon the understanding of the special priestly office.

The terminology of the "lay apostolate" has taken firm hold of the Roman Catholic Church during the last generation. Originally it occupied a subordinate position below the hierarchical apostolate. Thus Pius XI defined it as "the participation of the laity in the hierarchical apostolate."[14] This interpretation of the lay apostolate was fully in line with the thinking of the church concerning the hierarchical apostolic succession. But during the Second Vatican Council the concept of the people of God was forcefully freed from this narrow confinement. In the introductory chapter to the decree on the lay apostolate we read, "The Church was founded for the purpose of spreading the kingdom of Christ throughout the earth for the glory of God the Father, to enable all men to share in His saving redemption, and that through them the whole world might enter into a relationship with Christ. All activity of the mystical body directed to the attainment of this goal is called the apostolate, which the Church carries on in various ways through all her members. For the Christian vocation by its very nature is also a vocation to the apostolate."[15] It may well be true that this apostolate is still being considered an office that is carried on "in various ways," but in this document the primary emphasis is on "Christian vocation." This can only refer to baptism, because the royal priesthood which has its origin in baptism is described in the next paragraph (paragraph 3) in very adequate terms.

The statement that there are differences in the administration of the apostolate is based on the differences of the ministries which are performed in the body of Christ. This is a perfectly legitimate biblical concept. It does not interfere with the unity of the mission of the church. "In the Church there is a diversity of ministry but a oneness of mission."[16] There can be no doubt that this passage does not refer to the hierarchical mission of the church, for in *De ecclesia* we read, "Layfolk . . . is engaged in the Church and in the world, in their allotted role in the mission of the whole christian people."[17] In keeping with this statement the scope of the mission is described thus: "They exercise the apostolate in fact by their activity directed to the evangelism and sanctification of men and to the penetrating and perfecting of the temporal orders through the spirit of Gospel. In this way, their temporal activity openly bears witness to Christ and promotes the salvation of men."[18] This means that this passage speaks of an apostolate which is not a one-sided hierarchical apostolate, but an apostolate which is understood as having its origin in the mission of the people of God. The fact that there are various levels in this common mission which are based on various ministries and offices does not militate against the unity of the apostolate.

Thus the discussions of the Council about the lay apostolate have opened up once more the problem of a special priestly office within the church. The attention of the Catholic Church has been directed to an aspect in the doctrine of the church which during the Reformation had been attacked as representing a one-sided hierarchical idea of the office. Thus, for example, Luther emphasized again and again that the ecclesiastical office is so intimately intertwined with the congregation of God that the bearers of the office act "in its name."[19] With this statement Luther did not mean the modern concept of a democratically structured congregation which looks upon its officers as its executives, although he wanted to criticize a concept which looks upon the hierarchy as independent of the body of Christ as it carries out its mission for the church in the world. Not only the fact that the office is made for men must be recognized in this criticism, but also the reality of a congregation that has been called in baptism in which every believer on the basis of his faith must bear the responsibility on his part for the proclamation of the Gospel and the administration of the sacrament.[20]

Luther arrived at these conclusions because as far as he was concerned the authority *(potestas)* for the exercise of the apostolate is based on baptism. Against this definition it is clear that in the Roman Catholic Church the *"potestas"* is based on the consecration which takes place in ordination. Therefore when Luther says that the ecclesiastical office must be carried on "in our name," that is in the name of the people of God, he wants to indicate that *"potestas"* is not something that is added to baptism but is included in baptism. This *"potestas"* is not based on the consensus of the church but is bestowed in the sacrament of baptism by the Lord of the church himself. He, the Lord, has given this office and the congregation calls into this office its servants. By saying that this office belongs to "us" Luther wants to point to the ecclesiological meaning of the office, to the inclusion of the body of Christ in the functions of this office. This is the case so that Christ may be really Lord of this office and not a certain privileged hierarchy.[21] For Christ never exists without his body which is the church. It is a strange feature of Catholic thinking that also this statement is recognized again and again. There has developed throughout the centuries of history of dogma a bias according to which Christ is considered merely as the head of the hierarchy. The recognition that the church as a whole has a mission in this world raises a big question mark about this dogma without however casting radical doubt upon the formal teaching of the church as had been done for example during the period of the Reformation. In any case, the introduction of this new element of thought opens up some possibilities that the understanding of the Reformation will be more highly esteemed and will be considered to be of some value.[22]

## The Office of Christ and the Office of the Church

As the Father sent his Son into the world, in the same manner the Son sends the apostles into the world (Cf. John 17:18; 20:21). The combination of these two missions has a strange implication for Catholic theology, for this does not only lead to an identification of the bearer of the office with Christ, since for this identification other words of the Lord can be used (e.g. Luke 10:16; Matt. 18:18, etc.)[23] but Catholic theology considers that the parallel actions of the sending of the apostles and of the sending of the Son includes also the transference of the office of Jesus Christ to his apostles and their successors who are the bishops. In this way the ministry of reconciliation which has been entrusted to Jesus Christ is continuing. Thus the incarnation continues in the church based on the work of the apostles. Christ himself is present here on earth in the bishops and they continue his office. Thus Catholic theology builds its interpretation of the episcopal priestly office upon its understanding of the office of Christ.[24]

The documents of the Council give clear expression to this emphasis. The connection between the office of Christ and the office of the priesthood is described in the following way: "Priests in virtue of the Order they have received and the mission entrusted to them by the bishops are ordained to serve Christ their Master, Priest and King, and to share his ministry. Thus the Church on earth is constantly built up into the People of God, the Body of Christ and Temple of the Holy Spirit."[25]

In order that we may understand the Catholic concept of the priesthood it is important to shed some light on the close connection of this concept with Catholic Christology, for the office of the church is dogmatically described in analogy with the office of Christ.

From the passage that has just been quoted it is clear that the office of Christ is understood in the threefold way *(munus triplex)*. He is Master, Priest, and King. It was not until the last century that this threefold division was accepted in Catholic theology,[26] whereas it had played an important part in the old Protestant Christology. In the patristic tradition there was only a concept of a twofold office of Christ which certainly is more in harmony with the biblical statements, for in the New Testament Christ is called both King and Priest. These two designations are found in the identification of the Old Testament people of God with the New Testament people of God.[27] If we are looking for a biblical foundation for the transferal of the offices of Christ, then only this one parallel is found. In this connection it must be emphasized that these offices were not transferred to the hierarchy but to the people of God.[28] The transferal of the offices of Christ to the hierarchy is the result of a special interpretation by Catholic theology. This Catholic emphasis is closely connected with the narrowing down of the concept of the church. It is only logical on the basis of this emphasis that after Catholic theology had taken over the dogma of the three offices of Christ from Protestant dogmatics it applied this doctrine immediately to its concept of the priesthood.

The priesthood is thus a combination of the threefold office of

Christ—of the prophetic, priestly, and royal offices. The Catholic concept of the office ascribes to this office three authorities *(potestates)*, namely, the authority to teach, the authority to sanctify, and the authority to rule *(potestas docendi, sanctificandi et regendi)*. This authority originates with Christ who made the apostles participate in it *(participes effecit)*. The apostles have passed on this power to the bishops who are considered their legitimate successors. However, when the bishops pass on this authority in the sacrament of ordination to the priests they do this only "in a lesser degree" *(subordinato gradu)*. But even in this diminished passing on of authority it is still a participation in the authority of Christ. "The priestly office, joined as it is to that of the bishop, shares the authority by which Christ himself builds up, sanctifies and rules this Body."[29]

In Chapter II of the decree on the priesthood these three offices of the priests are described in some detail.

To the prophetic office, which on the highest hierarchical level is the *magisterium* of the church, corresponds on the level of the priesthood the proclamation of the Word of God (Par. 4). Even though we may be justified by objecting to the concept of the *magisterium* in this concrete application in the Roman Catholic Church, we must rejoice and confess with satisfaction that a valid foundation has been given to the ministry of the Word.[30] Whereas formerly the priestly office was one-sidedly described as an office of sacrifice, we must duly acknowledge that in this decree for the sake of the awakening of faith ( Rom. 10:17 *fides ex auditu* is quoted) the sermon of the priests has been given a central position. Of course, we could ask a number of questions about the meaning of this "priestly" proclamation, for certainly the decree does not mean only the call to the office of preaching, but it also applies here certain strictures to the sermon of the priest. Yet we will note with special recognition that the service of preaching is considered an essential part of the divine service and that the inner union between preaching and the administration of the sacraments for the sake of faith is emphasized. "Preaching within our Christian community, especially to those with little belief or grasp of the faith, calls for different methods. Instruction must be given while the priest is actually administering the sacraments. They are, after all, the sacraments of the faith which is born and nourished by the living word. That is especially true of the Liturgy of the Word during the celebration of Mass. The proclamation of our Saviour's death and resurrection, the response of the people, listening to that message and the actual offering by which Christ sealed the New Testament in his blood, form one complete whole. The faithful share in this offering by their prayers and by receiving Communion" (De presb., Par. 4). This definition is clearly a further result of the constitution on the sacred liturgy in which a more central role is assigned to the Word of God in the divine service and in the life of the Christian than we are used to assume from previous Catholic dogmatic statements.

The "priestly office" consists primarily in the administration of the sacraments through which the work of sanctification is carried out. "Priests through the ministry of bishops are consecrated by God to become in a special way sharers in Christ's priesthood and his ministers in celebrating the sacred mysteries. Christ exercises his priestly function unceasingly through his Spirit in the liturgy."[31] In the *Tridentinum* this special "priesthood of sacrifice" was based on the commandment of Christ during the eucharist, "This do in remembrance of me" *(hoc facite in commemorationem meam).*[32] Perhaps it is not completely accidental that in the description of the priestly office in the decree on the priesthood there is also a reference to the other sacraments. The Eucharist, the sacramental offering of Christ, is still at the center and everything else is grouped around it. "Converts under instruction are made ready step-by-step to share the Eucharistic Feast, while the faithful, already bearing the seal of Baptism and confirmation, are incorporated into the Body of Christ by reception of Holy Communion" (De presb., Par. 5). Here, too, the primary purpose of the priest is seen in leading the congregation to active participation in the service of God. The emphasis upon the Eucharist does not envisage the celebration as exclusively the priestly sacrifice of the individual priest, but as an obligation of the priest to lead his congregation to an understanding of this action by the church. This emphasis was caused by the pastoral concern of the Council, while at the same time it was an important land-mark in an official decree dealing with the priesthood. It might be interpreted in this way that "the priestly office" does not exist inde-pendently but evolves only on the basis of its ecclesiological context. If this is the case, it means clearly a change of emphasis which is expressed very cautiously, to be sure, but which is present nevertheless. This new emphasis could liberate the priestly office from its isolation and connect it more fruitfully with the priesthood of all believers than has been possible in the past.

The royal office of the priest is derived from the office of Christ as Head and Shepherd of the church.[33] This office is referred to as a special authority which in this document is not called in the traditional way the authority to rule *(potestas regendi)*, but a spiritual authority *(potestas spiritualis)* established for the edification of the congregation and patterned on the example of Christ. When the priest is described in this careful wording in his role as a leader of the congregation and when his obligation toward the poor and the weak is emphasized as a "sign of the messianic activity" (Luke 4:18), we must recognize an emphasis which tries to avoid the danger of clericalism.[34] For when we talk about the leadership of the church it is always difficult to see clearly that this "ruling" consists in serving. In this connection hardly another passage was used as often during the sessions of the Council and in its documents as Matt. 20:28: "Even as the Son of Man came not to be served, but to serve and to give his life as a ransom for many." However, the last part of this passage is quoted only infrequently, or at least it is not considered as determining the qualification of this ministry. If it had been quoted, the statements would have been more explicit. In that case, the position of authority of the church would not have been interpreted as primarily bringing "the church" and its message to the attention of the people by all means, but rather that she must give her life for it and suffer the rejection of the world directed against the church. For the Ruler of the kingdom of God himself was crucified and mocked in his royal dignity (Matt. 27:29). His suffering and death are essential parts of his royal office (John 18:33-37). All this must be considered when the royal, that is, the ruling office of the priests, and of course of the bishops, is being discussed.[35] To be sure, these references had not been clearly expressed, but the decree of the priesthood has avoided the clerical way of speaking and has thus pointed the way to the spiritual pastoral aspects of the office.

## Participation in the Office of Christ

Above we have indicated that the threefold division of the office of Christ is not part of the New Testament testimony, although elements for such a definition of the ministry of Christ can be found there. But whether we construct a Christology upon the twofold office of Christ which would be in accordance with the basic kerygma of the New Testament or upon a threefold prophetic, priestly, and royal office is a Christological problem which does not concern us here. However, the question whether the office of Christ as understood in the one or the other way can be applied to the office of the church must be answered in order to arrive at an understanding of the ecclesiastical office, and it must be asked here in a critical way. This is justified because in Lutheran dogmatics a justification for it has never been developed, although the *munus triplex Christi* had been accepted as orthodox doctrine.[36] This dogmatic development has taken place on a different plane which shows the signs of the Roman Catholic theology.

It is indeed surprising to find out that in recent times the so-called "Catholic" tradition which is part of the decree on the priesthood has also found entrance into ecumenical documents.[37] Is it possible that we are at the beginning of an ecumenical consensus concerning the doctrine of the ministry? Should we look upon this as recognition of truth and a sign of new hope in our dealing with one of the most difficult problems related to the mission of the church? A genetic investigation of the documents in question—if such an investigation could be carried out—would lead us to doubt the presupposition of this question. As far as I can discern these concepts have entered the ecumenical discussion by way of the high-church movement of the Anglican Church, which in turn has borrowed these ideas from the Roman Catholic dogmatics of the nineteenth century. Thus we are back at the same source. However, the fact that a doctrine concerning the office of the ministry has found a willing echo in the ecumenical work is also due to the Christological emphasis in modern Protestant theology. A Christological justification for the ministry is indeed quite attractive, but we must always recognize the limits of this doctrine in its ecclesiological application. Christology must not lose sight of the trinitarian context and must clearly recognize the specific situation in the history of salvation in which the ecclesiological office functions in relationship to the office of Jesus Christ. It is in this connection that there are definite reservations in the ecumenical movement in view of the continued study of the ecclesiastical office.[38] Our few critical questions point in the same direction.

Our primary concern is the necessity to clarify the concept of participation *(participatio)*. What do they mean when they say that the holders of the ecclesiastical office "participate" in the office of Christ? The decree of the Council is not interested in clarifying this question. The concept of participation is taken for granted, and this is the reason why the possibilities for misinterpretation continue to plague us.

For Protestant theology it is of basic importance that the historical work of Christ is recognized as having been accomplished at one time and in a unique way, that is, that the work of salvation has been wrought once and for all through his suffering and death on the cross, through his resurrection and his glorification. This is his own work which he can share with no one else. But Catholic theology is inclined to speak at this point of the participation of humanity in the work of Christ, for example in its mariology.[39] The Protestant point of departure for the understanding of the essence of the church and her ministry is the axiom of the exclusiveness with which the Lord has completed his ministry. For this reason, Protestant theology is careful and quite definite not to speak of the work of the church which she carries on in her ministry as a mediating activity. But this is exactly what is at the center of the definition of the priest in the Catholic interpretation.[40] *Lumen Gentium* does not avoid the claim, "They do share, at their own level of the ministry, the office of Christ, the sole mediator" (1 Tim. 2:5).[41] To be sure, in its mariological pronouncements the Council has defended itself against Protestant objections and has declared that there is a difference between the "role of the mediatrix" Mary and the office of the mediator Christ. It has declared that the two roles can be reconciled (without, however, giving theological reasons for this statement).[42] But in defining the doctrine of the participation of the ecclesiastical office in the office of Christ a similar statement is missing. Without such a statement the concept of participation is subject to the misunderstanding that Christ's unique redemptive work is continuing in the activity of the special office of the priesthood. To be sure, it is stated that the hierarchy acts only on the basis of the office of Christ, but it acts in such a way that it participates in it and cooperates with him. In this connection the words *cooperatio* and *participatio* are often used interchangeably.[43] The office of Christ which he carries on in the world after his glorification through the Holy Spirit is based on his unique work of redemption. The period in the history of salvation in which the glorified Christ builds his church today among us permits merely *a spreading* of this unique work of Christ.[44] This work of Christ must be proclaimed to all people in order that man may be incorporated into Christ through baptism. The body and blood of Christ which has been given and shed must be distributed so that people may be received into the communion of Christ and may become partakers of his salvation.

Taken in this sense "participation" means two things:

1. It is the incarnation of the presence of Christ in the proclamation of the Word and in the sacraments of Baptism and of the eucharist. This coming into the flesh is accomplished through the office of the church which, acting in the name of Christ, makes available his institution of the means of grace to the people so that they can partake in his salvation. The participation in the ecclesiastical office in this context is completely instrumental. Christ acts through people whom he has called to be his messengers. This work does not depend upon the person, but upon the office, the commission, and the mission by which Christ gives himself for the salvation of mankind. Thus the office has nothing to do with the person who holds the office. It is not at all important how a person stands before God, whether he has faith or whether he is an unbeliever, as long as he carries out his office towards his fellowmen according to the institution of Jesus Christ. The office is not qualified by the person who occupies the office. But also the opposite is true: The office does not make the person who occupies it acceptable before God. Priests and laymen are different only in view of the office which they occupy, but not on the basis of their personal qualities which are all the same in the presence of God. On this premise is based the

criticism of the reformers against the office as a sacrament, for a sacrament is a gift of salvation and the person who is called to an office does not receive salvation for himself but he receives the commission to become a minister of Jesus Christ. He merely proclaims through his office the salvation of Christ, namely the things that Christ has done for our redemption once and for all time. Christ's unique office becomes effective when today it is being applied through the office of his ministers to mankind.

2. When these means of grace which are given us through this office are accepted in faith, there takes place participation in the second meaning of the word. Then it is a matter of salvation of every individual. A person can take part in salvation, that is in the office of Christ, only when he has faith, and this faith is created through the proclamation of the Word and by the distribution of the sacraments and is kept alive by these means. This faith is on a different level than the office which a man occupies. The believer may be engaged in a secular calling or he may occupy an ecclesiastical office. In either case he is a priest in the New Testament meaning of the word. He participates in the office of Christ by dying with him and living in him. The death of Christ is manifested in his participation in the death of the Old Adam and the coming alive of the "new man," of the Christ-man who in faith gives himself to man as eternal life. This communion with Christ is the full communion in faith with him. There is no difference with the Lord Jesus Christ between a person who occupies an ecclesiastical office and a person who does not hold such an office. All offices, both secular and ecclesiastical, are forms of life in which the Christian life is mortified and renewed again according to the example of Christ *(mortificatio* and *vivificatio).*[45]

The rediscovery of the universal priesthood of all believers in Roman Catholic theology in recent years and its positive evaluation during the Second Vatican Council is of great importance for the understanding of the participation in the office of Christ. Unfortunately, the definition of the universal priesthood of all believers is often limited as far as the laity is concerned. Therefore its relationship to the priesthood of ordination is merely of pragmatic but not of dogmatic relevance. The universal priesthood of the laity, which has its basis in baptism and confirmation, is defined like the ecclesiastical office on the basis of the office of Christ as "priestly, prophetic and royal office."[46] In *Lumen Gentium* this participation of the laity in the threefold office of Christ has been described in detail.[47] With this description the universal priesthood of believers and the special priesthood of ordination are placed on the same level as far as their content is concerned. Therefore it is not enough merely to state, "There is an essential difference between the faithful's priesthood in common and the priesthood of the ministry of the hierarchy, and not just a difference of degree. Nevertheless, there is an ordered relation between them: one and the other has its special way of sharing the single priesthood of Christ."[48] What do they mean when they say in this context, "not just a difference of degree"? This statement presents problems which Catholic theology perhaps has never realized, but these are the very problems which the theology of the Reformation has attacked. Whether the reformers have answered this question satisfactorily is a different matter.

In a theology based on the Bible, however, the fact must be taken into account that this "participation in the office of Christ" which we call "the royal priesthood" includes the "occupants of the priesthood of the hierarchical ministry" as well as "the laymen." Participation in this sense is on the personal plane, that is, it is based on the relationship of faith. A "conformity with Christ" which is applied especially to the ecclesiastical office[49] does not exist. In following his occupation the priest finds himself in the same life of faith based on baptism through his dying and rising again with Christ as all lay people. Sanctification is the common calling of the people of God, where we find diversity of offices. This insight of the Council was unfortunately not utilized to its fullest extent, for the manifold services in the body of Christ (Rom. 12:4-5)[50] have nothing to do with any difference in "essence" or "degree."

There is, however, one difference, namely the ministry, the office whose bearer is Christ. This difference does not permit us to split the church into an estate of the hierarchy and an estate of the laity. Priests and lay people are united with each other in the body of Christ. This union is essentially not just a pragmatic working side by side with each other. Ordination to an office in the church means a calling to a special service in the body of Christ. The Council has correctly stated, "The priests of the New Law are by their calling and ordination set apart, to a certain extent, in the midst of the people of God. But the purpose of this is not to separate them from the rest of the people of God nor, indeed, from the rest of men but only to ensure that they are completely dedicated to the work to which God calls them."[51] How can we reconcile with this statement the concept of an *essential* difference between laity and priesthood? It is probable that the Catholic dogma of the sacrament of ordination is a stumbling-block which prevents the complete unfolding of the ecclesiology of the people of God, for in the sacrament of the ordination the personal relationship of the person called to the priesthood is being changed, a change which in the New Testament is attributed exclusively to the sacrament of baptism. This sacramental concept of ordination has come into conflict in the documents of the Council with the ecclesiology of the people of God (and especially with the reevaluation of the lay apostolate in the framework of this eschatology). Thus the traditional Catholic concept has come in flux. But we must ask the question whether an ecumenical dialogue should start at this point. Perhaps it does lead to a common understanding of the ecclesiastical office without which the church cannot live.

# Notes

1. Yves Congar, *Ministères et laicat dans les recherches actuelles de la théologie catholique romaine,* in: *Ministères et laicat* (Taizé 1964), p. 143.
2. There were several references to the fact that Catholic ecclesiology had become "hierarchology." Yves Congar, *Jalons pour une théologies du laicat,* Unam Sanctam 23, Paris 1954, p. 68.
3. *Constitutio dogmatica de ecclesia (Lumen Gentium),* Par. 20. In the text the constitution is given according to the English edition of the Catholic Truth Society, London, 1966.
4. *Decretum de presbyterorum ministerio et vita,* Par. 5. The text is given according to the English edition of Catholic Truth Society, London, 1966.
5. *De presb.,* Par. 12 and 13, cf. *de ecclesia,* Par. 21.
6. This possibility is admitted on the basis of the derivation of the individual sacraments of the church from the church as "Ur-

sakrament," Karl Rahner, *Kirche und Sakramente*, Freiburg 1960, p. 51.

7. *De ecclesia*, Par. 28.

8. *Ibid.*

9. This is clearly expressed, e.g., in the liturgical concelebration ordered by the Council. See: *De sacra liturgia*, Par. 57. It is an expression of the hierarchical communion (*De presb.* Par. 7 and 8).

10. E.g., K. Rahner, *Schriften zur Theologie*, Vol. II, Einsiedeln 1958, p. 351.

11. Cf. in this connection the detailed treatment of this theme by Y. Congar, *Jalons* . . . , p. 46 ff., where the author deals with the Reformation, recognizing and admitting the Catholic one-sidedness and the reaction of the reformers which emphasizes the unity aspect of the communion. He nevertheless concludes that Catholic hierarchical one-sidedness is not heretical because it retains the structure of the church. Over against this the reformers are called heretical because they attacked the structure of the Church. See esp. pp. 58 and 71 ff.

12. This is generally admitted by Catholic theologians, but the meaning of the terminology is underestimated for the dogmatic use of this insight. See Y. Congar, *Jalons,* . . . , pp. 173 and 177 f.

13. *De ecclesia*, Par. 9.

14. "Participatio laicorum ad hierarchicum apostolatum" (*Mens nostra*, of Dec. 20, 1929, quoted according to Fr. Dabin, *Le Sacerdoce Royal des Fidèles*, Paris, 1950, p. 491).

15. *De apostolatu laicorum*, Par. 2. English text according to the N.C.W.C. translation endorsed by the Bishops of the United States.

16. *Ibid.*

17. Cf. *De Ecclesia*, Par. 31 (under Laity): "pro parte sua missionem totius populi christiani in Ecclesia et in mundo exercent." In *De apost. laic.*, Par. 3, it is further stated: "Omnibus igitur Christi fidelibus onus praeclarum imponitur adlaborandi ut divinum salutis nuntium ab universis hominibus ubique terrarum cognoscatur et accipiatur."

18. *De apost. laic.*, Par. 2, text according to the N.C.W.C. translation endorsed by the Bishops of the United States.

19. E.g., in *De captivitate babylonica,* WA, VI, 564,12: "nostro nomine omnia faciant." Also V. Vajta, *Die Theologie des Gottesdienstes*, Stockholm - Göttingen, 1952, p. 196-221, esp. pp. 208 ff.—Concerning Luther's concept of the ecclesiastical office, see the important studies by W. Brunotte, *Das geistliche Amt bei Luther*, Berlin, 1959, and H. Lieberg, *Amt und Ordination bei Luther und Melanchthon*, Göttingen, 1962.

20. That this means not a democratic office but an office based on an ecclesiological foundation is proved by the fact that Luther does not diverge from the concept of office as instituted by Christ. This is clear, e.g., from the quotation in his treatise "Von Konziliis und Kirchen" where he says: "von wegen und im namen der Kirchen, viel mehr aber aus einsetzung Christi" (WA 50, 633,2).

21. W. *Brunotte*, *loc. cit.*, p. 165 and G. Pedersen, *Laeta libertas* (in: *Festskrift til K. E. Skydsgaard*, København, 1962), p. 125.

22. Of course this presupposes that this understanding of the reformers must do away with later Protestant falsification.

23. Pius XI uses in reference to John the expression, "alter est Christus" in his encyclical *Ad Catholici sacerdotii* 1935 (Denz. 2275).

24. Cf. P. E. Persson, *Kyrkans ämbete som Kristus-representation,* Lund 1961, p. 23 f.

25. *De presb.,* Par. 1.

26. A recognition of the history of the *munus triplex* in Protestant and Catholic theology is offered by P. E. Persson, *loc. cit.,* esp. pp. 247 ff.

27. More about this in my article, "Der Christenstand als königliches Priestertum" in: *Weltluthertum heute* (Nygren-Festschrift, Stockholm-Göttingen-Rock Island, 1950, pp. 350-373).

28. Paul Dabin, *Le Sacerdoce Royal des Fidèles,* Paris 1950, offers a collection of texts from the days of the reformers to the modern time.

29. *De presb.,* Par. 2.

30. Cf. Par. 4; also Pars. 13 and 19.

31. *De presb.,* Par. 5.

32. Denz. 938 and 949.

33. *De presb.,* Par. 6.

34. The influential Catholic weekly, *The Tablet,* in the issue of Jan. 22, 1965, has an article concerning the decree on the priesthood with the subtitle, "The Epitaph of Clericalism?"

35. For the understanding of the freedom of religion which caused a lively controversy during the Council this biblical documentation would have been of greatest importance. However, it was never mentioned.

36. A group of theologians in Uppsala has recently maintained this threefold concept of the ecclesiastical office. See the volume of treatises, *En bok om kyrkans ämbete,* by Hj. Lindroth, Stockholm, 1951. The above-mentioned work by P. E. Persson brings a detailed critique on this position.

37. *The Fourth World Conference on Faith and Order. The Report from Montreal,* 1963, edited by P. C. Rodger and L. Vischer, London, 1964, p. 64, informs of such theological orientation. The formulations appear, however, in the context of pneumatology which is missing in the documents of the Vatican Council.

38. This was read in the meeting of the Faith and Order Commission, 1964, Aarhus. The minutes with the critical remarks are published in Faith and Order Paper No. 44, Geneva, 1965, p. 48.

39. See *De ecclesia,* Ch. VIII.

40. Thomas Aquinas, *Summa Theol.* III, g. 22, art. 1: "proprium officium sacerdotis est esse mediator inter Deum et populum."

41. *De Ecclesia,* Par. 28.

42. *Ibid.,* Par. 60.

43. Here the concept of the *cooperatores Dei* (1 Cor. 3:9) is interpreted by Catholic theology in a much wider sense than is permitted, according to the biblical text. Anthropological and Christological presuppositions play a more important part here than the Pauline text.

44. The Protestant theologian has better access to such thoughts in which there is an emphasis on the eschatological limitation of the hierarchical power, and on the aspect of distribution (as e.g. K. Rahner, *Schriften zur Theologie,* Bd. III Einsiedeln, 1956, p. 293 ff.) than to thoughts which emphasize the hierarchy as a protective wall around the unique

work of the mediator Jesus Christ (e.g. Y. Congar, *Sainte Eglise*, Paris, 1963, pp. 218 ff.). We are, however, certainly influenced in our criticism by the fact of the historical phenomenon of the "hierarchy."

45. The implications of the twofold participation are also found in Congar, *Ministères et laicat*, 1964, p. 144, where a distinction is made between the "personal" and the "public" office. The first is common to all; the latter is reserved for the special ecclesiastical office. A more detailed description would perhaps lead to some clarification concerning the question that is of relevance to the first meaning. The second would lead to some divergency which has dogmatic implications.

46. *De apostolatu laicorum*, Par. 2, cf. Par. 10.

47. *De ecclesia*, Pars. 34-36. These texts, as so many others, show the decisive influence which Congar had upon this Council through his various publications. His book concerning the theology of the lay apostolate is based on this threefold scheme.

48. *De ecclesia*, Par. 10: "Essentia non gradu tantum," is a literal reproduction from an address by Pius XII of November 2, 1954, published in *Acta Apostolicae Sedis* XLVI, 1954, p. 669.

49. This concept is closely connected with the sacramental character of ordination in Catholic dogma. This is also apparent from *De presb.*, Par. 2, in the following formulation: "sacerdotium Presbyterorum initiationis christianae Sacramenta quidem supponit, peculiari tamen illo Sacramento confertur, quo Presbyteri, unctione Spiritus Sancti, *speciali charactere signantur et sic Christo Sacerdoti configurantur*, ita ut in persona Christi Capitis agere valeant."

50. *De ecclesia*, Par. 32.

51. *De presb.*, Par. 3.

Chapter V

# The Attitude of the Council Toward Religious Orders and Discipleship

## Monasticism and Reform in the History of the Church

The Second Vatican Council has repeatedly affirmed its desire to seek for renewal on the basis of the Gospel and the idea of service. Any renewal of the church can only be achieved by an about-turn in current thinking and the acceptance of new ways of thought. The churches which have come into existence since the Reformation have chosen the motto "Ecclesia semper reformanda," and Roman Catholic Christians do not want to be outdone in the quest for renewal and reform. It is only natural that evidence of the working of a spirit of renewal should be sought in the church before the Reformation in order to demonstrate the existence within the Catholic sphere of many imposing examples of a creative and constructive approach to the task of renewal.[1]

In this connection we are reminded of the revitalizing power of monasticism in various epochs of church history. Monasticism has long been regarded by Protestant church historians as an alien ascetic influence within Christianity, deriving from the pessimistic dualism which flourished in many various forms in the early centuries of the Christian era. Through the writings of such men as Adolf Harnack, Karl Holl, and Ernst Troeltsch, a change in this biased judgment on monasticism has been effected.[2]

97

Although there are many instances of degeneration in the ascetism practiced by the early Christian monks, it should not escape recognition that one of the primary motives for the pursuit of the monastic life was love for God and his holiness.[3] It was not by coincidence that monasticism made its appearance in church history at the same time as the church was becoming a recognized power within the Empire. The victory of the church, due to its change of fortune under Emperor Constantine, put a great temptation before it in its relations to the world. Monasticism gathered all the forces which were opposed to this temptation by virtue of its desire for an effective and uncompromising application of the Gospel. In the early church the spirit of renewal became concentrated most effectively in the Benedictine reform movement and in the evangelization carried out by the Celtic and Anglo-Saxon missions.[4] The Cluniac reform movement developed during the general decline of the church and of civilization after the disintegration of the Carolingian empire. The rule of the reformed monasteries was basically that of St. Benedict to which additions were made, the aim being to achieve an inner spiritual renewal among the monks. This inner renewal soon began to have social and cultural consequences.

As Cluny's period of greatness drew to a close about the time of the first crusade new centers of a spiritual order of knighthood began to grow up which were full of action and vitality. Many new monastic foundations originated in France, which was also the home of the Cluniac movement. This in itself is sufficient evidence of a thread of continuity in the monastic reform movement. The Cistercians thought of themselves as a movement of renewal within the tradition of *Cluny*. On the one hand they were very critical of Cluny, but on the other they carried on its tradition. And the strict observance of Benedict's rule is the fundamental principle of the Cistercians.

Bernard of Clairvaux as the leader of a renewed monasticism initiated a second stage of Christianization. Now a great effort was made to reach the secular world. These efforts to influence bourgeois society were continued intensively by the Mendicant Orders of Francis of Assisi (himself a layman) and Dominic. The Benedictines, Cistercians, and Premonstratensians were more or less bound to their cloisters which were usually far removed from the centers of population. The Mendicant Orders recognized that the changes which had come about in the social structure called for a new kind of preacher, teacher, and missionary. Francis was deeply disturbed by the attempts that were made to modify his first unwritten rule. As an obedient son of the church he submitted to the attempts made by the Curia to approximate the Franciscan Brotherhood to the older orders. But he suffered much under the changes introduced into his rule and failed to see the need for them. The case of Francis is a very good example of how the power of a monastic reform government can cause such an upheaval in the institutional church that the reaction of the leading officials is hostile.

Even Martin Luther's development as a reformer cannot be understood without having in mind the fact that Luther made up his mind to pursue the monastic life in order to find the answer to his religious questions, and it is significant that he joined the Augustinian Eremites who were known for the strictness of their rule. The rule of the Augustinian Eremites followed that of the Augustinian Canons, which in turn was based in broad outline on Benedict's rule. It was through his monastic observance that Luther came to the insights which led to his becoming a reformer, a matter to which consideration will be given later. At the same period there were numerous brotherhoods and communities living under a semireligious discipline all searching for a renewal in the life and preaching of the church. It is an astonishing fact that twice as many religious orders were founded between 1524 and 1544 as in the two previous centuries. A statistical survey of new foundations of orders for men reveals that in the sixteenth century there were fifteen new foundations as opposed to one in the fifteenth, and four in the fourteenth century.[5]

The continuity in the tradition of monastic religious life can be clearly traced in the reform movement centered around Ignatius Loyola, who acknowledged his debt to the Benedictine Cisneros of Montserrat, the Carthusian, Ludolf of Saxony, and the Augustinian Canon, Thomas à Kempis.[6] The reform carried out within the Roman Catholic Church during the sixteenth century undoubtedly began with efforts to reform the religious orders and culminated in the Council of Trent. The Council would never have been possible but for the theological thinking undertaken within the orders and their programs for reform of monastic life. The Council of Trent entrusted new social, charitable, and educational responsibilities to the orders and thereby contributed in some measure to their inner renewal. This, however, is not the place to enter into further discussion of the contribution made by the orders to the Counter-Reformation, or of the changes in monastic life in modern church history.[7]

Monasticism played a less important role than the hierarchy and theology in the renewal of Catholicism after the Enlightenment. The Jesuits were banned for decades not only by individual European states but even by the Curia itself; only after thirty and more years in the wilderness were they permitted to reorganize themselves in the year 1814. The secularization of countless monasteries and convents had many serious consequences for monasticism. But more serious than the external threat was the impact on the religious orders of the economic and intellectual changes in society. What role remained for the orders to play in a secularized world? What justification could be found for their peculiar position midway between a radically secularized and anticlerical sphere, on the one hand, and a hierarchically centralized church on the other? The monasticism of the nineteenth and especially of the twentieth century has not sought to evade these questions, but there has been an absence of definite instructions from both the Pope and the Council. The attitudes to renewal which have evolved out of the practical experience of the religious orders and out of the literary debate that has been going on, needed to be carefully examined and given the official authorization of the church.

## Seeking a Theology of the Life of Religious Orders

Already before the Second Vatican Council, bishops, faculties of theology, and members of the religious orders themselves had emphasized the necessity of making the reform of the life of the religious orders one of the principal themes of discussion in the Council. Yet the first mention of the subject in any conciliar document occurs in the record of the debate on the paragraph dealing with the universal call to holiness in the schema "De Ecclesia" which refers to the special function and purpose of the religious orders.[8] Several of the Fathers expressed themselves in favor of a biblically-based renewal of the spirituality of the religious orders. The use of the somewhat ambiguous description of the religious life as the "state of perfection" came in for criticism. If one can speak of a state of perfection, it can only refer to the calling of *all* Christians. To live according to the evangelical counsels is a duty incumbent on all Christians whatever their calling, and even if the religious life is thought to be the most radical application of these counsels, this duty is no less universal.[9] This criticism is given no expression in the conclusion of Chapter V of the decree, nor is it mentioned in Chapter VI which is devoted to the religious. No attempt is made to develop a theology of the religious life which aims at practical reforms. Nevertheless, it is possible to discern certain fundamental principles of the religious life. The religious life rests upon the evangelical counsels of poverty, chastity, and obedience which are consecrated to God. The religious do not constitute an intermediate state between the laity and the clergy in the hierarchical structure of the church. "It is the case rather that a number of Christ's faithful are invited from the clerical and the lay states to enjoy a special gift in the life of the Church and to advance, each in his own way, the Church's mission of salvation" (Par. 43, De ecclesia).

Just as this paragraph emphasizes the charismatic character of the religious life as a gift of grace, coming as a call of God to enter this life freely, so the next paragraph (44) discusses the relation between the vows and the evangelical counsels on the one hand, and on the other hand the connection between baptismal grace and the evangelical counsels and the ordering of all religious life within the church. Nothing is said about the unique character of the vows.[10] The emphasis is laid on the role of the religious life within and for the church as a whole.

"The evangelical counsels bring about a special union of their adherents with the Church and her mystery, by means of charity to which they are the guide. The spiritual life of these adherents must therefore be devoted also to the good of the whole church." So the taking of the vows of poverty, chastity and obedience is "seen to be like a sign which has the power of effectively attracting all the Church's members to a lively performance of the duties of the Christian vocation. It must do so" (Par. 44, De ecclesia).

From the Protestant point of view, this approach should be welcomed. It excludes any individualistic interpretation of the struggle for perfection, and avoids drawing any distinction between the religious and *all* Christians in that struggle. But it still maintains that the religious life is a clearer imitation of the life of the Son of God; on this point Protestants must beg to differ. Paragraph 45 goes on to discuss the relation between the hierarchy of the church and the religious orders.[11]

In the concluding section some admonitory advice is given, but it scarcely does justice to the real difficulties confronting the religious life in the modern world. The main object would appear to be to protect the religious against any too critical assessment, for the statement says: "No one should think that their consecration makes religious strangers to their fellow men or unprofitable citizens here on earth. Even if in some cases they have no direct contact with their contemporaries, they keep their company at a deeper level in the heart of Christ. They give them spiritual cooperation to ensure that the building, which is the State, has its foundations in the Lord and is aligned on him, to prevent frustration in the work of those who are engaged in building it" (Par. 46, De ecclesia).

These statements, which are apologetic in tone, needed to be expanded and developed. The original document on the renewal of the religious life, entitled "*De statibus perfectionis,*" contained a hundred pages; but after the first session it was reduced to thirty pages under the title "*De Religiosis*"; and in the third revision following the second session it shrank to a mere four pages. At the beginning of the third session certain paragraphs were added. The final decree consisted of twenty guiding principles which can be subdivided into four groups: (a) Renewal called for by the contemporary situation (1–10); (b) Communal life and external forms such as seclusion and habit (11–13); (c) Education of the Novitiate (14); (d) The function and the coordination of the communities (15–20). Although these statements stressed the need for the renewal of the religious life in accordance with the evangelical counsels, the decree met with more criticism than approval when it was debated in the Council.[12] Cardinals Döpfner, Suenens, and Bea were particularly critical of the slender theological basis of the schema.

Döpfner made four points which deserved a fuller consideration than was in fact accorded to them. (1) Spiritual renewal (Return to the sources of the spiritual life and to the simplicity of the Gospel). (2) The adaptation of the religious life to the demands of the present day (The need to find a form of obedience which commended itself to the mature people of today). (3) The education and training of the religious. (4) The problem of the types of orders (The overcoming of institutional narrowness). Döpfner complained that the renewal movement within the church had not yet penetrated far enough into the monasteries and convents.

In a similar vein the general superior of the Congregation of the Holy Cross, Germain-Marie Lalande, suggested that the present crisis in recruitment for the religious orders might well be because youth regarded the monastic institutions as too traditionalist and out of touch with life today. The decree on the religious life should really have given more adequate expression to the Council's desire for renewal. Several of the Fathers remarked upon the absence of any mention of the numerous brotherhoods and communities of laymen not bound by the monastic vows.

Pietro Fiordelli, Bishop of Prato in Italy, asked that the decree should make special mention of the communities of laymen, since these had been accorded solemn recognition by Pius XII in 1947. Their members made a valuable contribution to the apostolate of the church. These members did not want to be equated with the religious; on the other hand they could not be counted as laymen since they practiced the evangelical counsels in the world. Quite apart from the fact of their rapidly growing numbers and significance (1964, 16 lay communities under papal direction; 60 under episcopal direction; and 300 without official sponsorship), which entitles these lay communities to serious consideration, is the question of their theological basis, which should have received attention in the Decree.[13]

In this connection it is interesting to note the different assessment of the status of the members of these lay communities made by two such noted theologians as Hans Urs von Balthasar and Karl Rahner. Whereas von Balthasar[14] thinks of the members of the lay communities as laymen, Rahner[15] insists that the combining of a secular life with a life lived in accordance with the precepts of the Gospel through membership within one of these lay communities constitutes a new development of the religious life which was not so apparent formerly and which merits theological reassessment. Rahner formulates his view in this way: "The evangelical counsels which form the basis of a form of life through taking vows recognized by the church, also determine the form of life in the lay Communities and define the special position of their members (as a permanent way of life in the Church and recognized by the Church as such)."[16]

In the ecclesiastical documents which deal with the lay communities[17] Rahner and von Balthasar are in general agreement that the members of these lay communities live "in the world" and are not religious from the standpoint of Canon Law. Rahner, however, identifies the substance of life within the religious orders, and he bases this contention on the vows that are required of all intending members of the lay communities, which would seem to differentiate them from the laity in the theological sense. Laymen in the theological sense must possess the spirit of the evangelical counsels, but in their case this spirit is not expressed "in the outward ecclesiological form which is concerned with methods rather than with the spirit of the world-conquering love of the Crucified Christ."[18] These reflections of Rahner[19] naturally imply a reconsideration of the apostolate of the laity as distinct from the position of the religious and from the position of members of lay communities.

The decree "De Religiosis" should undoubtedly have paid more attention to these problems which are burning topics in contemporary theology. It is not in the least surprising that in the 122nd full assembly on the 14th of November only the last of the first fourteen guiding principles received the necessary two-thirds majority. Principles 15–20 were approved with the required majority in the 123rd full assembly, but the commission that had been considering these had to take account of numerous objections which were referred to it. In the 143rd general assembly held on the 6th of October 1965, Enrico Romulo Compagnone, Bishop of Anagni, submitted the report on the schema concerning the religious orders. He rightly described the new text as deeper in its conception and permeated by a spirit of greater pastoral concern, and he felt that this complied with the wishes of the full assembly held on the 12th of November 1964. More than 14,000 Modi had been presented and these had been reduced to 500. Four new paragraphs (9, 10, 11, and 25) were added. The bishop reminded the assembly that the schema should be considered in connection with the dogmatic constitution on the church (chapter 6), the decree concerning the pastoral office of a bishop, and the decree concerning the missionary task of the church (Chapters 1, 3, and 4).

It is not necessary to consider here each separate voting. Only once did the number of votes against rise as high as 57 and that was in the vote on the tenth principle, "Concerning Lay Orders." This raised the question of recognizing their full equality with religious orders, and their right to seek ordination to the priesthood for their members when need arose. The final result of the voting on the whole schema was decisively positive. There were 2142 votes cast, and probably a third or more were cast by members of religious orders.[20] There were 2126 in favor, only 13 against and three votes that were invalid. The final outcome of the voting had almost the authority of a plebiscite. The new paragraph 11 concerned itself primarily with the lay communities, and thus goes some way to fill a gap that was noted earlier.

The striking thing about this decree is its repeated insistence upon the ultimate norm of the religious life which is to be found in the Gospel, namely *the imitation of Christ* (Paragraph 2 and elsewhere). Furthermore the decree stresses the binding character of the intention of the founder of each order. There is no questioning of the common basis of all religious life constituted by the evangelical counsels. These, when they form the substance of special vows, represent a unique dedication which is an extension of the baptismal dedication and brings this to its fullest expression (5). At this point the question arises whether or not the christocentric relation which is the essence of discipleship can be properly expressed if, in fact, it is based on the evangelical counsels. Protestants welcome what the decree has to say about love for God, and about the sources of the spiritual life (6). The more it is stressed that the precondition of discipleship consists in being loyal to Christ, the more the document commends itself to Protestants.[21] But one cannot wholly escape the impression that the decree represents God's initiative and help too much as cooperating with the natural human will. This impression is confirmed when the vow of obedience is interpreted as the complete dedication of the will of the individual.[22]

## The Reformation and Monasticism

Luther did not primarily direct his criticism to the outward signs of monastic decadence. Strict observance was still to be found along with a good deal of laxity—indeed Luther had attached himself to a strictly observant order. His main criticism of monasticism was the result of his understanding of the principles of the system, and he realized the impossibility of self-justification through the monastic life.[23] The practice of the evangelical counsels of celibacy and poverty over and above the Ten Commandments, which are obligatory upon all Christians, still does not guarantee the gift of the grace of God. Despite all, God's grace remains absolutely free. According to Luther, it was impossible to reconcile the monastic vows based on the evangelical counsels with the freedom that is received in Christ. At some stages it appeared that Luther might be able to purge the monastic ideal of all its Pelagian tendencies by combining it closely with baptism and justification.

From 1518 to 1519 he continued to recognize the validity of monastic vows. He argued that the vows were taken freely. In his sermon on the Sacrament of Baptism in 1519 Luther appears to understand monasticism as the expression or rather outward sign of the death that is symbolized in baptism. Luther draws the conclusion here that the man who, to a greater degree than in the married state, "seeks more suffering, and by much exercise would speedily prepare himself for death and soon attain the goal of his baptism, let him bind himself to chastity or to the spiritual order. For the spiritual estate, if it is as it ought to be, should be full of torment and suffering in order that he who belongs to it may have more exercise in the work of his baptism than the man who is in the estate of matrimony, and through such torment quickly grow used to welcoming death with joy, and so attain the purpose of his baptism."[24] This positive assessment of monasticism on the basis of baptism was not his last word, and Luther's attitude changed after he had looked more carefully into the question of the *vows*.

In 1520, while Luther was turning over in his mind the problem of the Sacraments, it struck him that the monastic vows were based only on human tradition, and that monasticism, as it was then practiced, served only the end of self-justification. The more he pursued the thought of the "Freedom of a Christian," the clearer it seemed to him that the monastic vows were directly opposed to that freedom. They were to be thought of together with the Law, as being contrary to the freedom which Christ has brought. Luther pressed this conclusion upon his readers untiringly. He now doubted whether the vows could ever be taken in a state of true Christian freedom. Yet in spite of his doubts he still allowed in both sets of theses "De Votis" (published in 1521) that a person could take the vows in good faith. Although we are free from the Law and from the religious vows these still exist as *legitimus usus;* but no one should take vows that are contrary to his Christian freedom.

In February 1522 Luther published *"De votis monasticis iudicum"* which expressed his final conviction with regard to the monastic vows.[25] He dedicated this work to his father, to whom he now conceded that there could be no vows which were opposed to, or could claim superiority over, the universal commandments such as the command to love one's parents. Luther now radically rejected the division of Christianity into the two classes of those in the state of perfection and those remaining in imperfection. God never commanded anyone to take a vow. Vows are, in fact, sinful in character when they do not arise from faith. They are opposed to the commandments which demand faith (1st Commandment), and the praise and confession of God's name (2nd Commandment), but which do not require the taking of any vows. The eternal vows of obedience, chastity, and poverty are in any case wrong means for attaining blessedness. Furthermore, they are opposed to human reason! "What does the celibate give to God when he offers him chastity which is not in his power nor ever can be, because it is God's gift alone, which a man can receive but cannot offer."

The weightiest argument against the vows is that of the freedom of the Christian man. From this it would seem as if Luther had rigorously dispensed with all vows in making this judgment on the religious life. But this is not the case. The eternal vows anticipate the freedom and grace of God, and therefore they must be rejected.

But that is not the case with vows which are temporary, provided that they spring from the freedom that comes through faith. So Luther, despite his radical rejection of any notion of self-justification through the religious life and his rejection of the eternal vows, still admitted the possibility of monasticism understood in the evangelical sense. This possibility will be discussed later. Luther, then, addressed a challenge to Roman Catholic theology which could not be ignored. He asked whether the Gospel can be split up into commandments and counsels, or whether it is more truly a gift to all and an obligation upon all.[26] This question merited a thorough consideration and reply from the Catholic doctrinal authorities, and in this aspect at least we must be critical in our approach to the statement of the Vatican Council.

## Monk and "Layman" Share the Same Call to Discipleship

Only since about the middle of the third century have there been three distinct classes or estates recognized within the church, namely those of the laity, the clergy, and the religious. The monk is not a clergyman although he may become one. "His status is not determined by his office or his function, but by his profession and his way of life."[27] Whereas the distinctions between clergy and laity began to appear even in New Testament times, the status of the monk first becomes clearly distinguishable from that of the layman at the time when he sought to fulfill in a special way the Gospel's call to perfection which is made to *all* Christians. The separation of the two groups was due to historical rather than to theological causes. Therefore the Reformation opposed the view that the doctrine of classes or estates had any part in the divinely appointed structure of the church. The difference between the estate of the religious and that of the laity was deepened by the clericalization of the monastic orders. The outcome of the process of giving the monastic life a clearly liturgical direction (especially by St. Benedict) was that there were few monks in the West who were not also clerics, or at least did not live in the same kind of liturgical discipline as the clergy. This development entailed very serious consequences for the view that was taken of the "lay state."

During and after the time of Emperor Constantine many special privileges were accorded to the clergy. Bishops, priests, and monks were given very extensive immunities, and priests and monks separated themselves from the simple believers, whose life was regarded as worldly.[28] It was forgotten that the aim of the Christian calling was the same for the laity as it was for the clergy and monks. Medieval Christendom was strongly influenced in its thinking by the monastic system. It was the Reformation which rediscovered what had been obscured under this all-pervading influence, namely that Christianity was a religion for this life and should not be understood simply in terms of the eschatological and monastic interpretation of it. Catholic theologians have long been aware of the need for a theology of the laity in which the status of the laity within the church is seen as something more than a "concession." Yves Congar prepared the way for this development by his outline sketch of a theology of the laity.[29]

It is now generally agreed that *"The Laity Also Constitute Part of the Church,"*[30] though it is still believed that the estate of the laity differs from that of the ecclesiastical hierarchy and that of the religious. The layman is the Christian who remains in the world and is given a task to carry out there. Karl Rahner's impressive formulation states:[31] "Accordingly the layman is the Christian who remains in the world. Not in the sense that his vocation is secular . . . but in the sense that the layman has a specific task to do in and for the world which determines his status within the *Church* (not simply in civil life). Seen in this way the layman is *no longer* a Christian who has nothing to say in the Church, and nothing to do but be the passive object of the Church's (clergy's) pastoral concern for his salvation, and who, *therefore,* is concerned with worldly matters which have a secular but no religious significance, and which would engage his attention just as much if he were not a Christian. To be a layman in the Church and to hold that status as a title to membership means that as a member of the Church he holds a special position, namely that of being an instrument and function of the Church there, where the *world* is (this of course refers only to the lay *Christian* as *distinct from* the clergy and the Religious)."

Today the phrase "the apostolate of the laity" is heard everywhere and it occurs with such positive emphasis in the documents of the Vatican Council that it would appear almost as if the "priest-hood of all believers," which was such a burning concern of the Reformation, has now found general acceptance. But it must be remembered that Roman theology still maintains a distinction between the two estates of the laity and the religious, and Protestant theology is unable to accept any such distinction. Moreover, it cannot accept any such division of the whole of life into "Christian" and "worldly" spheres. We cannot choose to live our lives in one or the other of these spheres, nor is it possible to live a life "more" directed towards the sacred reality than is the "normal" life of the layman who is fully alive to the world in following Christ. No one has expressed this more forcefully than Dietrich Bonhoeffer.[32] "To have part in Christ means that we stand at one and the same time in divine and in human reality. . . . This does not mean there are two spheres but *only one*, in which Christ is expressed and in which divine and human reality are joined together."[33]

This states and underlines the misunderstanding upon which *medieval* monasticism rested. The error lay not in the recognition that Christ called men to discipleship and thereby involved them in a struggle with the world. Luther affirmed the worth of life in the world and even associated the call of Christ with our worldly vocation. "The return of Luther from the monastery to his 'vocation' —in accordance with the New Testament—was the hardest blow struck against the world since the days of the Early Church" (Bonhoeffer).

The Christian today, however, is clearly in a different position from the Christian of the Middle Ages. The tendency towards a mass-society and a mass-church has resulted in loss of personality and in a weariness in our calling. The machinery of bureaucracy and the progress of technology in work have reached such a highly developed stage that it is often difficult to discover the Christian significance of one's worldly "vocation." Under such circumstances it is easy to see why those who seriously desire to be Christians are showing new interest in the possibilities of community-living and even in the monastic life. The situation which originally gave rise to monasticism seems to have recurred. Even the old established orders are alive to this situation, and they are anxious to open the way to those who feel the call without obliging them to receive ordination and become priests. This relaxation of institutionalism can be seen as an attempt to do justice to the concept of the priesthood of all believers.[34]

The question remains, however, whether monasticism as an estate can be thought of as a "higher" form of discipleship than that pursued by other chosen members of the church of Christ. Is it possible to maintain that the monastic life is a Christian life in the fullest sense, as described in the chapter concerning the laity (in the Constitution on the Church), where the characteristic of the religious life is said to be that it affords a clear and outstanding example of the fact that only through the spirit of the Beatitudes can the world be transfigured and brought to God? Every single disciple is called to follow Christ and to holiness. Division of the way of perfection into two different estates is not justified. This does not exclude the possibility of *communal* life in seeking to follow Christ, even a communal life similar in form to the monastic life. But such a form of life is only a different (not a better) attempt to be obedient to the call of discipleship. There are no guarantees for a better or more certain success in attaining the goal of all Christian striving. The doctrine of the religious life is an understandable consequence arising out of a particular historical situation in which the church found itself. This doctrine cannot be said to have produced only good results in the history of the church, and on this ground alone it should not be perpetuated. The most fundamental objection to it is the New Testament view of the Christian church and the call to discipleship which comes to all Christians without distinction, and to which all are enabled to respond.

## Christian Monasticism Today?

Luther's rejection of monasticism was sharpened in the confessional documents of the Reformation. The articles of the Augsburg Confession, Article XX (De fide et bonis operibus), XXI (De cultu sanctorum), XXIII (De coniugio sacerdotum), XXVI (De discrimine ciborum), and XXVII (De votis monachorum), show severe criticism of the Catholic ideal of life on the basis of the Article concerning justification by faith alone (Article IV). Article XX contains not only the rejection of asceticism (fasting, pilgrimages,

rosaries, joining a religious order), but also, from the outset, sounds
a positive note indicating the reconstruction effected by the Reformation, as Luther himself had expounded it so forcefully in the
"Freedom of a Christian." All Christian conduct was no longer
directed towards the realization of righteousness, for righteousness
is realized through the justification which God accomplishes in
Jesus Christ. The purpose of morality is no longer to give the
Christian life stability, for that rests on God's mercy alone. Luther's
view of marriage is accepted, in which marriage is regarded as a
natural state which makes the exaltation of celibacy seem empty
and godless. Nevertheless, the Augsburg Confession does allow
that "few people possess the gift of celibacy." Here the state of
celibacy is understood as a charisma, and in this sense it is approved
by Luther himself. But this charisma cannot be institutionalized.
Chastity is a gift of God and is not at man's disposal, because he
cannot anticipate circumstantial changes. Celibacy can only continue
to be chosen so long as it remains possible to practice it. Nor are
poverty and obedience (to monastic superiors) any more defensible
as "evangelical counsels" than chastity.[35] The Sermon on the Mount
cannot be understood as an exposition of the evangelical counsels;
over its directions is written Matthew 5:19—what follows is by way
of commandment not counsel. There is nothing in the New Testament about works of supererogation.[36]

In the recent attempts to set up religious brotherhoods and communities the criticism voiced at the Reformation has been taken
into account. Poverty and community of goods are not regarded as
ends in themselves, or as a special form of holiness. Celibacy is
chosen in order to be free to serve Christ and one's neighbor, and
even obedience to the rule or to the prior is practiced for the sake of
unity within the community.[37] The conceptions of the individual
communities today are in the nature of things, widely different.[38]
It seems safe to say, however, that they all came into being because
of a growing awareness in many Christian circles of an emergency
arising because the state churches were swamped with large numbers of "baptised" Christians; but entry into a community is not
thought of as a legal requirement for salvation. All these new communities seek to set an example for Christian living in the world,

and seek to make the church visible as such. They regard themselves as Christians among Christians and not as superior Christians.

Max Thurian of Taizé[39] recognizes that the married and unmarried states are both equally justified possibilities, but he claims that we are called either to the one or the other. The question is only whether our "calling" should be expressed through lifelong vows. The answer given varies from community to community, but as far as Taizé is concerned the answer is clear and precise. Taizé uses the expression *"commitment"* (engagement) in order to avoid any suggestion of merit that might be attached to the word "vow." Yet in practice "engagement" means the same as "vow." Roger Schutz, the prior of Taizé, leaves us in no doubt that he believes that in principle the engagement is final and irrevocable. He writes:[40] "For all those who have entered the monastic life, the final acceptance of the commitment to celibacy means that they become men with only one love." He himself raises the question: "When marriage and celibacy make such demands, how can we bind ourselves for life?" And in reply to his question he says: "When we commit ourselves to Christ, He commits himself to us. That is a conviction born of experience; it confirmed a call to us, which perhaps only the person who receives the call can ever fully understand." In the directions of the Taizé Rule[41] the provisional character of the rule is mentioned. Should not this understanding of the rule apply just as much to the "commitments," which are, in practice, vows? The freedom of the Christian man is held to be the essential precondition of all commitments. This means in effect that the communities which have sprung up on Protestant soil have a biblical basis and remain true to the Reformation insights.

The Second Vatican Council is equally insistent that the vows of poverty, chastity, and obedience must be taken freely. Protestant thinking remains unable to accept the view that the three "evangelical counsels" present a better way to achieve perfection; yet despite this continued difference of opinion, a remarkable degree of unanimity has been achieved in the dialogue concerning the ways of following Christ, which holds out much promise for the future.

# Notes

1. Cf. Hans Küng, *Konzil und Wiedervereinigung, Erneuerung als Ruf in die Einheit*, 6th Imp., 1960, 53 ff.
2. Cf. F. Wulf S.J., "Die Stellung des Protestantismus zu Askese und Mönchtum in Geschichte und Gegenwart," in *Geistliches Leben in der heutigen Welt*, 1960, 194-218: also W. Nigg, *Vom Geheimnis der Mönche*, 1953.
3. Cf. U. Ranke-Heinemann, "Die Motive für die Entstehung des Mönchtums nach dem Selbstverständnis der ersten Mönche," Thesis, Munich, 1954. Later published under the title, *Das frühe Mönchtum, seine Motive nach den Selbstzeugnissen*, Essen, 1964.
4. Cf. St. Hilpisch, *Geschichte des benediktinischen Mönchtums*, 1929: Th. Bogler, *Mönchtum in der Entscheidung*, 1952.
5. Cf. Léo Moulin, *Le Monde Vivant des Religions*, Paris 1964. See Appendix.
6. Cf. Hugo Rahner, *Ignatius von Loyola als Mensch und Theologe*, 1964: F. Marxer, *Die Inneren Geistlichen Sinne, Ein Beitrag zur Deutung Ignatianischer Mystik*, 1963.
7. Cf. Jean Canu, *Die religiösen Männerorden, Aschaffenburg* 1960: also H. Mulert and E. Schott, *Konfessionskunde* 3rd Ed. 1956, 322 ff.: also P. Meinhold, *Ökumenische Kirchenkunde*, 1962, 223 ff.
8. Cf. in the English Edition Catholic Truth Society 1966, Chapter V, 57 ff. and especially 62 ff.
9. Cf. "Die Reform der Orden," in *Herder Korrespondenz*, March 1965, 269: See also B. Albrecht, *Stand und Stände: Eine theologische Untersuchung*, 1962, 80 ff.

and 108 ff. (Rätestand und Ordenstand.) See further E. Ranwez, *Concilium* No. 9, 1965, 748 ff. Ranwez argues that the evangelical counsels concerning poverty, chastity, and obedience are not the only evangelical counsels and that these other counsels apply to all Christians.
10. Cf. B. Häring, "Das Gesatz Christi," *Moraltheologie*, 1954, 766 ff.
11. Cf. especially Andreas Boni, O.F.M. "De religiosorum conditione iuridica in Constitutione Dogmatica," "De Ecclesia," *Concilii Oecumenici Vaticani II*, Antonianum, Fasc. 2, 1965, 244-258.
12. Cf. *Herder Korrespondenz*, March 1965: L. A. Dorn and G. Denzler: *Tagebuch des Konzils. Die Arbeit der Dritten Session*, Nuremberg and Eichstätt, 1965, 341 ff.
13. Cf. J. Beyer, S.J., *Les Instituts Séculiers*, 1954: *Études sur les Instituts Séculiers, Textes et Études theologiques*, Desclée de Brouwer 1963.
14. "Wesen und Tragweite der Säkularinstitute" in *Civitas* II, 1955/6, 196 ff., see also *Der Laie und der Ordenstand*, 1949.
15. "Laie und Ordensleben. Uberlegungen zur Theologie der Säkularinstitute" in *Sendung und Gnade. Beiträge zur Pastoraltheologie*, 3rd Ed., 1961, 359 ff.
16. *Op cit.*, 362.
17. A.A.S. 39, 1947, 114-124; 40, 1948, 293-297.
18. *Op. cit.*, 383.
19. Rahner addresses himself to this subject in *Schriften zur Theologie*, Vol. II, 3rd Ed. 1958, 339 ff. "Uber das Laienapostolat."
20. Cf. *Presseinformationen* No. 16, 17, and 20 from 6-12 October, also K.N.A. Nos. 60-62.

21. Paragraph 12.
22. Paragraph 14.
23. Cf. B. Lohse, *Mönchtum und Reformation*, 1963, also "Die Kritik am Mönchtum bei Luther und Melanchthon," in *Luther and Melanchthon*, being papers delivered to the Second International Congress of Luther Studies, 1961, 129 ff.; R. H. Esnault, *Luther et le Monachisme aujourd'hui*, Geneva, 1964.
24. *Luther's Works*, Vol. 35, p. 41.
25. Cf. W. A. VIII. 573-669.
26. Cf. F. Wulf, S.J., *Geistliches Leben in der heutigen Welt*, 1960, 34-98; Self-denial and self-sacrifice as exercises in following Christ and as marks of the new life in Christ; see also E. Ranwez, "Drei Evangelische Räte" in *Concilium*, No. 9, 1965, 748 ff.
27. Y. Congar, *Der Laie, Entwurf einer Theologie des Laientums*, Stuttgart, 3rd Ed., 1964, 26.
28. Y. Congar, *Priester und Laien im Dienst am Evangelium*, 1965, 242 f.
29. Paris, 1952.
30. Title of a book by Louis-Marie de Bazelaire, Aschaffenburg, 1959.
31. *Schriften zur Theologie*, Vol. II, 343.
32. *Nachfolge*, 1937; *Ethik*, 1963. especially 208 ff.
33. "Ethik," *op. cit.*, 210.
34. Cf. E. von Severus in *Mönchtum in der Entscheidung*, edited by Th. Bogler, Maria Laach, 1952, 18.
35. Cf. Catholic point of view; E.

von Severus, "Zu den biblischen Grundlagen des Mönchtums" in *Glaube und Leben*, No. 26, 1953, 113 ff.: E. Heufelder, *Die Evangelischen Räte*, 1953: C. Feckes, *Die Lehre vom christlichen Vollkommenheitsstreben*, 2nd Ed. 1953: A. Schulz, *Nachfolge und Nachahmen: Studien über das Verhältnis der neutestamentlichen Jüngerschaft zur urchristlichen Vorbildethik*, Munich, 1962.
36. Cf. Article on the "Evangelical Counsels" by Franz Lau in *RGG*, 3rd Edition, II, 785-788.
37. Cf. E. Biot, O.P., translated by W. J. Kerrigan, *The Rise of Protestant Monasticism*, Baltimore, 1963; J. B. D. Cotter, "The Monastic Idea in Protestantism Today," in *The Church Quarterly Review*, April/June, 1963; 218 ff.; W. Schleiter, *Evangelisches Mönchtum? Entwicklung und Aufgabe der Bruder- und Schwesternschaften in der Kirche*, Stuttgart.
38. Cf. The self-description edited by Lydia Präger, *Frei für Gott und die Menschen*, 2nd Ed. 1964. : S. von Kortzfleisch, *Mitten im Herzen der Massen*, Stuttgart, 1963.
39. *Ehe und Ehelosigkeit*, 2nd Ed., 1957.
40. *Das Heute Gottes*, French Edition 1959, German: 1961, Herder Bücherei 1963. 2nd Ed. 1964, 91 f.
41. *Geistliche Weisungen im Anschluss die Regel von Taizé*, Gütersloh, 1963, 77.

Chapter VI

# Some Main Trends in the Renewal
# of Roman Catholic Missiology

"The scheme on mission is no more than the airport from which
the plane can take off," one of the bishops from Africa explained in
private during the fourth session of the Second Vatican Council;
"the airport will be forgotten, as soon as it has fulfilled its function
and the plane is going at cruising height." There can be no doubt
that this expresses the general mood in the aula when the missionary problems were debated, at any rate among the people engaged
in missionary work. Missionaries do not normally think much about
theories and papers, and they often tend to underestimate the importance of such things. At any rate, there is now a *Decree on the
Church's Missionary Activity*, and thereby Roman Catholic missiology has got a new start which will no doubt determine much
missionary thinking and acting in years to come.

## I. The Background of the Decree "Ad Gentes"

The fact that this decree is the first conciliar text in history to
deal directly with the missionary outreach of the church is in itself
of great importance and will have decisive consequences. For the
first time the Roman Catholic Church is teaching "in council" on
the nature of its mission to the world.

116

This decree must be understood against its background. An official statement like this ought perhaps to have its own meaning independently of time and space, but this is most certainly an empty theory in the case of this Decree, which is by nature a number of remarks on a very specific situation against a very specific background.

The background is first of all the crisis which affects Roman Catholic as well as Protestant missionary activities just now. This crisis is not just a result of external forces. It is not created first of all by the new era. Not colonialism and its end, not nationalism and its beginning, but the achievements of missionary enterprise itself have created the crisis.

## 1. Plantatio ecclesiae

*"Plantatio ecclesiae"* has been the motive for all *"*churches in mission" in the past centuries, i.e. all churches that believed they were churches. A number of missionary societies did, however, represent the tendency to separate the kingdom and the church so strictly that the churches no longer could be regarded as churches in any genuine sense. In those societies, of course, *"plantatio ecclesiae"* could not be an explicit motive.

Yet, by a strange irony of history, even those societies did in fact plant churches. They hoped to see apostolic *ecclesiolae* grow up as the result of their sowing the Gospel; but in practice a number of quite ordinary churches did spring out of the soil in Asia and Africa. These "hard facts" were difficult to accept. The triumphant period of the first "apostolic" mission gradually disappeared into a more realistic way of thinking, and in this the *"plantatio ecclesiae"* motive was gradually accepted by the majority of missionaries. Now and again reactions against this came up, and new "apostolic" movements had a try, but they in turn had to accept the church as their aim if anything was to result from their missionary zeal. This continuing "call to realism" from the "harvest fields" also had repercussions for the "home base." The "sending" societies or churches were thereby recalled to a more genuine and realistic ecclesiology.

The Roman Catholic Church too has had its Romantic period, and the aftereffects have been and are hard to digest. The return to realism has however started, and we are now seeing the repercussions in the sending churches and societies. The *ecclesia triumphans* is no longer a popular notion among the Roman Catholic missiologists. The *ecclesia peregrinans,* the *ecclesia in via* is much more favored.

The period of planting churches all over the world has had important consequences for the development of the Roman Catholic Church as a whole. It has contributed to the development by which the Roman Catholic Church has become very Roman. Missionary work has always been frustrating. It needs much discipline and concentration and paternalism. The Roman Catholic missionaries found all of this in the Congregatio de Propaganda Fide under the direct rule of the Roman pontifex. This centralization was closely connected with the expansion of the Western world into "all the world." The exercise of papal selfhood through the Portuguese and Spanish powers and later through the Propaganda and its machinery was one of the important reasons for the decisive concentration on the papal authority in 1870. That year was the year in which European imperialism (Russian, British, German) reached a climax, and the spiritual emperor in Rome had both the inclination and the ability to compete with the secular emperors.

In that same period the Roman Catholic Church seriously lacked missiologists who could "demythologize" this development. In the Protestant world there were at any rate some missiologists (Warneck and his able group of colleagues) who were able to demythologize the "caesareopapism" exercised by German and English imperialists and colonialists. Therefore in the Protestant churches the development toward self-supporting, self-governing, self-propagating churches had started before the middle of the 19th century and was able to grow steadily. The same development can, of course, be found in the Roman Catholic Church, but both later and less strongly. The papal selfhood was a hindrance for the selfhood of the churches which were planted all over the world. Only with the acceptance of this decree has a decisive and outspoken change been accepted by the church as a whole.

## 2. Communio ecclesiarum

The planting of the church succeeded. That is the great fact of our era of church history. We have by now grown accustomed to it, but in reality it is a great and surprising fact with important consequences for the whole life of the whole church. It is because of this fact that the missionary enterprise is in its present crisis. If the intrinsic aim of mission is to plant the church, what then when the churches are planted? Already 100 years ago Protestant missiologists had expected "the beautiful death" of the missions, when the house had been built. This "euthanasia" was postponed, however, by the fact that there were plenty of "regions beyond," where new churches needed to be planted. There are still certainly a few "white spots" on the map of the church, but they are now so few that they are losing their influence on missionary thinking. One can, of course, always ignore facts, and crowds of Protestant "free-lance" fundamentalist missionaries are trying nowadays to realize a "fools' paradise," a paradise which was lost long ago.

Yet even the responsible missionary enterprise is in a crisis today. It is changing radically and it must change, since the situation has changed. The churches exist. The churches *are* present all over the world. But for what purpose are they present? What is the intention of their existence? What is their mission? The metamorphosis of the missionary enterprise lies just in the simple change that missiology is trying to give as an answer to these questions: The churches are there for mission, they are present for each other and for the sake of the world, they exist for others.

This means a new stress on *communio ecclesiarum,* and mission becomes the definition of this *communio* existing in fraternal love and in *diakonia* for the world. In the Protestant churches the emphasis on the three-self formula has now been transferred to another formula: "The whole church with the whole Gospel for the whole world." This is how the *communio ecclesiarum* perspective is expressed. The same thing has now happened in Roman Catholic missiology and is expressed decisively in the decree. The whole active presence of the whole church is now coming into focus, and thereby the world college of bishops is forced to become an episcopacy for the whole world.

This idea, however, is dynamite for the papal selfhood. By it the Roman period of the history of the Roman Catholic Church has been put to an end. This fact is only gradually and partially realized as yet, since the Western dominance of the world, to which the Roman centralization definitely belongs, is still a reality which blurs the fact of the coming universal society. But those who have ears can hear that a new word has been spoken, not least in the Second Vatican Council. That word speaks about the church as the *communio* of all churches in this world, headed by their bishops. The collegiality, so much spoken of at the Council and still so little practiced, is but one expression of the completely new situation.

The dilemma of the Congregatio de Propaganda Fide is another example. Its parallel in the Protestant world was the International Missionary Council, which represented the missionary societies, even though it tried to get indigenous leadership involved in its conferences and committees. This was acceptable in the period of the *plantatio ecclesiae*, but it became intolerable in the period of the *communio ecclesiarum*. The International Missionary Council had to be integrated into the World Council of Churches (1961) which represented the *communio ecclesiarum* for better or for worse.

In a way the situation is different in the Roman Catholic Church. The Propaganda has always been in principle a part of the church itself, but this has been theory, not reality. Up till now only the Pope's own authority has expressed the unity between mission and church. The coming senate of bishops and the regional conferences of bishops will make a real integration possible between church and mission, but a change from inside will also be needed. This change will have to deal with the missionary perspective of the local congregation, of the priesthood, of episcopacy as such, and certainly glimpses of such a change can already be seen in the decree.

The way in which the Congregatio de Propaganda will change its policies will indicate how far this change has gone in reality. A gradual reformation of the outlook of the "congregation" so that it can function as the instrument for the "inter-communion" of the churches, as a clearinghouse for the "two-way traffic" between the members of the whole family of churches in mutual service and mutual inspiration will be the decisive sign of the necessary change. The present *jus commissionis* can develop into a *jus communionis* so that the churches themselves locally and regionally will decide what help they can give and what help they need. That would mean the realization of actual catholicity in a church which has up till now been more Roman than Catholic.

The development towards such a *communio ecclesiarum* has come to the forefront in the last few years, but it would not be fair to forget that it is rooted in a reorientation which started many years ago and was accepted by papal authority at an early stage. Pius XI, in his *Rerum Ecclesiae*, maintained—in spite of all the regulations in canon law—that *all* bishops share the burden of the missionary obligation with the Pope. Pius XII, too, understood that the mission of the apostles continues in all the bishops in communion with Rome. But, of course, he did not see the consequences of this insight. One of the consequences will no doubt be a revision of canon law, whose vision has up till now been mainly confined to the situation of Europe and America, so that the understanding that the missionary obligation rests upon the bishops collectively or *collegialiter* is totally missing. The need for active participation by all bishops from all the churhes in the total mission of the whole church is more important than the fact, so well registered in the canons, that for 1,500 years the bishops have not been responsible for the missionary outreach of the church.

### 3. Incorporatio mundi

Previous to the *plantatio ecclesiae* period an earlier period can be described by the words *"plantatio fidei."* That tradition, which was under the inspiration of the school of G. Warneck, was a comprehensive attempt to understand missionary activity as the propagation of the faith to all non-Christians. As a result it was not much interested in canon law and not at all ecclesiastical in its outlook.

The outspoken *"plantatio ecclesiae"* period between the two world wars was an attempt to reach a more typical Roman Catholic missiology. This approach was therefore ecclesiastical, hierarchical, and juridical, as was the main trend in the Roman Catholic Church as a whole in that period. The nature of mission was determined according to canon law. Since juridical concepts change in history, the understanding of mission had to be accepted as a variable one.

In that period the aim of missionary activity was to reach not only non-Christians but also e.g. Protestants, since they belonged canonically under the jurisdiction of the Congregatio de Propaganda Fide. The planting of the hierarchical church was seen in a strict way as the real task of mission. All subjective or spiritual aims were secondary to that.

This stress on *plantatio* was later on modified somewhat by a similar stress on "*consolidatio ecclesiae*," since the churches already planted still belonged under the Propaganda, but this addition only strengthened the stress on the external task. This line of thinking became the basis for the missionary encyclicals of Pius XI and XII.

This same trend is still very much alive in Roman Catholic missiology and can easily be found in the decree. But what is important is that a third tradition is arising, based on the new understanding of the meaning of the *communio ecclesiarum*. The signs of the new traditions to be found in the decree and in other Council texts belong, of course, to the new orientation from and after John XXIII. This "*aggiornamento*" of the church is marked by an attempt to get rid of any purely ecclesiastical orientation and to escape the tyranny of canon law. Of course, canon law is not burnt. But during the sessions of the Council so much spite against the canonists was expressed that a bit of burning might have been appropriate now and then.

At any rate, strong tendencies to move from an ecclesiastical to an ecclesiological orientation have been felt in modern Roman Catholic missiology, for instance in the decree; there is then a clear and repeated attempt to drop juridical definitions in favor of an understanding determined by factual conditions and problems in the modern world.

The best intentions from the "*plantatio fidei*" period seems to enter the scene again. Together with the emphasis on *plantatio* and *consolidatio ecclesiae* there is a real interest in what can be called "*incorporatio mundi*." The opening up of the church towards the world is at the same time an invitation to the world as a whole to become a part of the church, to be re-membered in the one body. Only in this way can the church grow into fullness. To plant the church and to consolidate its life and mission is still very important, but so is the growth of the total life of the church. The motive of growth plays a decisive role in modern Catholic missiology, and it is stressed that the church needs the whole world—the separated brethren as well as the Jews and the non-Christians—for this growth.

## II. On the Origins of the Decree "Ad Gentes"

However, the general background in the situation of the church at large must be distinguished from the specific situation at the Second Vatican Council, the direct background for the decree.

The sentences with which this paper started probably express the opinion of the majority of fathers in the Council. "It could have been much better, but it *could* certainly also have been worse." The reality of this statement was proved in the history of this decree. It *had* really been much worse!

The detailed story of its different stages cannot be told here. It has best been described in *Zeitschrift für Missionswissenschaft und Religionswissenschaft*, 50. Jhrg. Jan. 1966, part 1, pp. 3 f. by Josef Glazik and in *Herder Korrespondenz*, February 1965, part 5, pp. 232 f., and December 1965, part 15, pp. 723 f. To begin with, both the preliminary commission on missions and the later Council commission on missions were headed by Cardinal Agagianian and were under the influence of the traditional "Congregatio de Propaganda Fide" thinking.

In March 1963 it became clear that the main part of the material of the commission would be taken over by other Council commissions. This was, of course, a hopeful development, since it meant that the missionary perspective was accepted and integrated into the whole life of the church, but it did not make the task of the commission on missions easy. Also the schema which resulted from the redrafting remained within the traditional approach. What was going on in the Council had not yet influenced the thinking of the commission on missions in any important way. Consequently it underwent a series of vigorous attacks, sent in as letters, since the text had not yet been dealt with in the aula. Even members of the commission participated in the opposition, so that it became obvious that the schema was not a result of genuine teamwork in the commission. The commission therefore had to have another try. It worked hard in the last weeks of 1963, and the result was a completely new and much better schema, which was supported by practically all the members of the commission. This draft was accepted by the coordination commission in January 1964 and was sent to the fathers. At this time the opening up in the Council's thinking was obvious, and the fathers were very frank in their criticism. They pointed out that the emphasis was still on missions, not on Mission. They also criticized the predominant clericalism and institutional one-sidedness. This would have led to a redrafting and to a schema pretty close to the one at which the Council finally arrived. But already on April 23, 1964, the coordination commission had decided that all those schemes which had not yet been presented to the fathers should be reduced to short statements in the form of propositions.

So the commission again had to change the direction of its work. Since the Constitution on the Church had by then accepted from the commission on missions a draft and made it its own paragraph 17, in which the essence of missionary theology was presented, this whole normative area was left out. In the *"schema propositionum"* only 14 short declarations on "the missionary activity of the church" were put forward.

When this mini-schema was presented to the fathers it met vigorous opposition. It was known that this schema was not according to the wishes of the commission, but the result of different maneuvers backstage. As another result of these maneuvers the pope himself for the first and last time during the Council appeared in the aula in order to pacify the opposition. This happened on Nov. 6, 1964. He argued for the acceptance—with minor changes—of the schema and spoke favorably of the common missionary obligation of the church. The fathers, however, were not so easily pacified. The discussion became sharp, now and then offensive and vehement, at any rate very outspoken. The great Cardinals from northern Europe together with the Asian and African bishops were the leaders of the opposition in the aula. After the list of speakers was finished no one needed to ask *"placet"* or *"non-placet."* The fathers were only asked if they wanted a full schema put before them and not just a short declaration, and the great majority answered in favor of this proposal.

The majority of the commission on missions were happy to return to real work again. They now had behind them a solid and outspoken episcopal consensus to work on. The traditionalists from the Propaganda were pacified and the different backstage maneuvers had been proved to be against the will of the fathers. The commission had a fine new start, in which its own leading minority was politely set aside. A sub-commission was elected with Bishop Johannes Schütte (SVD) as its leader, to be responsible for the redrafting. Already at the beginning of April 1964 its proposal was discussed by the full commission. The draft from the sub-commission was somewhat watered down by the commission, but the drafters accepted this, knowing that once more the voice of the fathers would be raised.

The resulting text was a clear-cut Vaticanum II scheme, closely connected with the Constitution on the Church. It was sent in and accepted as the basis for discussion which took place in the fourth session from the 7th till the 13th of October, 1965. After a genuine and challenging discussion, in which all the deteriorations of the schema were pinpointed, the text was accepted by an overwhelming majority as the basis for modifications. Shortly afterwards it underwent the last comprehensive revision, in which for example a whole new chapter on "the young churches" was added (3). In the final vote all chapters and parts were accepted by a great majority except the part which dealt with the reform of the Congregatio de Propaganda Fide. One-third of the fathers disliked the influence which people behind the curtain had exerted in the last hours on that part whereby the radical reform of the "Propaganda" was left to the pope himself. On the 7th of December 1965 the whole decree on the Church's Missionary Activity was promulgated.

This development of the scheme on mission—to and from and up and down—meant that the decree which resulted never had a chance to develop out of a continuing process. It was made rather hastily and under some pressure. When it was dealt with in the fourth session, "the episcopal fatigue" was obvious. The fathers were tired, psychologically and maybe spiritually. There was no real discussion in the aula, no encounter between the differing groupings. The speeches went on as parallel lines, often repeating one another. The *"placets"* were given rather automatically. "Let us finish and go home," was the general mood. "This Council has already done what was possible, the rest is silence." The influence of the bishops upon the development seemed to dwindle—in spite of all the talk about collegiality. "Better go home before it disappears totally." "If this goes on I may turn Protestant." Such sayings were not just jokes. Behind them was a good deal of frustration.

It is important to know this special background. The scheme on mission did *not* receive the attention it had had a fair claim to receive. The scheme on mission should have been dealt with in connection with the scheme on the church. That would have given it a challenging setting. The fourth session was on the whole gray. The black weeks of the third session did not continue, but the price was a number of gray weeks without much excitement and fervor.

## III. Analysis of the Decree

It is very difficult to formulate a consistent opinion about the decree since it is not itself consistent at all points. Different schools of thought have contributed to it and the result is not always homogeneous. A synthesis has, of course, been aimed at, but time and circumstances did not allow for its growth into a more harmonious unit. As it is, however, it expresses in an honest way the pluriformity which characterizes present Roman Catholic missiology.

When attempting to analyze the text, one must also be aware of the fact that what is now on the table is not an attempt to make a complete treatise of the universal mission of the church. The decree is a description of some basic principles of missionary activity, and it puts forward those principles in a restricted and rather traditional way. In trying to keep a balance between the real avant-garde and the traditionalists the decree itself is a moderate statement without "dangerous" tendencies.

This is also seen in the way in which the crisis is dealt with. One certainly cannot call it dishonest, but on the other hand, there is no outspoken, honest, and open recognition of the really serious situation in which all missionary activities find themselves in these days. But this guarded cautiousness is something which Roman Catholic missiology shares with practically all missionary thinking.

### 1. Missio Dei and the ecclesia militans

The first chapter of the decree on mission is often understood as a sort of repetition of the second chapter of the Constitution on the Church, and it has been argued that this first chapter is therefore not necessary. This is a misunderstanding. In reality the introduction to the decree on mission goes behind the exposition in the Constitution on the Church and is itself the presupposition for that. The mission which is the mission of the church is basically God's mission, grounded in the Holy Trinity, participating in the *Missio Dei,* and thus mission is the basis of the church, so that one should speak about the church of the mission.

Archbishop Johann Baptist Zoa from Cameroun expressed this in the third session when he said that mission has its origin in the mission of the Word and of the Spirit. This mission is continued in and by the church, the church being the instrument for this mission. There is only one movement, which begins in the Holy Trinity and returns to the Holy Trinity, passing through the world and through history. Mission means participation in this movement, to enter into it, whereby the Word is brought to men in order to bring them to the Father and in order that they may cooperate with the Holy Spirit.

Mission as the continuation of the history of salvation, of the history of the works of God, beginning in the "fountainhead of love," the charity of God the Father, is very clearly expressed in Part 2 of the decree. Mission is participation in that *Missio Dei* which is a result of God's love to the world. But God calls men to share this life not only as individuals without any relation to one another, but as a people in which his children who had been scattered abroad might be gathered into one. Mission and unity and salvation therefore belong closely together. This is where *ecclesiology* begins. This was the starting point for the thinking on the church among the Christians of the first generations, and it has to be our starting point today. It gives us the right perspective for the church in the world.

The church turns to the world simply because it is her nature to do so as the church in mission. This must be expressed in the way *eschatology* is dealt with. That is, however, only partially done in the decree. Eschatology in the biblical sense is the story of the clash between the powers of this world and the kingdom of God which is now at hand. The church is by necessity placed in the middle of this clash, since it is the messianic people, created in these last days of human history as the means of God's salvation. The proclamation of the Gospel as the messianic tidings is the decisive obligation of the church, is the center of its eschatological action in and for the world, that action which is caused by Christ's own hidden lordship over the world. Looking forward in hope to the epiphany and apocalypse of Christ as Lord, the *ecclesia militans* awaits its liberation and its resurrection.

Certainly parts of this picture are to be found here and there in the decree. The church as the people of God, journeying along the narrow way of the cross, prepares the way for Christ's coming (1). The incarnation is understood as God's action to rescue men from the power of darkness and of Satan (3). But such passages are few and they have not been able to determine the atmosphere of the whole decree. The idea of growth has become so dominating that the real eschatological nature of Christ's mission is obscured. The rhythm of the apostolate is not slow (like that of a vegetable) but is an explosion (as in the parable of the seed), as Cardinal Meouchi from Beirut pointed out in the aula on the 7th of October 1965. Or as Cardinal Jaeger the same day put it: "The history of salvation is a drama of the deeds of light and darkness, and the church through her missionary activity shares in the passion of her Lord. Thus all appearance of frivolous optimism will be avoided and the reality of sin will not be overlooked."

The warnings were aimed at a revision of paragraph 9 which dealt with "Eschatological Aspects of Missionary Action," and some improvements were achieved. But that paragraph still is not at all what it should have been. Missionary activity is, however, in a fine way seen as the task of the church in the period between the first and the second coming of Christ, when the church will be brought together like a harvest from the four winds. Before Christ comes the Gospel must be preached to all nations. Missionary work is nothing other and nothing less than the manifestation or epiphany of God's plan and its fulfillment in the world and in history through which God manifestly brings about the history of salvation. Through the preaching of the Word and the celebration of the sacraments, the central and culminating point of which is the Most Holy Eucharist, this activity makes Christ, the author of salvation, present.

Christ is also present in the world. There his presence is secret, but still active, since all elements of truth and grace among non-Christians are caused by him. Nevertheless, even such elements need to be restored to Christ, for he overthrows the reign of the devil and conquers the manifold malice of sin. All such elements, when raised up, contribute to the glory of God, the confusion of the devil, and the happiness of men.

All this is understood as the movement towards eschatological fullness, since the people of God is thereby increased to the mature measure of the fullness of Christ so that the spiritual temple grows and is built up.

This is all very fine and beautiful, and yet, have not those sentences in fact lost the heart of the matter? The hidden presence of God is to be found in all elements of truth and grace, and mission work frees these elements from harmful influence and restores them to Christ. This is done with Christ's real presence in the Eucharist as its center. Mission work is thus in itself "nothing other and nothing less than the manifestation or epiphany" of God's plan. This way of speaking about hidden presence and real presence is common, but is it biblical? Is not the hiddenness which corresponds to the coming epiphany or apocalypse of the Lord his hidden presence in the messianic proclamation and action of his people? Is not this proclamation and action much more than restoration, elevation, and perfection? Are not these messianic realities God's own presence in the midst of a turbulent world at war against God and his Holy One? Is not, therefore, eschatological fullness something more than the increase of the church, even if it may also include such an increase?

In the October 1965 text there was a strong tendency to change the eschatological drama into an idyllic and harmonious pastorale. In the last text "the lion" was introduced, but its roaring was not allowed to spoil the peace and calm of the atmosphere.

A truly eschatological understanding of the missionary action of the church can only be gained when the living Word of God is taken as the center of the church in mission. The point is, however, that this is done in many other parts of the decree and would also fit in with the passage "on eschatology" (9) in a better way than the whole idea of growth which is spelled out in it now. If we take eschatology seriously, then growth certainly has meaning, for growth is eschatologically the result of the new creation, a *creatio ex nihilo*. That which was nothing is taken in by Christ and recre-

ated into the new being, his body. The "no" before the "yes" cannot
be evaded without losing the eschatological horizon. And the "yes"
can never be accepted without the proclamation of the living Word
of God, the Gospel of his favor and love.

## 2. Proclamation and salvation

"God can, in ways known only to Him, bring men, who through
no fault of their own do not know the Gospel, to the faith—for
without faith it is impossible to please God" (7). This statement
from the decree corresponds to the statement in *Lumen Gentium*
(16) in which it is said that "those also can attain to salvation who
through no fault of their own do not know the Gospel of Christ or
His Church, yet sincerely seek God and moved by grace strive by
their deeds to do His will as it is known to them through the dic-
tates of conscience. Nor does Divine Providence deny the helps
necessary for salvation to those who, without blame on their part,
have not yet arrived at an explicit knowledge of God and with
His grace strive to live a good life. Whatever good or truth is
found amongst them is looked upon by the Church as a preparation
for the Gospel. She knows that it is given by Him who enlightens
all men so that they may finally have life."

After a period where the juridical viewpoint was dominant and
external norms were favored, the tendency is now the opposite. One
often gets the impression that in modern Catholic missiology all
mankind somehow belongs to the church, although in different degrees and at different levels, since no man is without any relation
with God.

On this background the question inevitably comes up whether
or not mission has become superfluous. Why take the means of grace
to people, when their own genuine intention and good deeds can
mean salvation for them? Mission can at any rate easily be understood as a possible extra, an additional help. But who will risk
life and health in missionary activity for so little? Recruiting for
mission becomes problematic on this basis. Missionary bishops and
leaders of religious orders, of course, felt this very strongly and spoke
up in the aula against any watering down of the missionary motive,
and consequently in the last texts a much stronger argument for

missionary work was put forward. It was done by stressing three aspects:

1. *The theocentric argument:* Missionary work has to be carried on not for man's sake, but for God's glory. *Deus vult.* It is God's will (7), he has commanded his disciples to go forth. It is therefore a matter of obedience to be the church in mission. Mission happens for the glory of God.

2. *The ecclesiocentric argument:* Missionary work happens because full salvation requires visible and external grace and community. Salvation is not individual salvation, but corporate union with God and other Christians. Mission is this *"incorporatio mundi,"* and without mission this *incorporatio* does not happen. The church in mission is therefore still in a real sense the sacrament of salvation (1 and 5). In mission mankind is not just told that it is already saved, but salvation achieves its effect everywhere (3), the church in mission is the means of salvation (6) for without unity there is no salvation (4 and 15). Consequently, it can still be said that "those persons cannot be saved who knowing that the Catholic Church was founded by God through Jesus Christ as something necessary, nevertheless refuse to enter it or to remain in it."

3. Thus the *jus sacrum evangelizandi* is still valid. There is only salvation in Christ, and Christ is in his church, but Christ can move beyond his church. He is not imprisoned in it. The right of the church to preach the Gospel is also its duty to follow its Lord beyond the frontiers of the church into all parts of the world with the living Word of God.

In the last text this very important perspective is vindicated much more strongly than in any other edition of the scheme and probably more strongly than in any other Roman Catholic text at all. In practically all parts the decree speaks about the preaching of the message, of the Word of God, of the Gospel (1, 3, 4, 5, 6, 7, 8, 12, 13, 15). This proclamation has to be the task of the whole church, of the laity, of the priests, and of the bishops (20, 23, 24, 39).

There is not the slightest chance of lessening the importance of this Gospel orientation in the decree. What was lacking in the Constitution on the Church is found explicit and consequent in the decree on mission, even if other tendencies, which cannot easily—

if at all—be combined with this Gospel orientation, are also found. All this means that the *presence* of the church in the world is rightly understood not only as *praeambula evangelisationis,* but first of all as evangelization. "The Church fulfills its mission when . . . it becomes fully and actively present to all men and peoples so as to bring them by living example, preaching, the Sacraments and other means of grace, to the faith, freedom and peace of Christ" (5). Even if the disciples when immediate preaching of the Gospel is impossible can "in a certain sense make Christ present" (6) through their silent witness, the missionary activity has to be understood in that it makes Christ present through preaching of the Word and celebration of the sacraments (9). And this same thing is said very explicitly thus: "It is not enough for a Christian Community to be present and established in some nation. Nor is it enough for it to practise the apostolate of example. It is established and is present in order to announce Christ to its fellow-citizens by word and deed and to help them to receive Christ fully" (15). Then "the whole community of Christians can become a sign of God's presence in the world, and the active presence of the laity can thus make the Gospel grounded in the character, life and work of the different people of the world" (21).

"Plantatio ecclesia" is not enough, not even with "consolidatio ecclesia" added. The church must be present *in order to* be missionary, *in order to* announce Christ to the world.

### 3. The apostolic continuity

"The duty of spreading the faith and doctrine of salvation by Christ is imposed on the church by Christ's explicit command . . . ," this is the beginning of a significant statement in paragraph 5 (The Church sent by Christ), whose first phrases seem to indicate that the church as such and as a whole represents the apostolic continuity in its missionary perspective. The following phrases, however, run: "which the Order of bishops, assisted by their priests and in union with the Successor of Peter, the Supreme Shepherd of the Church, inherited," whereby it seems to be stated that only the bishops represent this same continuity. The next phrases, however, go on: "This duty is also imposed on the Church by reason of the life which Christ bestows on its members."

In paragraphs 1 and 2 the whole decree starts with the assumption that "the Church has been divinely sent to the nations to be the sacrament of salvation" and that the "pilgrim Church is missionary by its very nature." The reason for this is the participation in the *Missio Dei*.

When the commission on mission had to begin anew after Nov. 6, 1964, it took in advisers and theologians of a rather progressive type, and the first draft from the sub-commission, presented to the whole commission in March 1965, started, in the same way as did the Constitution on the Church and the so-called schema 13, from the "people of God" before moving on to the hierarchy. But "for certain reasons" (which probably was the attitude of Cardinal Agagianian and his group) it became necessary to stress the hierarchical aspect to such a degree that this balance was lost again.

After the discussion in the aula in October 1965 the opinion was expressed by leading members of the commission that it would now be possible to go back to the original text and develop the mission of the whole church, also the mission of the laity in their own right, not only in cooperation with and as helpers for the clergy. Cardinal Alfrink, for example, said that the text hobbled between two concepts and expressed the hope that this ambiguity would be cleared up. For him the missionary obligation lay with the whole people of God under the leadership of the hierarchy. Consequently, it is wrong to speak as if missionary activity is committed only to the hierarchy, while the rest of the faithful are merely capable of cooperation with the bishops. Other bishops had spoken in the same way and asked for the same change in emphasis.

Bishop John Schütte—the head of the drafters—in his presentation of the schema on November 10 declared that "a special effort had been made to establish a proper balance between the fact that Christ's mandate to preach was given directly to the Apostles and their Successors and the request of many fathers that there should be a greater emphasis on the missionary vocation of the whole people of God."

No doubt an attempt was made, but without much success. The last text, it is true, speaks strongly about the general missionary vocation, but this vocation is still seen as a sort of cooperation with and assistance to the bishops. It has been explained in this way: "The mandate entrusted to the apostles and the impelling graces of the Holy Spirit are complementary, not competing." But that explanation cannot do away with the fact of hierarchical one-sidedness in the decree. The church as such is not understood as the continuity of the apostolate. The words about "the apostolate of the laity" are mainly rhetoric and are not expressions of an *aggiornamento* of the concept of the apostolate.

This assessment is clearly supported by the way in which the words apostolic and apostolate are used in the decree. A few representative instances will suffice: "Since the Church's life is *apostolic,* the Catechumens should learn actively to help in the work of evangelization and of building up the Church . . . " (14). "Congregations (orders) working for the same *apostolic* aim should not become too numerous to the detriment of both the Religious Life and the *apostolate*" (18). "The laity endeavour to establish the rule of justice and charity in civil life through their civic and *apostolic* activity . . . " "Through their truly Christian life, families become seed-beds of the *apostolate* of the laity" (19). "Associations and groups should be established through which the *apostolate* of the laity may be enabled to permeate the whole of society with the Gospel spirit" (15). "The *apostolate* of the example is not enough, Christ must be announced" (15). And finally: "It is part of the function of a bishop, as the ruler and centre of unity in the diocesan *apostolate,* to promote missionary activity . . . all missionaries are subject to his jurisdiction in their various activities which are connected with the exercise of the sacred *apostolate*" (30).

It is evident that only in the last instance is the term apostolate used in the full meaning. The previous quotations used the terms apostolic and apostolate in a secondary way, more or less as synonymous with the general and vague meaning of missionary.

On the other hand, there are instances in the Decree where "missionary" is so loaded with meaning that it seems to be the real decisive norm and reality in the life of the Church: "Missionary work is intimately connected with the nature of the Church: this work propagates the Church's saving faith; it perfects the Catholic unity of the Church by extending it; it sustains the Church's apostolic zeal; it exercises the collegial goodwill of the Church's Hierarchy; it gives proof of the Church's holiness, which it causes to radiate and develop" (6). This citation is extremely interesting since in it the "notes" of the Church from the creed are interpreted as "open" concepts, able to grow. In missionary work the "Catholic unity" (which must include both *catholicity* and *unity*) is perfected by extension, the *apostolic* zeal is sustained and the church's *holiness* is developed.

If "missionary" had been used in this sense in the whole decree it would certainly have meant a breakthrough in Roman Catholic missiology and probably in missiology as such. In this sense missionary work is certainly no extra in the life of the church, but is the church itself in its growth.

The interesting passage from 6 says about missionary work that it "exercised the *collegial* goodwill of the Church's hierarchy." This is the positive side of the hierarchical dominance in the decree on mission. Through this one-sidedness the missionary obligation is very clearly put on the shoulders of all bishops as a part of their collegial duty.

"The task of proclaiming the Gospel everywhere on earth belongs primarily to the Body of Bishops" (29). "It is part of the function of a Bishop, as the ruler and centre of unity in the diocesan apostolate, to promote missionary activity" (30). "All Bishops, as members of the body of Bishops which succeeds the College of Apostles, are consecrated not just for some single diocese, but for the salvation of the entire world . . . the extension of the Body of Christ is the responsibility of the whole College of Bishops" (38). In such sentences the prerogative becomes an obligation, and suddenly the right context for all hierarchical claims is seen in radical clarity.

This approach was spelled out in the aula already in the third session by Cardinal Bea, who, quoting the Constitution on the Church, stressed that all members of the episcopate college together have the task of preaching the Gospel to the whole of mankind. And in fact this is the necessary consequence of the *"communio eccle-siarum."*

The strength of the papal centralization has been its obvious importance for the evangelization of the world. In our time the *communio* of bishops, the college of bishops, has the same importance for the announcement of the Gospel to all mankind. Only if this is taken seriously can the new collegiality gain real importance in the life of the church.

In connection with this the missionary obligation of the *"younger churches"* must be seen. Chapter 3 "on Particular Churches" was added late and deals with this problem as a whole. A true independence is urged but at once the corollary interdependence is stressed as strongly. "The young churches should remain in close communion with the whole Church" (19), and this should take place as a mutual exchange of forces in order to increase the life of the Mystical Body.

The direct missionary obligation of the local young church is brought forth clearly. Each particular church is sent to those who are living in its territory, and it has to be the means of pointing out Christ to others. This is so for the bishop, who should first and foremost be a herald of the faith so that he may lead new disciples to Christ (20). And this is so for the local priests who should join forces with the foreign missionaries with whom they form one college of priests . . . in order to preach the Gospel to those outside the church. And it is so for the whole laity, for whom the missionary obligation is given as an apostolic vocation.

It is stressed that the young churches should participate as soon as possible in the universal missionary work of the church by sending their own missionaries to proclaim the Gospel all over the world, even though they themselves are suffering from a shortage of clergy. For their communion with the universal church will be brought to perfection only when they themselves take an active part in missionary zeal towards other nations (20).

A number of the practical consequences concerning such Joint Action for Mission are developed in the decree, and even the idea of a sort of taxation of all churches for missionary purposes (proposed by Cardinal Frings from Köln in the third session) is put forward (38). When the hierarchy is understood as the direct continuity of the apostolate, and when the hierarchy is specified as the episcopate "in college" then of course the consequence will be that the collegiality also will become a necessity in practical leadership. During the long period when the missionary enterprise was directed by the papal authority the *Congregatio de Propaganda Fide* as such had a key position. This in itself could mean anything, depending on how the leadership of the Congregation was composed. Until now in practice only the Roman Cardinal members of the Congregation have exercised this leadership, since they were always on the spot. This, of course, has meant that the staff has had a disproportionate share of the actual influence, since the Roman Cardinals definitely do not know too much about the missionary situation all over the world. The secretaries no doubt have exercised their influence with great ability and goodwill, but certainly their rule was not an expression of the catholicity of the church. Because of the development of the collegiality of the bishops on the basis of the *communio ecclesiarum,* a change in the leadership of the Congregation had to come. The 1964-1965 sub-committee which drafted the new schema intended to propose a radical change of the Congregation, whereby the collegiality of all bishops was realized also in the leadership of missionary activities and whereby the insight of those actually engaged in missionary work was applied to revitalize the mission of the church.

This was done partly but not mainly under the pressure of Asian and African bishops. The main impetus seems to have come from the leaders of the religious orders who wanted to have closer liaison with the congregation and to bring into it more competence and local expertise. The commission therefore proposed that the *"Dicasterium constituatur membris selectis ex omnibus illis qui in opere missionali collaborant . . . "* and all these *"statutis temporibus convocandi, collegialiter sub auctoritate Summi Pontificis supremam gubernationem totius operis missionalis exerceant."*

On "higher authority" this proposal from the commission was questioned, and with grudging consent of the leaders of the commission (not all members seemed to have been informed about the change) another edition was suddenly distributed with these sentences: *"Hi omnes, statutis temporibus convocandi, supremam gubernationem totius operis missionalis participent."* Nothing about collegiality and only participation in, not exercise of, leadership.

The reaction from the Asian and African bishops was strong and bitter. A number of strange maneuvers took place on this issue, some of them certainly below any decent standard.

Bishop John Schütte openly declared at a press meeting that the amendment was a serious weakening of the schema, a weakening which was not wanted by the commission itself and which seemed to be against established policy. But in order not to endanger the whole schema the change had been accepted. But he and others would be happy if some of the fathers in the Council would come out for the stronger version. He described the problem in this way: "The Curia is the executive instrument of the Pope, the Council is the adviser of the Pope. A conflict between the executive and the advising organ is possible and is only to be solved by the Pope himself." In the end both parties had to give in, and the text is the result of such a compromise. It states (29) that there should only be one competent Roman Congregation for all the Missions and for all missionary work, namely the one "for the Propagation of the Faith." This Congregation should direct and coordinate both missionary work and missionary aid throughout the world, though the rights of the Eastern Churches should be respected. It is stated that this Congregation, together with the Secretariat for Promoting Christian Unity, should seek ways and means of bringing about and guiding fraternal cooperation as well as harmonious living with the missionary efforts of other Christian communities, so that the scandal of division may be removed as much as possible.

The delicate point of leadership is dealt with in this way: Selected representatives of all those who collaborate in missionary work would have an effective part with deliberate vote (!) in the direction of this Congregation. They should be Bishops from all over the world—after consultation with the Episcopal Conferences—the Heads of the Missionary Institutes and of the Pontifical Mission Aid Societies, chosen in ways and under conditions to be determined by the Roman Pontiff. All these (!) should be called together at fixed times to exercise "*supremam ordinationem*" of all missionary work under the authority of the Sovereign Pontiff.

The balance in the compromise seems to be in favor of the reformative wing, although the vague formulations will allow for quite a lot of influence from the "*status quo*" minded wing. There is no longer any mentioning of "*collegialiter*," but the facts implied in this term will have a fair chance of becoming a working reality in the Congregation.

## 4. Where is the frontier?

In the *Ecumenist*, Nov.-Dec., 1965, p. 11, Peter Hebblethwaite stated: "What has happened is that a dynamic conception of the Church has replaced a static conception. Post-tridentine theology, in the main, saw the Church first and foremost as a structure, an institution, with well-defined frontiers: you were either within or without and you knew the difference. In this view the missionary was easily defined as someone who tried to reach out to people who were beyond the boundary. He was known, significantly, as a *foreign* missionary. Conversion consisted in bringing people within the boundary, or to put it the other way round, in extending the boundaries to include new people."

Today the frontiers are definitely not well defined. Today it is very difficult to know the difference between those who are within and those who are without. Today the missionary is not at all easily defined and the meaning of conversion has become very ambiguous. And this is so both in Protestant and in Roman Catholic missiology.

This uncertainty is on the whole a result of the lack of a clear answer to the question: Where is the frontier? The term "foreign mission"—which was an expression of awareness of the difference between within and without—has lost its meaning today, since there is no longer a Western home, in which the church lives its traditional life, and a "foreign" world, into which the church has to send its expeditions or missions in order to plant the church.

The clear distinction between the Western world and the rest of the world has dwindled, and the fact of the *communio ecclesiarum* now means that the home base of the mission is everywhere in the world. The only frontier to work with is the frontier between the church and the world, and it is in principle the same everywhere in the *"oikumene."* But in this way "mission" tends to become the term indicating the church itself in its growth and in its movement into all secular realities of society. Thereby, however, the exact and urgent sense of mission may be lost. When everything is mission, the result may soon be that nothing is mission.

That danger is even more acute when, as in modern Catholic

ecclesiology, the possibility of salvation outside the church is accepted. Then the frontier becomes even more obscured and in reality tends to lose all importance.

A reaction against the general and indefinite use of the term "mission" was strongly expressed in the aula, not least by very "progressive" fathers. Cardinal Frings from Köln, for example, on behalf of the African and other missionary bishops already in the 3rd session wanted to maintain the strict meaning of mission and rejected the word mission in connection with the work in areas which are now dechristianized. Mission must mean the preaching of the Gospel in places where it has *not yet* been preached.

And Bishop Jacob Moynagh from Nigeria spoke on the same line and argued that when the difference between missionary work in the real meaning and the normal pastoral activity of the church is done away with, the mission will suffer much. The urgency of the real missionary activity will not be clear any longer if the concepts are not distinguished from one another. Also Cardinal Bea stressed that the cherished task of the church is still the preaching of the Gospel to those who have not yet heard of Christ.

The missionary is no longer characterized by his leaving his own country but by his going to those who have *not yet* heard the Gospel—whether he is autochthonous or foreigner (23). This consensus, however, did not influence the traditional territorial distinctions. These distinctions were maintained in so far as legal matters were concerned.

Therefore no clear-cut definition of "mission" was reached in this Council. The important and wide definition from paragraph 6 has already been mentioned. According to that, mission means the growth of the church in unity, holiness, catholicity, and apostolicity. A similar definition is given in paragraph 9: "Missionary work is nothing more nor less than the manifestation or Epiphany of God's plan and its fulfilment in the world and in history, through which God by means of the missions manifestly brings about the history of salvation." Mission according to this understanding is the church itself fulfilling its task. But at the same time, of course, more formal and legal definitions are found in the schema, whereby the more specific meaning of mission is expressed.

## IV. De Ecclesiae Habitudine ad Religiones Non-Christianas

In several parts of *"Ad Gentes"* the attitude of the church to non-Christian faiths is described. Whatever elements of truth and grace are found among non-Christians are understood as a secret presence of God. The task of missionary work is not to deny the reality of these elements, but to free them from the contagion of evil and restore them to Christ, who is their author (9).

Restoration, correction, and elevation are the key words of this understanding. The attitude of the church to other expressions of faith in God is that of sympathy. The task is never to reject and condemn, but to uncover the seeds of the Word in the different religious traditions (11).

By sincere and patient dialogue the communication of the Gospel has to take place, so that people can grow in insight and be brought under the dominion of God the Savior, whom they already have met and know about.

The same approach is found in *"Lumen Gentium."* The ability, riches, and customs in which the genius of each people expresses itself have to be fostered and not denied. Taking them to itself, the church purifies, strengthens, elevates, and consecrates those elements and thus brings back all humanity and its possessions to Christ who is the source of everything and is to become the head of everything (13).

Since in reality "the whole of mankind" belong somehow to the Catholic unity, since all men are called by the grace of God to salvation (13), there is no definite frontier between the church and the non-Christians. All are related in various ways to the people of God (16). First of all, the *Jewish people* is mentioned as the people to whom the testament and the promises were given and from whom Christ was born according to the flesh. It is stressed that on account of their fathers this people remains most dear to God, for God does not repent of the gifts he makes nor of the calls he issues (16).

This theme is developed with strength and clarity in that passage of the declaration on the relation of the church to non-Christian religions which deals with "the Jewish religion." The spiritual bond between the people of the New Testament and the people of Abraham is seen as a decisive part of the mystery of the church, since the beginnings of the church's faith and of her election are already found among the Patriarchs, Moses, and the Prophets. The "exodus" of the chosen people from the land of bondage is seen as a foreshadowing of the salvation of the church. The basis for the relationship between the church and the Jewish people is the cross of Christ, on which he reconciled Jews and Gentiles and made them one in himself.

Faced with the tendency to consider "Jewish" a synonym for Anti-Christian, the declaration states the fact that not only Jesus himself, but also his mother and his apostles and the majority of the first disciples were Jewish. As Gregory Baum expressed it: The Pharisees were not more Jewish than Mary, the high priests not more Jewish than the apostles, and Judas not more Jewish than the first congregation in Jerusalem.

The Jews did not, for the most part, accept the Gospel, but God's gift and call are irrevocable. The church awaits that day on which all peoples will address the Lord with a single voice and serve him shoulder to shoulder. In this eschatological way the hope for the salvation of "whole Israel" is confirmed.

In the present situation mutual knowledge and respect, common studies and fraternal dialogue are recommended. This can happen and ought to happen, since it is not permissible for Christians to attribute to all Jews, neither those alive when Jesus was killed, nor the Jews of today, the guilt for his sufferings and death. The Jews should not be presented as rejected by God, and therefore they should not be rejected in any way by the church.

Any kind of hatred, persecution, or display of anti-Semitism, directed against Jews at any time and by anyone, is "deplored" by the fathers. Some misgivings were created because the first texts had "condemn," for which "deplore" was substituted. This can, however, be interpreted, as is done by Gregory Baum, to mean that the church can only condemn the sin of others, but when it has itself been a part of such sin it has to "deplore" it.

This is, however, an interpretation given by a representative from the most open and honest wing of the theologians at the Council; certainly the opposite wing would not support such an interpretation. Because of the statement on the Jewish people a maximum of diplomacy was used by the administrators of the Council, who on the one side had the skeptical Jewish public, always ready to conclude that the Council did not dare to repent honestly, and on the other side the Arab pressure groups wanting to stop any utterance which might be interpreted as a political acceptance of Israel. In spite of this pressure, the Council succeeded in tackling the most important issues at stake, even if at some points the last text represents a weakening of the first drafts. A passage from the earlier drafts, in which the word *"deicidium"* as an accusation against the Jews was condemned, was dropped, and that aroused a rather bitter Jewish reaction. But in fact that deletion cannot be considered important. The meaning is still in the declaration, even if the actual word is not there.

The Jews are in this way seen as a part of God's plan of salvation, but the same—although in another way—is said about the *Muslims,* since they acknowledge the Creator, profess to hold the faith of Abraham, adore the one merciful God, who on the last day will judge mankind ( *Lumen Gentium* 16). Though they do not acknowledge Jesus as God, they revere him as prophet. They also honor Mary, his virgin mother. At times they even call on her with devotion.

The traditional quarrels and hostilities between Christians and Muslims should, therefore, be forgotten, so that all can work for mutual understanding in order that justice, freedom, and peace can be achieved for the benefit of all mankind (Declaration 3).

The Eastern religions, too, are mentioned in a very positive way. Thus in *Hinduism,* men contemplate the divine mystery and express it through an inexhaustible abundance of myths and through searching essays into philosophy; they seek freedom from the anguish of our human condition either through ascetical practices or profound meditation or a flight to God with love and urgency. Again, *Buddhism* in its various forms realizes the radical inadequacy of this changeable world; it teaches a way by which men, in a devout and confident spirit, may be able either to acquire the state of perfect liberation, or attain the supreme illumination by their own efforts or through higher help.

As a whole, the church in such texts as these stands forth as the mother of mankind, with an open heart to all faiths. It rejects nothing that is true and holy in the religions, but rejoices in everything which can be seen as a reflection of the Truth which enlightens all men, Christ who is the fullness of religious life, in whom God reconciled all things to himself (2).

Apart from what the Council *said* on the missionary obligation of the church, it was in itself a great contribution to the missionary activity of the church, since through all its sessions the Catholic fathers were reeducated and given a missionary outlook. For months they sat down and listened to one another and to the theological experts in order to be able to fulfill their task. The Western bishops for the first time really met the bishops from Asia and Africa and Latin America and so the church universal became a functional reality for them. Outlooks and opinions were thereby gradually changed.

Thus the manifold character of the Catholic Church, its pluriformity in life and thinking, became a fact evident to all, and was accepted as such. The Catholic communion of churches (in the plural!) was before the fathers and its factual consequences were accepted. Each church must have its own image and life according to that in order that it can really incarnate itself in the whole life of mankind. Not the Roman and Latin church alone, but the church of Christ must be at the center. This was probably the real and decisive contribution of this Council.

## Chapter VII

# The Declaration on Religious Liberty

### 1. Significance

For Protestant ecumenical leaders, the Declaration on Religious Liberty was the Second Vatican Council's "most welcome accomplishment" (Dr. Fry, Chairman of the Central Committee of the World Council of Churches), "especially praised" (Dr. Visser 't Hooft, General Secretary), "most impressive document" (Dr. Eugene Carson Blake, nominee for the General Secretaryship).[1]

This is true from only one perspective. From other points of view, at least half a dozen conciliar documents can be considered more important. However, as Catholic bishops in the debates at St. Peter's often emphasized, the statement on religious liberty was a *sine qua non*. Without it, a large part of the world would continue to agree with the 19th century English historian, Macaulay, that Roman Catholicism involves " . . . a complete subjection of reason to authority . . . and, above all, a merciless intolerance."[2] The Council's stands in favor of ecumenical openness and the humble service of mankind would not have been credible, and its impact on those both inside and outside the church would have been greatly reduced.[3]

Further, this was probably the most difficult of the Council's steps towards renewal. However much Macaulay may have exaggerated, he was, of course, right that the Roman Church insists on ecclesiastical authority more than any other major Christian body. This makes liberty particularly difficult for it to acknowledge. With the emphasis

145

on authority, goes the claim that Rome and those in communion with it are the one true church, the one church whose dogmas cannot be in error and therefore cannot alter. This declaration certainly appears to threaten these positions; it at the very least seems to change the official teaching of the past more drastically than any other of the Council's actions. Successive popes have condemned religious liberty, not, to be sure, with full dogmatic force, but with a solemnity which falls just short of that.[4]

Yet the pressure to change was immense. It came, not only from countries such as the United States, where Catholics have long affirmed their devotion to religious liberty, but also from Communist lands where the church finds it difficult to protest repressive governmental action unless it can affirm its own belief in freedom for others.

It is thus easy to see why the battle over religious liberty was severe. If the Roman Church can repudiate its official position on such a matter, the number of points on which it cannot change, on which it cannot have been in error, is drastically and unpredictably reduced. Vast areas become uncertain, and the authority of the church and its claims to uniqueness and immutability would seem to be seriously undermined. This has led even some non-Catholic commentators to predict that Catholicism will suffer serious losses as a result of this declaration.[5] This, certainly, is what the conservatives fear. It was this which made their struggle against the declaration longer and more bitter than against any other of the Council's documents, except possibly the section on the Jews in the Declaration on non-Christian religions.

Rather than recount the details of this story, and of the long and difficult process of formulating the declaration, we shall confine ourselves in this chapter to analyzing the weaknesses and strengths of the final version.

As the document is brief, easily available and has been widely reported, we shall not summarize it, but plunge immediately into analysis.[6]

## 2. Weaknesses

Perhaps without exception, the weaknesses can be attributed to efforts to guard against the dangers (both real and imagined) feared by the conservatives. The first of these dangers is that religious liberty be equated with "indifferentism," with the view that it makes no difference to what religion or church one belongs; or, more specifically, that men are not morally obligated to become Catholics to the degree that they find the truth. To protect against this, a strong reaffirmation of traditional Roman claims was inserted into the introduction of the last draft of the declaration: "We believe that this one true religion subsists in the catholic and apostolic church. . . . All men are bound to seek the truth, especially in what concerns God and His Church, and, when known, remain in it. . . . Religious freedom has to do with immunity from coercion in civil society, [and] leaves unimpaired the traditional doctrine on the moral duty of man and society toward the true religion and one church of Christ" (No. 1).

These additions were widely protested: they were said to weaken the affirmation of freedom. However, when one reads with the same kind of technical precision with which a jurist reads the law—and this must be done, for what we have here is a carefully composed statement of official policy—one sees that the change is in form, not substance. The previous draft expressed the same teaching, though more briefly and pallidly: "The principle of religious liberty leaves intact the Catholic doctrine of the one true religion and of the one church of Christ." In short, what is affirmed is freedom from social, political, legal, and psychological pressure, not from the moral obligation to adhere to the true religion and the true church.[7] A Protestant need not quarrel with this, because, unless he has been influenced by secular relativism, he also opposes religious indifferentism. He also believes in the absolute obligation to adhere to the truth once this is known, even though, for him, this involves the rejection of Roman claims, not their acceptance, as for the Catholic.

Nevertheless, as some Catholics also recognize,[8] it is unfortunate that this doctrine was expressed so starkly in this particular place without any of the qualifications found in the Decree on Ecumenism, the Constitution on the Church, and the Declaration on non-Christian religions. In these is expressed genuine respect for what, from the Roman Catholic point of view, are the partial truths of other churches and religions. Without similar expressions of respect the acknowledgment that their adherents have full rights to religious freedom sounds grudging, and the declaration loses in psychological effectiveness.

A second defect of the declaration is more serious. Past sins of the church against religious liberty are only indirectly acknowledged, and the degree to which the present teaching represents a radical change is minimized. On the first point, all that is said is that "in the life of the people of God . . . there has at times appeared a way of acting that was hardly in accord with the spirit of the gospel or even opposed to it. Nevertheless, the doctrine of the church that no one is to be coerced into the faith has always stood firm" (No. 12).

From the point of view of Roman Catholic presuppositions, this is technically true. It is not the church which has acted against the spirit of the Gospel in its treatment of heretics, Jews, and others, but rather sinful men within the church. Further, persecution has always been explained, not as an effort to coerce conscientious dissidents or unbelievers, but as a means of protecting the gullible multitudes from dangerous teaching, or as pressure on those who act, not from honestly held convictions, but in bad faith.[9]

Nevertheless, for more than a thousand years the visible, institutional church, and not simply men within it, appeared to all the world to be officially and fully committed to positions such as that of the Theodosian Code of 380 A.D.: "The church, despairing of his [the pertinacious heretic's] conversion, makes provision for the safety of others and, having cut him off from the church by excommunication, relinquishes him to the judgment of the secular arm to be eliminated from the world by death."[10]

Confession needs to be made for this shameful record, and it could have been done. The Decree on Ecumenism, for example, asks pardon for the wrongs inflicted on "separated brethren." Something similar could have been included in this document. Bishop Beran of Prague, who has spent many years in Communist prisons, asked the Council to do this: "The Catholic Church is today expiating the defects and the sins committed in her name against religious liberty in past centuries, such as the case of the priest John Huss in the 15th century. . . . Thus even history admonishes us that in this Council the principle of religious liberty and the liberty of conscience must be proclaimed . . . in a spirit of penitence for the sins of the past." Bishop Baraniak made a similar request on behalf of the entire Polish hierarchy, as did also Cardinal Rossi in the name of 83 Brazilian bishops.[11]

There is little doubt, further, that those in the Secretariat for Christian unity chiefly responsible for drafting the declaration would have liked to comply. Their failure to do so vividly illustrates the tenacity of the opposition and the difficulty that the Catholic Church as a whole still has to admit its wrongs and its changes explicitly and publicly.

It does not behoove Protestants, however, to be self-righteous even on a point like this. We too easily forget that the churches of the Reformation also adopted the infamous position of the Theodosian Code during the first period of their existence.[12] We forget that many of our churches accepted religious liberty reluctantly, that it was forced upon them by outside, often secular, developments. We cannot pride ourselves because they yielded to these pressures more quickly than the Catholics, for in part this was the result of their weakness and lack of the size and the organizational means to resist as persistently as did the Roman Church. Further, even when the principles of indifferentism have been rejected, its spirit has had an influence. Protestants are not likely to feel as deeply as do even those Catholics who are fully committed to religious freedom that "there is truth which it is not possible, without guilt, to fail to attain," and that, as a consequence, heresy "is much more of an absolute threat to human life than all other occurrences in face of which people today still feel the use of force to be justified. . . . "[13] As a consequence, our tolerance of error is all too likely to be rooted in indifference rather than in active Christian love. Lastly, we frequently lack a keen awareness of the unity and continuity of the church. Our confession of the sins of our fathers (including Luther's and Calvin's) is too facile unless it is wrung from hearts which deeply sense the oneness of the family, of the people, of God in all times and places.

It is not in a condemnatory spirit, then, that we come to the third and most fundamental criticism of this declaration. The grounding provided for the affirmation of religious liberty (as distinct from the affirmation itself) is questionable, not only from a Protestant perspective, but also from the point of view of much contemporary Roman Catholic thought. A different approach could have been chosen, and the question arises whether one of the reasons the present one was adopted was because it makes it easier to avoid explicitly acknowledging the sins of the past and the degree to which the Roman Church is now changing its position.

There were at the Council two different schools of thought on how to explain the reasons for affirming religious liberty. One is sometimes referred to as the "French school": its approach is theological, stressing revelation. The other was called the "American school," largely because of its most distinguished exponent, Father John Courtney Murray, S.J., and it is more juridical, utilizing a modernized version of traditional natural law theory. The final document reflects the influence of both approaches, but the second predominates.[14]

Both approaches agree (as indeed do the studies of this topic sponsored by the World Council of Churches)[15] that the right to freedom from social coercion in religious matters is not directly revealed and is not explicitly found in Scripture, even though it is rooted and implied there. However, one approach emphasizes the strength and clarity of this revelational foundation much more than does the other.

This stress on revelation creates greater difficulties for a traditionalist Catholic position because it suggests, at least by implication, that the church has in the past tragically misunderstood or failed to see the consequences of the faith for freedom. It is, therefore, so to speak "safer" to argue, as does the declaration, from a historicized version of natural law theory. According to this, although the moral exigencies of human nature are unchanging, men become aware of their full range only gradually as a result of historical developments. It is only in modern times that the demand for religious liberty has been fully articulated, and so now "This Vatican Council takes careful note of these desires . . . and proposes to declare how much they are in accord with truth and justice" (No. 1).

The pattern of argument, in short, is that of discerning and responding to "The signs of the times." This pattern is appropriate to a pastorally-oriented council concerned with the *aggiornamento*, the "up-dating," of the church, and it is much in evidence in other council documents, especially in the Constitution on the Church in the Modern World. However, in reference to religious liberty, it lends itself to attempts to excuse the church's failures.

Thus it becomes possible to argue (though the declaration, fortunately, does not itself explicitly do this) that the church is not really to blame for its past transgressions against religious liberty because, after all, the very idea of a universal right to religious liberty has only recently developed. Even the nineteenth century popes who condemned religious liberty can be thus absolved because at that time religious liberty in Europe (contrary to the situation in English-speaking countries) had not yet been clearly distinguished from indifferentism, from the view that men possess a "moral," not simply legal-social, right to believe what they please.[16]

Another advantage for traditionalists in this approach is that, because it starts with a non-theological, natural law right to liberty, it is easier to avoid the question of freedom within the church.[17] From the point of view of the internal reformation of Catholicism, this latter question is crucial. To be sure, the declaration has implications for this because what it has to say about the importance of "responsible freedom" (No. 2) and of deciding on the basis of "one's own judgment" (No. 8) presumably applies, not only to those seeking "the true religion," but also to those within it. Yet this point is not developed, and consequently the role of the "Christian faithful" in the church is made to sound more passively submissive (No. 14) than in a number of other council documents. If, in contrast, the declaration had started with revelation and Scripture, this silence would have been more difficult because the Bible is chiefly concerned with evangelical freedom, with the liberty of the Christian man, and it is from this perspective that the teaching on social and civil liberty would then have had to be developed.

It is not only the primacy given the argument from reason and natural law which can be criticized, but also some of its details. For example, the medieval scholastic "two-storied" picture of reality is perhaps most apparent in the declaration than in any other of the Council's documents. It speaks of the transcendent realm of "eternal, objective, and universal" laws and truths in which men "participate . . . through the mediation of conscience," and then describes religious liberty as the right to non-interference in the search for these transcendent truths (No. 3).[18] The rather negative notion of free-

dom and heteronomous concept of law suggested, even if not required, by these formulations is neither biblical nor modern. This
impression is somewhat modified by the stress on human dignity as
the foundation of freedom. Yet would it not have been better to
speak, as some bishops proposed, in terms of the right and "obligation to search for the truth about the self, the meaning of life and
its destiny,"[19] and of human dignity and freedom as arising from
the "call to communion with God" (as does Chap. 1 of the Constitution on the Church in the Modern World)?

Because of this natural law approach, the section on revelation
is confined to showing that the scriptural testimony harmonizes with,
rather than requires, freedom from external coercion in religious
matters. It asserts, first, that this is "consonant" (No. 10) and "fully
congruent with the freedom of the act of Christian faith" (No. 9).
Secondly, Christ and the apostles "rejected all carnal weapons and
were gentle and respectful" (No. 11). Consequently, the church
"recognizes and supports religious liberty as consonant with the dignity of man and divine revelation" (No. 12). Thirdly, there is "harmony" *(concordia)* between the freedom of the church to carry out
its duties of proclaiming the Gospel and bringing men to Christ and
"the religious liberty which is to be recognized as the right of all
men and communities and sanctioned by constitutional law" (No.
13; cf. No. 14). There can be no quarrel with any of these points. The
only question is whether they go far enough.

Although it would be totally misguided to suggest that the Roman
Church has not, in this declaration, fully committed itself to religious
liberty, yet one could wish that this had been affirmed as something
demanded by, and not simply in agreement with, revelation. As long
as this is not done, there will persist in some minds the question
whether it is not at least theoretically possible for the Catholic position to be reversed (as has happened in reference to the traditional
teaching on usury, and perhaps now also on birth control, both of
which have also been based on natural law). Even apart from
such farfetched fears, is it really theologically permissible to speak
as if revelation by itself were inconclusive in this matter? Can there
be any doubt that the church's violations of religious liberty are
contrary to revealed truth, to what the declaration itself speaks of
as the "Kingdom [which is] established, not by blows, but by hear-

ing and witnessing to the truth, [and which] grows by the love whereby Christ, lifted up on the cross, draws all men to Himself" (No. 12)? Are Christians not obligated to acknowledge this, and thereby confess that the churches have sinned, not only when judged by modern insights into human dignity, but also by the scriptural witness to the Word of God?

## 3. Strengths

In concluding the discussion of the reasons given by the declaration for religious liberty, it must be emphasized that it is not the natural law argument as such which is objectionable,[20] but rather the emphasis on it at the expense of the appeal to Scripture and revelation. Considered by itself, the appeal to the insights of moral reason accessible also to non-Christians greatly strengthens the document. In the first place, the declaration is, in part, addressed to all men, and so must make use of arguments which can appeal to Christians and non-Christians alike. Secondly, and even more important, both honesty and humility demand that Christians recognize that the church has learned much in this area from non-Christians. It is in large part they who have taught us that human dignity involves the "natural" right to religious freedom. It may be that they have come to see this in part because their consciences have been sensitized by centuries of Christian influence, but this has often occurred despite ecclesiastical resistance. Sometimes even professed enemies of Christianity force us to turn anew to the Word of God and see more clearly what it implies.

All this is at least suggested by the declaration's acknowledgment that the demand for religious liberty has developed largely apart from express faith in Jesus Christ. Protestants would do well to learn from this. The *sola scriptura* means that the Bible alone is the supreme *norm* of the faith and should not be arrogantly interpreted, as Protestants sometimes do, to imply that it is the only *source* of moral and theological insight. God also acts and teaches outside the church. As the Bishop of Metz put it at the Council, "Human development can also be an action of the Holy Spirit."[21]

With the exceptions noted, the bulk of the argument in favor of religious liberty is the same as that used by non-Catholics, and so need not detain us further. The main point, which is clearly and effectively expressed, is that civil society must protect freedom of conscience and action in religious matters because these have to do with men's relationship to God and so totally transcend the competence of the state (Nos. 2-8).

We have spent all this time on the reasons for, rather than the affirmation of, religious liberty, because it is the former which are questionable. Yet it is the affirmation which is important. It would have been possible, as some bishops suggested,[22] to dispense with reasons altogether and simply affirm the principle. Catholics can, if they wish, argue for religious liberty in other ways, but from henceforth the official and authoritative teaching of their church forbids them to deny it. Also non-Catholics are chiefly interested, not in the formulation of the theological and natural law foundations, but in the concrete, practical character and consequences of the religious liberty to which the Roman Church has now committed itself. Does it adequately oppose the violations of the rights of others of which Roman Catholics have continued to be guilty, especially in countries such as Spain and Colombia?

The answer is "yes" almost without qualifications. At nearly every point, the declaration presents as strong and comprehensive an affirmation of the right to religious liberty as do the statements of the World Council of Churches.[23] The exceptions chiefly have to do with the lack of complete explicitness that this includes the right to disbelief,[24] the right not to be religious. However, even though this right is not proclaimed *espressis verbis*, it is clearly implied when the document says that "within due limits" (which are later satisfactorily specified), "no one is to be forced to act against his conscience, nor impeded from acting according to his conscience whether privately or publicly, whether alone or in association with others" (No. 2)

Another point at which a similar problem arises is when the declaration states that governments ought "to help create conditions favorable to the fostering of religious life" (No. 6). In a document of this kind, meant to apply to vastly different conditions throughout the world, it is, of course, impossible to specify concretely what this means, but it does raise the question of whether the rights of the non-religious are not being overlooked. Is it really the business of government to favor religion over non-religion? However, just previously, it is clearly said that "the civil power ought, by just laws and other appropriate means, to safeguard the religious liberty of *all*" (No. 6). If emphasis is placed on this phrase, then this particular danger is reduced.

A caveat can perhaps also be entered in regard to the warning against the wrong kind of proselytizing, against "any manner of action which might seem to involve coercion or dishonorable or unworthy persuasion, especially when dealing with poor or uneducated people." It is quite correctly said that this "must be considered an abuse of one's right and a violation of the right of others." However, it is not clearly specified that this limitation is moral, not legal. It would have been helpful to say this, because any attempt to enforce this limitation by government action would be likely to imperil the right which religious communities have, and on which the declaration emphatically insists, "not to be hindered in their public, oral or written, testimony or teaching of their faith" (No. 4).

In confining our reservations to these minor points, we do not mean to suggest that everyone will be satisfied by this declaration. There are many Protestants, especially in the United States, who think that full religious liberty necessarily involves an American type of separation between church and state. They think it wrong for any religion to be in any sense legally established, or for the government to offer support to church schools even when this is done for all, not simply one religious group.

The declaration, however, says, on the first point, that "If, in view of peculiar circumstances . . . special civil recognition is given to one religious community in the constitutional order of society, it is at the same time necessary that the right of all citizens and religious communities to religious liberty should be recognized and observed" (No. 6). It is noteworthy that establishment is described as *permissible*, not as something which the Catholic Church considers desirable either for itself or others. The declaration says that the Catholic Church has no objection to established churches as long as the religious liberty of other groups is not infringed. This, in effect, sanctions the non-Catholic English or Scandinavian types of state church, but not the arrangements which have prevailed in such Catholic countries as Spain or Colombia. While some Americans might object, clearly most Protestants agree with such a view.

The same is true of the state assistance to religious schools which this declaration favors. It says that religious liberty involves "the right of parents to make a fully free choice of schools and other means of education without, as a result of this free choice, having unjust burdens imposed upon them either directly or indirectly" (No. 5). The Catholic, of course, thinks that he is unjustly burdened when the state taxes him for its own secular schools and does not equally support parochial schools. Once again, while most Americans object to this position, it is acceptable to the Protestants in many other countries who welcome governmental support of their schools and programs of religious instruction.

Probably the most difficult problem in reference to religious liberty is to define its limits. According to the declaration, a "civil society has the right to protect itself against possible abuses committed under the pretext of religious liberty" in order to preserve public peace and public morality, that is, public order (No. 7). It is true that societies find this necessary, as for example, when religiously based practices such as polygamy, or snake-handling, or refusal of smallpox vaccination have been forbidden by governmental action. These limitations of freedom are hard to define precisely, and this declaration probably does as well as any when it concludes: "For the rest, the usages of freedom must be fully maintained in society so that the freedom of man is respected as far as possible and is not curtailed except when and insofar as necessary" (No. 7).

Even after having satisfied themselves that this is as strong and forthright a proclamation of religious freedom as could be desired, Protestants will still want to know how quickly its provisions will be put into effect in those countries where the rights of non-Catholics have been violated. Even with the best of will on the part of the Roman authorities, this may happen slowly. First, in places like Spain and Colombia, the repressive legal measures are incorporated in concordats, in treaties with the Vatican, which are part of the law of the land, and cannot be unilaterally revoked by the church. The new official Roman Catholic position in favor of changing these concordats and other laws which infringe religious liberty, seems likely to produce quick action, at least in Spain, but, juridically speaking, whatever the church may do, it is quite possible for oppressive measures to remain in force for a long time. In reference to the infractions of liberty resulting from the intolerance of the Catholic masses in some places, the task of the church is educational, and its success largely depends on the attitudes of local priests and bishops. As past history shows, Roman Catholics do not always act like the well-disciplined army which some Protestants imagine, and so it may take considerable time for the spirit of this declaration to have its full effects in all parts of the church.

Nevertheless, in the words of the Catholic theologian Yves Congar, this declaration "will re-create a climate of trust in many countries and in many circles. It will act quickly or slowly in those nations which are at present tyrannical or engage in persecution. A universal opinion in favor of true religious liberty, sanctioned by law, will be more and more created in the world."[25]

This may not always be to the external advantage of the Catholic Church, especially where it has depended on an unchristian authoritarianism, but, as the declaration says, "it will make no small contribution to the creation of an environment in which men can without hindrance be invited to Christian faith, embrace it of their own free will, and profess it effectively in their whole manner of life" (No. 10).

# Notes

1. *Ecumenical Press Service* No. 45, Dec. 16, 1965, p. 6, and *New York Times*, Dec. 10, 1965, p. 8.
2. T. B. Macaulay, "Milton" (1825) *Critical and Historical Essays*, Everyman's Library Edition, London, 1924, I, p. 173.
3. For example, Cardinal Cushing of Boston went so far as to say that if the Council did not make a pronouncement on religious liberty, the ecumenical movement would collapse (*Herder Correspondence*, 1964, p. 202 and K.N.A., Sonderdienst zum II Vatikonischen Konzil, March 18, 1964). Robert McAfee Brown,

from the Protestant side, put it this way: "The reason a statement on religious liberty is so important is because . . . the Catholic Church is not fully trusted on this point. Whether rightly or wrongly, non-Catholics do not believe the Catholic Church has yet made up her mind about religious liberty, and they are fearful that the church may still espouse a position of intolerance, persecution, and penalty for the exercise of a faith not Roman Catholic" (*Observer in Rome*, New York: Doubleday, 1964, p. 174).
4. Some of the most conspicuous ex-

amples of this are cited in A. F. Carrillo de Albornoz, Roman Catholicism and Religious Liberty, Geneva: World Council of Churches, 1959, pp. 58-60. His citations are from Gregory XVI's *Mirari vos*, 1832 (cf. H. Denzinger's *Enchiridion Symbolorum*, 30th ed., nos. 1613-1615), Pius IX's *Quanta cura and Syllabus*, 1864 (cf. Denzinger, 1689-1690, 1715, 1777-1780), and Leo XIII's *Immortale dei*, 1885 (Denzinger omits the strongest passages, but cf. 1867, 1868 and 1880).

5. E. G. Steward Hughes, *Commonweal*, 1965, and, in the words of the Catholic Michael Novak, in *The Open Church*, New York: Macmillan, pp. 299-300: "it seems credible in the light of public knowledge . . . that the people of certain countries are so poorly educated in their faith that religious liberty might be interpreted among them as freedom to vote Communist, or otherwise to oppose their clergy."

6. The most easily available English edition of the document is in *Council Documents of Vatican II* to be published by McGraw & Hill in New York.

7. It is useful to summarize here points made at various places in the remainder of this chapter regarding the exact nature of the liberty with which this document is concerned and its distinction from other kinds of freedom.

It is concerned with affirming (a) a natural right to freedom in religious matters from constraint by men, society, and the public powers to act *against* conscience, (b) or to be prevented from acting *according* to conscience, which latter, in turn, involves (c) the right to manifest religious opinions in word and conduct either individually or in association with others, (d) insofar as this does not violate the necessities of public order.

This external, civic or social freedom must be sharply distinguished from (1) the internal personal freedom of self-determination, (2) the freedom to adhere to or reject the moral law— rejection of which, to be sure, results in moral bondage, (3) the evangelical or Christian freedom from sin and the law which is given by grace and the Gospel, and (4) the freedom of the church to carry out its tasks.

Most of the arguments against the declaration in Council were based on rather simple-minded confusions between these various types of freedom. For example, the declaration's praise of civic religious freedom was interpreted, quite wrongly as implying freedom from the moral law, and the insistence that freedom must be legally protected was attacked as superfluous because personal self-determination (e.g., the capacity either to believe or not believe) can be neither guaranteed nor abolished by law.

8. E.g., G. Cottier, *Etudes*, 322, p. 456 and R. Rouquette, *ibid.*, 323, p. 536.

9. E.g. the *Codex canonicis* sums up the Catholic theological and magisterial tradition in opposition to compelling anyone to become a Catholic when it says, "Ad amplexandam fidem catholicam nemo invitus dogatur" (c. 1351). The way in which this is combined with a denial of religious liberty is briefly and clearly explained as the "first view" in J. C. Murray, S.J., "The Problem of

Religious Freedom," *Theological Studies* XXV, 1964, pp. 503-575. In German, "Die religiöse Freiheit und das Konzil," *Wort und Wahrheit*, 1965, 409-430.

10. xvi. 1.2 (The English translation from C. Pharr, *The Theodosian Code*, Princeton, N.J.: Princeton University Press).

11. In speeches given respectively on Sept. 20, 17 and 20, 1965.

12. Indeed, a case can be made out for the view that the Protestants were in their principles often more intolerant than the Catholics, as Lord Acton has done in his famous essay, "The Protestant Theory of Persecution" (originally published in 1862, reprinted in *The History of Freedom and other Essays*, London: Macmillan, 1907, pp. 150-187). For references to the Protestant use of Roman Law and the Theodosian Code in heresy trials, see R. Bainton, "The Development and Consistency of Luther's Attitude to Religious Liberty," *Harvard Theological Review* XXII, 1929, pp. 107-149, esp. pp. 139-140.

13. Karl Rahner, *On Heresy* (New York: Herder and Herder, 1964), p. 18.

14. See Carrillo de Albornoz, *op. cit.*, pp. 27-40, for a summary of the kind of arguments emphasized by the first school, and Thomas T. Love, *John Courtney Murray: Contemporary Church-State Theory* (New York: Doubleday, 1965), for a complete exposition of Murray's writings in this area, which are scattered in many journal articles.

15. A statement of this point, together with references, is to be found in A. F. Carrillo de Albornoz, *The Basis of Religious Liberty* (New York: Association Press, 1963), p. 56.

16. Perhaps the fullest development of this argument is to be found in four long articles, referring especially to Pope Leo XIII, by John Courtney Murray, *Theological Studies* XIV & XV (1953-1954). See the criticism of the "pragmatism" (happily transcended by the council's declaration) to which this leads, A. F. Carrillo de Albornoz, "Religious Freedom: Intrinsic or Fortuitous?" *Christian Century* LXXXII, 1965, pp. 1122-1126.

17. It should also be observed that this is the point at which the declaration seems most directly to conflict with previous councils (not simply popes). Religious liberty involves freedom "to leave a religious community" (No. 6), but this is hard to reconcile with Canon 14 of Session VII of the Council of Trent (Denzinger, 870). Further, the Vatican Council denies that one who has "accepted the faith" through the Roman Catholic Church can have a "just cause" for doubting it (Denzinger, 1794). This would appear to justify Catholics in regarding those who leave the Roman Church as being in "bad faith," and would seem to authorize at least the psychological pressures on them which the declaration decries (No. 2). It is incumbent on Catholic theologians to explain how the teaching of these passages can be reconciled with this declaration.

18. As the footnotes of the declaration point out, this section very closely follows the teaching of St. Thomas Aquinas, *Summa Theologica*, I-II, q. 91, a.1 and q. 93, aa. 1 & 2.

19. Rouquette, *op. cit.*, p. 532.
20. This is not to endorse any particular theory of natural law, but, as is indicated in what follows, simply to say that it is appropriate in a document of this kind to utilize arguments additional to those derived from revelation.
21. Rouquette, *op. cit.*, p. 542.
22. This was true in the third session especially of some American bishops, e.g., Cardinal Ritter in his speech of Sept. 23, 1964.
23. This emerges from an examination of *Main Ecumenical Statements on Principles concerning Religious Freedom,* Geneva: World Council of Churches, 1965. The judgment of the World Council's "Secretariat on Religious Liberty," as indicated by its confidential reports, appears to agree with this opinion.
24. *Main Ecumenical Statements,* p. 37, citing the New Delhi, 1961, "Statement on Religious Liberty."
25. *Informations catholiques internationales,* Oct. 1, 1965, pp. 3-4.

## Chapter VIII

# The Theological Basis of the Pastoral Constitution on the Church in the Modern World

The Second Vatican Council addressed itself not only to the non-Roman-Catholic churches and to the non-Christian religions but also to mankind as a whole. It considered the broadest spectrum of the very difficult problems confronting the world today. This was a new step forward in the history of the councils; and it deserves very close attention. The result of the Council's deliberations are presented in the "Pastoral Constitution on the Church in the Modern World."

The Council attributed great significance to this task, and correspondingly addressed this Constitution directly to all men: The Council "addresses itself not only to the sons of the Church and to all who invoke the name of Christ, but to the whole of humanity. For the Council yearns to explain to everyone how it conceives of the presence and activity of the Church in the world of today" (2 and *passim*).[1] This characteristic is all the more significant in view of the fact that even though the "Decree on Ecumenism" deals with non-Roman-Catholic Christians, it does not address them personally but addresses the members of the Roman Catholic Church,[2] just as the "Decree on the Church's Missionary Activity"[3] and the "Declaration on the Relationship of the Church to Non-

Christian Religions"[4] are not directly addressed to the adherents of these other churches and religions, but rather instructs the members of the Roman Church. These texts are indeed extremely meaningful to non-Roman-Catholics and non-Christians but they receive only indirect knowledge of their content. The "Pastoral Constitution on the Church in the Modern World," however, speaks directly to the people whom it seeks to help and renew socially (3). It proposes to enter into direct dialogue with them (3 and *passim*). This intention resulted in important problems of basic methodology.

The text begins with a preface describing the purpose of this Constitution followed by an introductory statement dealing with "The Situation of Men in the Modern World." The body of the Constitution is divided into two major parts: Part I treats "The Church and Man's Calling" and Part II discusses "Some Problems of Special Urgency." In Part I, the church develops its teaching about man, the world in which man lives, and the church in relationship to both. In Part II, the church more closely considers various aspects of life today and human society, emphasizing those questions and problems which seem especially urgent today. As a result, although these topics are presented in the light of basic doctrinal principles, they contain some elements that have a permanent value, while others are of value only in our specific historical situation.[5] Thus, the first section discusses primarily the unchanging dogmatic presuppositions, while the second section applies these presuppositions to the solution of contemporary problems.

The Pastoral Constitution thus begins by analyzing the modern world and spelling out the problems confronting us today. In answering these questions, it first presents its basic doctrine of man and then discusses the most urgent problems one by one. The structure of this outline corresponds to a widespread apologetic method. It is recognized, however, that this method carries with it the danger that the partners in the conversation assume that the questions for which one has an answer ready can be taken for granted. The second and opposite danger is that one partner so formulates his answers to meet the concerns of the partner in this dialogue that the Christian witness is weakened. Obviously both of these can happen at once. For this reason, the first three sections of the following discussion follow the Constitution's own outline. In the 4th and 5th sections, however, we shall reverse this procedure and begin with the witness of the New Testament and on this basis ask to what extent the statements of the Pastoral Constitution on the relationship between Christ and the world, as well as between the church and the world, correspond to the position of the New Testament. The final section will evaluate the unique character of this new type of "pastoral constitution."

## I. Questions Raised by the Situation of Men in the World Today

Following the Preface, the Constitution begins by describing the situation of men in the world today. This presentation is continued and specific topics are discussed in the two following sections, for example, the discussion of atheism in sections 19 and 20 of Part I and the discussion of specific contemporary situations at the beginning of each chapter of Part II. "We must therefore recognize and understand the world in which we live, its expectations, its longings, and its often dramatic characteristics" (4).

"Today, the human race is passing through a new stage of its history. Profound and rapid changes are spreading by degrees around the whole world" (4). These changes have their source in the "intelligence and creative energies of man" and in turn have their own effect upon him. This "social and cultural transformation . . . has repercussions on man's religious life as well" (4). In these sections, special attention is given to the development of the natural sciences and of anthropology and sociology; these sciences have made it possible for us to change the earth, to develop a technology which reaches out into interplanetary space, and to plan the growth of humanity (5). In addition, special attention is given to the effects of the growth of industrial society on rural societies and the spread of large urban areas.

The comprehensive viewpoint of this Constitution draws our attention to the variety of problems which arise through these developments, not only between individual men or vocational groups, but also, for example, between the technically-developed

nations and the undeveloped nations, between those nations possessing atomic weapons and those without them, and between the
dominating economic systems and political power-blocs. Both
the general problem areas of urbanization and specific problems
such as the use of leisure time are discussed. Special attention is
given to the effects of these changes on religious life and to the
various forms under which atheism is spreading so rapidly in the
world today. The Constitution points out that one of the causes for
this lies in the failures of Christians themselves: "To the extent
that they neglect their own training in the faith, or teach erroneous
doctrines, or are deficient in their religious, moral, or social life, they
must be said to conceal rather than reveal the authentic face of God
and religion" (19).

The Pastoral Constitution expresses an open and positive attitude toward the modern world, similar to that expressed through
the inception of the dialogue with the non-Roman churches and
the non-Christian religions. The Constitution clearly points to the
manifold "tensions," "contradictions," "imbalances," "inequalities,"
"discords," "conflicts of forces," and "hardships" present in the
modern world. Furthermore, the decline of religious loyalty and
the spread of atheism are by no means overlooked. And yet these
matters are never referred to in a spirit of panic; rather the Constitution heeds the warning of John XXIII in his speech opening the
Council. John warned against viewing modern times in terms of
darkness and ruin. "We feel we must disagree with those prophets
of gloom who are always forecasting disaster as though the end
of the world were at hand."[6] Without in any way overlooking the
difficulties and dangers of the present world situation, the modern
world is affirmed; and the "difficulties," "contradictions," and "discords" are interpreted primarily as symptoms of the transition to a
better condition of humanity. The positive acceptance of the concept of progress is especially typical of this attitude. Without overlooking the difficulties connected with cultural, technical, and
economic progress, progress in all these areas is explicitly affirmed
and contributing to it is regarded as a duty. The "Decree on the
Instruments of Social Communication" also considers the dangers
which are involved in the use of mass media to be relatively small
in comparison with the possibilities of effective working which

they present to the church.[7] Scientific and technological progress
is regarded primarily as a divinely-willed development of the
creative capacities which God has given to man; and the political
and economic difficulties in international relations are in this context
regarded as an evidence of increasing consciousness of the unity of
mankind. Thus, the severity of the conflict between the ideologies
of atheism and of freedom and between ideologically oriented
political power-blocs, the intensity of the new nationalism of formerly colonial peoples, as well as the conflicts between the races,
are considered within a total context that is basically hopeful.

Corresponding to this view the Constitution in discussing the
effects of the changes in the world on religious life equally emphasizes the purification of religious life and the intensification of
personal and active involvement in the faith "on the one hand,"
and the decline in religious loyalty and the growth of atheism "on
the other hand" (7). In so doing, it does not fully take into account
the new forms under which the increasingly rapid spread of atheism
and the experience of the absence of God which destroy religious
loyalties attack the modern world with previously unheard-of fury.
It is also noteworthy that the Council separates the confrontation
of atheism from the confrontation of Communism and almost always engages in the latter only in an indirect manner. With all
due recognition of the cautious nature of this presentation and
the absence of a picture drawn in simple black and white, we must
still ask whether the intention of beginning the dialogue with all
men has not resulted in diluting the hard realities of life. This same
question was also raised by several fathers of the Council—and
indeed not only by those whose dioceses were directly involved or
who consider a dialogue with the temporal authorities impossible.

The Pastoral Constitution does not begin with a biblical or dogmatic understanding of the world, that only Christians could understand, but with the empirical realities of this world as seen by the
eyes of all men. What it presents, therefore, is less an analysis of the
deeper historical roots of the contemporary situation than a list
of phenomena. Modern natural science is named as the cause of
technological and social changes but no further investigation is
made of the complex interactions of the various factors involved
or of the spiritual roots of modern science. Indeed it would not have

been possible for this Constitution to have fulfilled that task. It does, however, investigate the effects of these phenomena on men: the confusion, the anxieties, and the questions which arise in men in view of the situation in the world today. These questions are mostly specific questions about relationships between the sexes, a just social order, overcoming of the danger of war, and so forth. The questions that are raised are, however, not only secondary questions which are concerned with ways of coming to terms with external difficulties, but the Constitution also recognizes that in these troubles, confusions, and anxieties man has begun to doubt himself. "In the face of the modern development of the world, an ever-increasing number of people are raising the most basic questions or recognizing them with a new sharpness: what is man? What is this sense of sorrow, of evil, of death, which continues to exist despite so much progress? What is the purpose of these victories purchased at so high a cost? What can man offer to society, what can he expect from it? What follows this earthly life?" (10). The Constitution probably overestimates the extent to which modern men are aware of this ultimate question. It is likely that many today have repressed it far more effectively than the Constitution assumes. Faith can admittedly recognize this ultimate question as the dynamic power behind atheism and as the pathos of the nihilism of our time, but many modern men no longer consciously ask this question. The Constitution thus does not begin with the questions which God asks of modern men through his revelation but with the situation of the world today and the questions which are asked by men who are confronted by it.

## II. The Presuppositions for Answering These Questions

The Pastoral Constitution addresses itself to all men. It proposes to enter into dialogue with all of them—whether they are members of the Roman Church or other Christians, whether they are adherents of non-Christian religions, or skeptics or athiests—and it seeks to answer the penultimate and ultimate questions which they ask in the situation of the world today. What arguments does it use to do this? And what universal human presuppositions does it bring to bear on these questions?

(a) The common starting point is the empirical reality of our age, as it is visible to everyone in cultural, economic, social, and political phenomena.

(b) Then the anxieties, yearnings, specific questions, and questions of ultimate meaning which the situation in the world today forces men to ask are presupposed as the common experience of all.

(c) It is also presupposed that all men in common possess a "godlike seed" (3), "an eternal seed" (18), that they hear God's voice speaking within them and know God's law in the depths of their conscience (16), that they all share in the natural law which God has given to all men and which reason can recognize as a demand, as well as that all men are confronted by God's witness to himself through creation (17).

(d) In addition, the Constitution refers to men's knowledge of "permanent" (4) and "universal values" (57), even though the awareness of these values is somewhat shaken. "For insofar as they stem from endowments conferred by God on man, these values are exceedingly good" (11). The use of the ideas "of truth, goodness, and beauty" (57) and "ancestral wisdom" (56) may be considered in this context.

(e) In addition to the possibilities of knowing God which are given to all men, the awareness of God's law, and the knowledge of values, the Constitution presupposes that grace is at work not only in Christians, but also in all men of good will and that the Holy Spirit "in a manner known only to God" offers to every man the possibility of being associated with Christ (22).

(f) Finally, the Constitution argues on the basis of biblical statements about creation, about God's saving work in Jesus Christ, about the church, and about the eschatological perfection of this world. Frequently the Christological and eschatological statements appear at the end of individual chains of thought.

The arguments which the Pastoral Constitution uses in addressing itself to modern men are thus manifold in nature and have quite different philosophical and theological sources. The exact meaning of these concepts (for example, of values) is often somewhat imprecise. Conceptions taken from phenomenology, natural law, the philosophy of values, and the history of salvation, are used alongside one another without being fused in any kind of systematic unity. It is clear that the Constitution seeks as far as possible to relate to the presuppositions of the men to whom it speaks and thus to begin the dialogue. However, it is also clear that the Council does not limit itself to universally accepted presuppositions but uses arguments which are not immediately acceptable to everyone and thus makes a transition from dialogue to teaching. This is true particularly of the biblical statements dealing with the history of salvation (f); but it is also true of the assertion that all men of good will are in some hidden way spiritually associated with Christ (e).

But even where the argument is based on God speaking to every man in his conscience and on that natural law which has been given to all men (c), the Constitution does not presuppose that these divine commands are actually known by all men in their true form. Thus, the Constitution frequently refers to the fact of the erring conscience. Values too (d) "are often wrenched from their rightful functions by the taint in man's heart and hence stand in need of purification" (11). Thus, the questions of men are first revealed for what they really are in light of God's revelation in Christ. The natural law must be interpreted in the light of the Gospel; and only in this light do we have true knowledge of the "principles of justice and equity" which right reason demands (63). The values of men are to be assessed in the light of the Christian faith and to be related to their divine source (11).

This variety of arguments is held together by the idea that revelation agrees with the experience of men, particularly with their experience of themselves (13) and that the message which the church brings corresponds to "the most secret desires of the human heart" (21). However, the meaning of the questions which men ask and of the most secret desires is finally revealed only in the light of God's revelation in Christ. Thus, the church in this Pastoral Constitution confronts men not only through statements about Christ, but also functions as the teaching church even when it argues on the basis of that conscience, natural law, and so forth, which are the common property of all men. This raises the question whether the Constitution adequately presents God's saving act in Christ by using it as one argument alongside of others in its dialogue with mankind. How are non-Christians to understand this argument? Since only faith can understand the foolishness of the cross as the revelation of divine wisdom, we must ask whether this Constitution, addressed as it is to all men, ought not more strongly seek to create faith. Ought it not ultimately proclaim Christ?

In terms of content, the Constitution's answer to modern questions begins with a discussion of the doctrine of man. "The pivotal point of our total presentation will be man himself, whole and entire, body and soul, heart and conscience, mind and will" (3). By beginning with the doctrine of man rather than with the doctrine of God, the Constitution recognizes that modern men do not ask questions about God but instead ask, "What is man?" In Part I, Chapter I deals with "the dignity of the human person"; Chapter II deals with "the community of mankind"; and Chapter III deals with "man's activity throughout the world." Thus Part I begins by answering the ultimate questions about the meaning of human existence. In Part II this becomes the basis for answers to the specific penultimate questions of this age.

Many of the elements of the statement of the doctrine of man in this Constitution are familiar to us from the philosophical doctrine of man which the Roman Church has taken over from classical and modern philosophical thought and uses in its basic dogmatic theology. This is true, for example, of the statements about reason, conscience, freedom, and assertion of the personal value and equality of all men as well as that he is created to live with other men in community.

At the same time, however, the doctrine of man is developed on the basis of the biblical history of salvation. Thus it does not begin with a philosophical statement but with the creation of man "to the image of God." This is understood as meaning that man is "capable of knowing and loving his Creator, and was appointed by Him as master of all earthly creatures that he might subdue them and use them to God's glory" (12). His creation for life in community is also based on the biblical statement about his creation "as male and female" (12). Under the influence of evil, man has rebelled against God and now attempts to achieve his goal without God. As a result he lives in conflict with his calling and in misery (13). In Christ, "the image of the invisible God," the mystery of man once again becomes apparent and the image of God, which was corrupted by the first sin, is once again communicated to the sons of men. Through his death, Christ has once again earned life for us (22); and through his Spirit he fulfills the Creator's intention that we live in community with other men by bringing us into the community of the church; he will someday make this a perfect community (32). The understanding of man in the Pastoral Constitution—like the understanding of the church in the Constitution on the Church—reflects a specific understanding of the history of salvation.

The Constitution does not fuse its dual understanding of man in philosophical terms and in terms of the history of salvation into a full systematic unity; here again we must distinguish between an understanding of man which is primarily determined on the basis of the creation and another which is more Christocentric. However, by and large, the emphases are in many ways more biblical that is often customary in Roman Catholic theology. In contrast to the widespread understanding of man in Roman Catholic theology as a rational being, who is made up of a body and an immortal soul, the Pastoral Constitution is concerned with the totality of man; and his value is found not only in his spirituality but also in his material nature. As a result, the relationship between husband and wife is viewed in a new way and the significance of our bodies for our relationships to other people is clearly emphasized at other points. In contrast to the widespread attempt to distinguish nature and supernature in man and to describe the primal state, the fall, and redemption, in terms of the possession, loss, and renewed reception of supernatural grace, which sees the "pure nature" of man as a constant and unhistorical factor, this Constitution places man into the context of the history of salvation and thus more strongly concentrates on his historical nature. As a result, the changes in the structures of social life and of man's dominion over nature are also more clearly seen.

## III. The Significance of the Pastoral Constitution's Answers for the Church and for the World

Part II bears the title "Some Problems of Special Urgency." Under this general heading the five chapters of Part II draw the conclusions of the basic anthropological statements of Part I and give instructions concerning men's behavior in specific situations of modern life. One is impressed by the comprehensiveness and breadth of the answers given to the most varied urgent questions of today: to problems of marriage and of the family, of culture, of economics and society, of national life, and finally of international relations and world peace. The only problem excluded is that of contraception, and thus no answer is given for the urgent problem of the population explosion—at this point the Constitution simply refers to a papal decision which has not yet been given.

It is not our task at this point to discuss in detail the answers Part II gives to current problems, since these answers are to be described and evaluated in a special section of this volume. I shall only refer to some of the most important. There is a significant shift in emphasis in the understanding of the goal of marriage from procreation to a personal relationship of love, in the context of which the problem of responsible parenthood is also seen in a new light. The Constitution shows a strong and positive attitude toward cultural, technical, and economic progress, the creative capacities of man, and the autonomy of culture and especially of the sciences. It supports the right of all men to share in this progress and emphasizes the need for a corresponding distribution of possessions, of work, and of wages among individuals and among the nations. It supports the free participation of citizens in creating a government based on law and determining the course of political events; and it supports a clear distinction between the tasks of the state and of the church. Finally, it soberly evaluates the new situation which has been created in the world through the discovery of atomic weapons and recognizes that the traditional distinction between a just and an unjust war is no longer adequate. It gives decisive support to a world government which will include all nations, to international organizations in the various social fields of nutrition, health, education, and labor, and to a universal economic order. This brief list is intended only to give the flavor of the rich content of these five chapters and to encourage the reader to study the full text. Each of these chapters is so interesting that it deserves the attention not only of the theologians but also of experts in the disciplines concerned and ought to be thoroughly analyzed by experts in marriage, culture, government, and economics.

The theological doctrine of man is of basic significance for each of these specific instructions. The individual discussions, however, are sometimes dominated by theological arguments based on revelation, especially on Christology, and sometimes more by rational arguments based on experience and natural law. The discussions of marriage and of culture in particular are dominated by theological arguments, whereas rational arguments are emphasized in the answers to economic, social, and political questions. However, the Christological basis is never completely absent. Thus, peace among nations "symbolizes and results from the peace of Christ who comes forth from God the Father," and is based on the reconciliation of men with God through the incarnate Son of God (78). Those whose lives are formed "in faithfulness to Christ and His gospel" and are "permeated with the spirit of the beatitudes, particularly of poverty" are expected to set an example by their support of social and economic progress (72). Cultural progress is to be supported in the confidence that "the mystery of the Christian faith furnishes . . . excellent incentives and helps toward discharging this duty more energetically and especially toward uncovering the full meaning of this activity, a meaning which gives human culture its eminent place in the integral vocation of man" (57). In all five of the problem areas dealt with, the Council more or less presupposes that Christ's law of love is the basic principle, and faith in Christ a stimulus and help for responsible action.

The answers which the Pastoral Constitution gives to the specific problems of our age are undoubtedly very significant for Roman Catholic Christians. This becomes clear when we compare these answers with those which previously were ordinarily considered to be "Catholic." Many previous positions which the Roman Church had once taken, for example, on natural science, progress, the sovereignty of nations, conscientious objectors, and so forth, against which some modern concepts could assert themselves only through difficult struggles are now abandoned. In the Pastoral Constitution as well as in the "Declaration on Religious Freedom," the Roman Church has corrected itself in noteworthy ways. In this as in other decrees the emphasis on the continuity of the church and of its tradition admittedly hindered the Council from explicitly pointing out such corrections. Thus, for example, only restrained references are made to the conflicts between the Roman Church and modern scientific development. In opposition to this, some of the fathers of the Council demanded that the Council rehabilitate Galileo. Actually, however, the corrections go far beyond those matters which the text of the Constitution explicitly designates as corrections. The notes of this Constitution extensively document the continuity of the Roman Catholic position on social questions with numerous references to the social encyclicals of the popes from Leo XIII to the encyclical of John XXIII, *"Mater et magistra."* It would be interesting to compare Chapter III, which deals with economic and social life, with each of these earlier encyclicals. We would expect to find a more progressive attitude on many more specific questions than the quotations in the notes of the Constitution lead us to expect. In any case, the Pastoral Constitution calls the members of the Roman Church out of a religious and cultural self-sufficiency and out of a secluded social and political conservatism to energetic involvement in responsible service of the whole of humanity.

The specific answers given by the Pastoral Constitution are also of significance for non-Roman churches. For they answer the very same questions which interest these churches; and the answers given by the Constitution are in their essential points similar to or even identical with those given by the assemblies of the World Council of Churches in Amsterdam (1948), in Evanston (1954), and in New Delhi (1961). This nearness and convergence of the separated churches in their new understanding of the Christian's responsibility for the world will not only strengthen the ministry of each individual church but will also reduce the scandal which

Christianity gives to the world around it through the history and present reality of its divisions. In fact, cooperation among the separated churches is most likely to occur in scientific, economic, social, and political areas. Here the world, which already sees the truth of the Christian message as disproved through the divisions of the church, can most easily observe a fellowship among Christians. In addition to this, that false religious introversion which withdraws from the current problems of humanity is also at work among the non-Roman churches. The vital forces in these churches will therefore be glad to know that the Pastoral Constitution so energetically calls Christians out of self-isolation to responsible action on behalf of the world.

Other questions are raised, however, when we ask about the significance of the Pastoral Constitution for the non-Christian world. In its answers to the various cultural, economic, social, and political problems of our time—with the exception of the peculiar characteristics of the Roman Catholic understanding of marriage and its reservations about birth control—the Council has to a large extent adapted itself to those positions which many people today feel are necessary. In correcting earlier positions of the Roman Church, it has given far-reaching approval to the autonomy of the sciences, to the basic principles of social and economic planning, to the democratic form of government, and to the basic principles and goals of the United Nations. The Council admittedly provides a theological foundation for these basic principles that is different from that current, for example, in scientific research, in the planning of the economy, and also in the United Nations. However, the specific directions themselves are very close to the principles which are currently accepted as valid and contain little that is new.

Naturally this far-reaching agreement does not mean that the principles of the Council have no value. The value of these answers, however, lies less in the fact that they point toward very new and unusual paths of action than that they support and strengthen the threatened structures of order in this world. Given the present world situation in which the relationship of the powers is so changeable, the powers of the United Nations are so weak, and social change occurs so rapidly, the significance of this support should not in any way be undervalued. However, one can hardly say that the Roman Church has here opened up specifically new paths to mankind which were previously hidden from non-Christians. At this point the church with its principles does not go before mankind as a leader, rather it adapts itself in the essential points— even though it does so on the basis of its own theological rationale— to that which many men already recognize as necessary quite apart from having any Christian convictions. In addition to this, it is noticeable that this chapter of the Constitution, corresponding to the make-up of the responsible commission of the Council, is to a large extent determined by Western, and specifically European, thought. The specific principles correspond more to the practical possibilities of Western man than to those of people living in Asia and in Africa.

Now, however, the Constitution addresses itself not only to Christians but also to all men. Can non-Christians understand it? Certainly they will be able to understand many of the specific prescriptions for action. These, however, are based on a theological doctrine of man, and this is ultimately rooted in the doctrine of Christ. However, only faith can recognize that Jesus is the Christ and Lord. Once again we must raise the question: Is it, in conversations with non-Christians, enough to quote the Bible constantly? Is it not necessary to be much more concerned about the actual interpretation of the Bible? Is it enough simply and repeatedly to adduce Jesus Christ as one argument in a list of other arguments for participating in the life of the world? Ought not the Constitution directly and personally proclaim and offer Christ to non-Christians? For "faith comes from hearing" (Romans 10:17). What are non-Christians supposed to think about Jesus Christ when the Constitution undertakes to give specific instructions in dealing with the situation of the world today by referring to Christ and then is hardly able to say anything else than what many rational men today consider to be necessary even though they do not share this faith? Does Jesus Christ really confront non-Christians as the Lord in this Pastoral Constitution, the one text of the Council which explicitly addresses itself to them?

## IV. Christ and the World

In the three previous sections we have followed the structure of the Pastoral Constitution and taken as our starting point the questions raised by the situation of the world today. Now we shall begin with the New Testament statements about Christ and the world, as well as about the church and the world, and on this basis raise questions about the Council's understanding of the church in the world as presented in this Pastoral Constitution. Our presentation of the New Testament statements must be limited to theses on only the most important and fundamental principles of the New Testament.

(a) The Pauline epistles and the Gospel of John describe the world as God's creation. Through rebellion against God, however, this world and mankind in particular has been subjected to the lordship of the powers of corruption and is under divine judgment. The coming of this judgment means that the world is coming to an end. "The form of this world is passing away" (1 Cor. 7:31); "the world passes away, and the lust of it" (1 John 2:17). The fact that the world still stands in spite of being subject to judgment is due to the patience of God, the preserver, and to the love of the Redeemer.

(b) Out of love for this world, God has sent his Son and given him into death. In Jesus Christ, the salvation of God has broken into this lost world. Through this message of the kingdom of God breaking into the world, through his blessings, and through his woeful lamentations, Jesus has called men to decision. Men's reaction to this confrontation with the person of Jesus is decisive for their future salvation and judgment. In his death on the cross he took the sins of the world upon himself. However, salvation from the judgment of the divine wrath is not given to us simply through the fact of his death but rather through faith in the Crucified.

(c) Having risen from the dead and sitting at the right hand of God, Jesus is now the Lord. Everything is subjected to him so that he may subjugate all things to himself. However, the New Testament writings do not characterize him as the "Lord of the world." Christ is the Lord of the church, the fellowship of those whom he has called out of the world and whom he has through faith rescued from the bondage and judgment of this world. He is the head of the new creation. "He who believes in the Son has eternal life; he who does not obey the Son shall not see life, but the wrath of God rests upon him" (John 3:36).

(d) Christ will come as the judge of the world, both of the living and of the dead. "We must all appear before the judgment seat of Christ, so that each one may receive good or evil, according to what he has done in the body" (2 Cor. 5:10). Then he will accept the one and reject the other. Then all will recognize that Christ is the Lord. His coming will be the end of the world and the perfection of the new creation which began with his resurrection and which grows in a hidden way within the church. However, the New Testament writings do not speak of a "new world" that is to come, but of a "new creation" and of a "new heaven and new earth."

These biblical statements also form the basis of the Pastoral Constitution. In spite of this, however, the Constitution shifts the emphases in ways which cannot be overlooked.

The world is primarily understood as created by God and as loved by God in Christ. In this connection, the rule of sin and the demonic powers and the fact that the world is subject to judgment are strangely de-emphasized and God's wrath over the world is not mentioned.

We also must ask whether one ought not, within the context of the New Testament understanding of the world, speak less glibly of human values and freedom and of the autonomous character of culture.

The Pastoral Constitution says less about Jesus Christ as the Savior from the world than as the preserver of this world. His work of salvation is referred to particularly in connection with the overcoming of the immanent cultural, economic, and political difficulties of our time. The Constitution does not always adequately distinguish between salvation from these immanent difficulties and salvation in the judgment of God, between social righteousness and the divine righteousness of the believing sinner, between the peace of this world and the peace which is given to us believers through God's act of reconciliation in Christ, as well as between human freedom in an immanent sense and the freedom of the children of God.

The future coming of Christ to judge the world is understood less as the end than as the perfection of this world. No mention is made either of the sufferings and catastrophes which the New Testament says must precede his coming or of the Antichrist, in whom the world's rebellion against God is concentrated. The "signs of the times" (4) are not interpreted as signs of the end of the world and of the coming of Christ. Through the use of the concepts of evolution and of progress, the struggle between the world and Christ and the nearness of Christ's sudden breaking into this world are underemphasized; and the progress of this world is related to the coming of the kingdom of God in such a way that—although it must be admitted that they are not equated with one another—earthly progress is nevertheless described as being of "vital concern to the kingdom of God" (39) in a way that is foreign to the New Testament writings.

As strange as the New Testament understanding of the world may at first seem to us, we must still ask whether this Constitution would not have seen the present situation of the world with all its dangers more clearly if it had avoided weakening of the New Testament statements as it did by accommodating itself to modern evolutionary concepts. This was probably due less to American than to French influence and especially to the influence of the evolutionary-cosmic conceptions of Teilhard de Chardin.

## V. The Church and the World

(a) The church is the people of God who have been called out of the world, who believe in Jesus Christ, who have been baptized into his death and incorporated [auferbaut] into his body through the Lord's Supper. They are in the world; but as people who have been set free from the bondage of this world through Christ, they are admonished: "Do not conform to this world" (Romans 12:2), and "Do not love the world or the things in the world" (1 John 2:15). On the contrary, faith is the victory which overcomes the world (1 John 5:4).

(b) As the people of God called out of the world, the church is sent into the world by God to proclaim Jesus Christ to all men as the only way of salvation. The world hears this preaching of the cross as a foolish and scandalous message that contradicts the wisdom of this world and requires faith. Thus, wherever the Gospel is proclaimed with authority, life and death decisions are made. Just as Jesus came "not to bring peace, but a sword" (Matthew 10:34), so the preaching of the Gospel results in conflict and struggle, for the world resists the lordship of Christ. In the midst of this struggle, however, the peace of God is given to those who subject themselves in faith to Christ as their Lord, who worship him, and who go out to meet him as their coming Lord. Thus, the church as the witness of God is the means [*Organ*] by which God's rule breaks into this world.

(c) Faith in Christ recognizes that God preserves the world in spite of its being subjected to judgment so that the Gospel may be preached to it and many may be saved through faith. The church is, therefore, sent not only to proclaim the message of Christ but also bears responsibility for the preservation of the world. This responsibility is expressed in the New Testament writings by the admonitions to obey the governments and to disobey them when obedience to God requires this, by the admonitions to slaves and masters, and by other statements in the catalogues of virtues and vices and of the tables of duties. In these admonitions the church has properly recognized the systematic basis of its efforts to achieve a just and peaceable order of life both for believers and unbelievers.

(d) These two tasks of the church, proclaiming of the saving message of Christ and contributing to the preservation of this world, must be distinguished from each other. They do, indeed, belong together, for the one and the same God is both the preserver of this world and the one who rescues us from bondage to it. And the expectation of the coming of God's kingdom makes every act on behalf of our fellow men a matter of ultimate concern. But the proper and primary task of the church is to proclaim the message of Christ and not to maintain order in this world. Jesus Christ himself was sent to proclaim the kingdom of God and not to establish himself as a judge and divider of inheritance for men who were in con-

flict with one another (Luke 12:13f.). Through the proclamation
of Christ, the lordship of Christ breaks into this world. And the
church serves the world primarily as the instrument [Organ] of the
lordship of Christ.

(e) Thus, the church is not at home in this world. "For here we
have no lasting city, but we seek the city which is to come" (Heb.
13:14). The church in this world is on a pilgrimage, and as it
follows Jesus its way leads it through condemnation, persecution,
and suffering to glory. This is the way of the church by that same
divine necessity which made it the way of Jesus. Through this in-
security and weakness of the church in this world, the risen Lord
intends to manifest his power. "Beloved, do not be surprised at the
fiery ordeal which comes upon you to prove you, as though something strange were happening to you. But rejoice insofar as you
share Christ's sufferings . . . " (1 Peter 4:12).

Admittedly such statements of the New Testament are explicitly
considered in the "Constitution on the Church" and in the "Decree
on the Church's Missionary Activity." In the Pastoral Constitution,
however, which speaks of the church in the modern world, they
are peculiarly de-emphasized.

This Constitution says, "Christ, to be sure, gave his church no
proper mission in the political, economic, or social order. The purpose which he set before her is a religious one" (42). Then, however, the Constitution goes on to speak primarily about questions
of the structures of this world. The New Testament's understanding
of the relationship of these two tasks to each other appears to be
displaced. The primary emphasis is no longer on the scandal of the
preaching of the cross, the message that the believers have been
saved out of this world, but on the church's concern for the
preservation and the progress of this world. Christ is adduced primarily in support of this and he appears to be referred to here more
as an argument in support of this than in order to directly and
personally announce and promise his act of salvation and his judgment to all men.

Corresponding to this, the New Testament's understanding of the
church has been changed. Even though the title reads, "The Church
in the Modern World," little is said about the actual situation of the

church in the world. Rather, the church appears to stand in a peculiar timelessness over against a changing world and to instruct it. In this context, it seems to be normal for the church to live in a situation in which its freedom is guaranteed by the laws of the state; and the opposite situation in which this freedom is not guaranteed or in which the church is persecuted seems to be abnormal. But is it any real help for those who are oppressed and robbed of their freedom to be given instructions on dealing with the social and political structures which it is impossible for them to fulfill? Ought the church give them only a model pattern for an orderly human society? Is it not rather responsible to proclaim the promise of Jesus: "Blessed are you when men revile you and persecute you and utter all kinds of evil against you falsely on my account. Rejoice and be glad" (Matt. 5:11 f.); "Count it all joy, my brethren, when you meet various trials" (James 1:2); "Rejoice insofar as you share Christ's sufferings" (1 Peter 4:13)? The basic message of the church must not be a complaint about the injustice which it has experienced, but rather the recognition that it is an advantage to be able to suffer with Christ. For in the brethren who suffer, the risen Christ manifests his glory in the midst of the world. The Pastoral Constitution, however, refers only incidentally to the great parts of Christendom whose faithfulness while suffering subjection is the glory of the church today.

These criticisms would be less important if the title of the Pastoral Constitution read: "The Church and the Structures of the Modern World," or "Contributions of the Church to the Preservation of the Modern World." However, the title "The Church in the Modern World" or as it originally read, "The Presence of the Church in the Modern World," poses a much more comprehensive task. We may not overlook the fact that much of what we miss here is expressed in the "Dogmatic Constitution on the Church" and in the "Decree on the Church's Missionary Activity." There, however, direct instruction is given only to the members of the Roman Church. And even when the Constitution on the Church seems to clarify thoroughly the essence and the universal mission of the church both for the faithful and for the world, it actually does not speak directly and explicitly to non-Christians. Thus, the Council has been peculiarly reserved about directly proclaiming the Christ to the world—except, of course, if one wishes to understand the self-presentation of the Roman Church at the Council itself as constituting such a witness to Christ. With all recognition of the courageous attempt which the Council has made in its Pastoral Constitution, we would, in terms of the theology of the Reformation, still have to say: Law and Gospel are not properly divided. In all fairness, one would, at this point, admittedly have to add the confession that the World Council of Churches has in many respects also not adequately clarified the theological bases for the church's support of the structures of this world, for example, problems such as natural law, the two kingdoms, Christocracy, etc.

## VI. The Risk of the Pastoral Constitution

With its Constitution on the Church in the Modern World, the Second Vatican Council has taken a courageous step forward which is without precedent in the history of the councils. For what is at stake here is something different from the concerns which ordinarily appear in the decrees of the councils, that is, the fixing of doctrines and ecclesiastical structures, defining heresies and schisms, and overcoming unclarity and tensions within the church itself. This Constitution, however, addresses itself to mankind as a whole and seeks to clarify the problems of living together which today so urgently demand solution. It differs from the kind of decree which one usually expects from a Council in that it does not establish a dogmatic definition that is binding for all time; rather it clarifies and gives direction specifically in terms of the present situation which will be quite different 10 years from now and then will again require new consideration and direction. In awareness of the threatening situation facing the world today, the Council has given itself the task of speaking specifically to this situation and offering the help that is available through faith in Christ.

This task of clarifying the modern situation of humanity was naturally accompanied by many difficulties. The text of this Constitution implicitly presupposes the "Dogmatic Constitution on the Church" (2). One of the difficulties which arises from this is that the Constitution on the Church speaks of the church in general and timeless terms; this Constitution, however, speaks about a very definite historical situation of the church in the world which is, in addition, a completely new kind of situation, unknown at the time that the biblical writings were written or the earlier dogmatic decisions were made. If it is true, however, that the exceedingly complex situation of the modern world is not easy to comprehend, then it is a thoroughly difficult task to arrive at specific answers to modern problems on the basis of established universal dogmatic statements which, for the most part, were developed under completely different historical circumstances. In addition to this, there was the technical difficulty that this text unlike all the others was not prepared by a preconciliar commission, but was first developed during the Council—although some previously prepared materials were used. There was, therefore, less time to permit the text to ripen and to bring the various sections which had been worked out by the various subcommissions into a complete systematic and stylistic unity or balance. Furthermore, this Constitution deals with so many different problems of history, society, relationships between the sexes, politics, and so forth that hardly any father or theologian of the Council could consider himself competent to speak on all of these problems at once. As a result of this, competent laymen were utilized in connection with this Constitution far more than for the other texts discussed by the Council, but these laymen were granted neither the right to speak nor to vote in the Council.

The innovations involved in this procedure made many fathers of the Council uncertain until just before the final vote was taken as to whether the draft was really ripe for release or whether they ought not possibly to restrict themselves to stating a few basic universal principles or simply to making a declaration on the question of world peace and leave the rest of the questions or even the entire Constitution to be worked out by the post-conciliar synod of bishops which the Pope had made possible. There was also some concern as to how such a new kind of conciliar text ought to be titled, since further changes in the situation of the world would apparently put it out of date within 10 years. In terms of its size and the significance of its content, it seemed appropriate to refer to it as a constitution. On the other hand, to designate it a constitution seemed to assign too much importance to an attempt of this kind in which many of the statements obviously could not claim the ongoing significance of fundamental principles. As a result, more modest designations such as "A Conciliar Letter," or "Declaration," or "Exposition" were considered. However, the text of the Constitution seemed to be too significant and its theme too comprehensive for such titles. As a result, it was finally given the new title of "Pastoral Constitution," in which the designation "pastoral" is intended to express its specific address to contemporary mankind.

No one could claim that the Council has resolved all of the difficulties connected with the method and content of this task. Most of the fathers and theologians of the Council were themselves clear on this point while it was being drafted; and it is, therefore, no sign of any lack of respect for their work that we here refer to some of the questions which are not answered. For it is obvious that not all of these new problems could be solved within the few years during which the Council was in session and also that they have not yet been resolved in other churches, but are constantly being considered and discussed. We ought, therefore, all the more recognize that the Council, in spite of these difficulties, attempted to come to grips with the theme "the church in the modern world" and directly addressed itself to all men. The fact that the Council was willing to accept some imbalances in the text because of the urgency of the many problems, not only gives impressive evidence of its sense of responsibility in dealing with the situation of modern man, but also proves that it was prepared to take seriously the dogmatic statements of the Constitution on the Church describing the people of God as pilgrims. In fact, the church in this world does find itself on a pilgrimage in which it must, on the basis of its faith in the act of salvation which has taken place once and for all, constantly consider the specific steps that it ought to take next. In deliberately maintaining the temporary and open-ended attitude of the Pastoral Constitution, the Council came very close to the dialectical method of work practiced by the World Council of Churches. On the basis of this Constitution we may, therefore, explicitly recognize that the Council has become a partner in the common struggle of the churches, in which every church that lives in the midst of such a rapidly changing world must be involved.

# Notes

1. Numbers in parentheses refer to the sections of the "Pastoral Constitution on the Church in the Modern World." In this chapter the translation used is from *The Documents of Vatican II* (Published by Guild Press, America Press, and Association Press, and copyrighted 1966 by the America Press. Used by permission). Abbreviated: *Documents*.

2. Section 1, *Documents*, p. 342.

3. Section 1, *Documents*, p. 585.

4. Section 2, *Documents*, pp. 662-663.

5. See the explanatory footnote to the title (1), *Documents*, p. 199.

6. October 11, 1962. *Documents*, p. 712.

7. *Documents*, pp. 319-331.

# Part III
# Perspectives

Chapter IX

# The Council and the Essence
# of the Gospel

Two diametrically opposite answers may be heard among us to the question whether after the Council we are faced by a changed Catholicism. Some people say, with a slight undertone of self-satisfied superiority, that Catholicism has not altered in the slightest. Everything remains exactly as before. Others, full of enthusiasm, say, with an undertone of illusory expectation of an early inevitable reunion, that Catholicism has undergone a radical change from its very foundations; only some minor points, but nothing of fundamental importance, now separate us.

Both views are incorrect. From a historical angle, we must honestly say, on the contrary, that the significance of this Council is that it has succeeded in reviving Catholicism in a way that has hardly ever occurred throughout its long history, but certainly without in any way altering the *foundations* of the Catholic Church from which we dissociated ourselves in part. What seemed to us during the Council to be its weakness, that two opposing trends, one progressive and the other conservative, attempted to neutralize each other, may possibly be seen by future historians as its true importance.

As Protestants we are naturally inclined to regret that the progressive tendency, sympathetic to us and indeed inclined towards a rapprochement, was opposed by other conservative tendencies. But we must take into account in this connection that we cannot expect the same results from an admittedly *Catholic* revival, which

189

must and will remain on a Catholic basis, as from the Protestant Reformation.

It is inherent in any Catholic revival that there *must* be two trends in the Council, and that an attempt must be made to reconcile them. Of course, there is another point to be noted in this connection, that from the beginning to the end of the Council the progressive tendency was more strongly represented than the conservative.

If a correct assessment is to be made, I must next stress that it is wrong to consider only the texts. This leads to the danger of regarding the Council merely as a collection of *prepared texts*. This is not a historical attitude. More than in any other Council, it is apparent here from the entire proceedings of the Council that its impulse will have as much influence as its texts. It is therefore important that we were able to attend as observers. And it is particularly important that we were able to have copies of the first drafts of all the texts that were discussed—which, moreover, by now are not available—and could follow, through the discussions and amendments, the way in which the final definitive texts were arrived at.

Pope John XXIII himself expressed the opinion that the revival of the Catholic Church would be accomplished through the Council. He described its goal as follows, in his inaugural address on October 11, 1962: "The authentic doctrine should be studied and expounded through the methods of research and through the literary forms of *modern* thought. One thing is the substance of the ancient doctrine of the *depositum fidei,* and another is the way in which it is presented." He went on to say that both pastoral and ecumenical aspects of such presentation should be taken into account. He ordained that no heresies should be condemned, no fresh dogmas proclaimed, and no old dogmas revived.

How far has the Council changed the Catholic Church within the meaning of this definition? Is the result merely a modernization of the outward forms of Catholicism? Is it really just a formal accommodation of church doctrine to the modern world that has taken place? I would say outright that actually more than this has occurred. John XXIII himself was anxious for something more than a mere formal revision. By his distinction between changing form and enduring substance, he simply meant to refer to the problem to which I alluded above. There are important elements in Catholicism which could be revived—not only of a formal kind—and there are some which for dogmatic reasons are unchangeable. It was not entirely fortunate that the changeable factors were made evident only as outward forms.

In another connection the distinction between changing forms and enduring substance was inadequate. It should have been defined what now are changing factors and what is enduring substance. The whole problem lies here, for us Protestants as well as for others. The question is more difficult for Catholicism than for Protestantism, since not only the Gospel, but later elements of ecclesiastical tradition, and indeed the primacy of the Pope, lie at the heart of Catholicism, and this too must be cleared up.

The Council also suffered from the fact that questions of the relationship between the essential nucleus and the changing factors were not raised from the first, and indeed were not even noticed by many people, and so it happened that some people, even outsiders, to some extent superficially regarded the renewal simply as an adaptation of the church to the modern world, and that this really essential effort was compromised by the fact that it lacked a proper theological basis.

Like any reform movement, including the Protestant Reformation, this renewal of the church manifests itself as a side-effect of a real extremism, a fanaticism. Seen from this angle, the result is that people seek only adaptation, without any theological basis. If such a false renewal gains ground, the true renewal (or true modernization) will be irreparably harmed, because it must lead to a reaction on the part of the opponents of any Catholic reform, the opponents of the idea of the Council. Therefore any occasion or pretext for such a retrograde movement must be avoided. The reaction against any false renewal must come from the *friends* of reform, not from the conservative *opponents* of reform, as was often the case in the Council, where the reaction of the latter was always wrongly inspired. Our Reformers in the 16th century themselves took in hand the opposition of the fanatics.

If in the past abuses have arisen in the Catholic Church, in our view this is because it has become all too worldly, instead of subordinating the undeniably necessary entry into the world to a higher principle. The renewal of the Catholic Church cannot consist in further progress along this road of undue adaptation, but on the contrary must be a purification of what with the passage of time has permeated the church in all too worldly form, and a deepening of what constitutes the basis of faith.

Thus in fact throughout all the Council texts may be distinguished a great reduction and concentration, behind much dead wood, and a return to a biblical conception. The worldliness of earlier centuries, which Catholicism has maintained as a tradition, is just what is out of date today and what suffocates the essential nucleus which at all times should have wider influence through its own strength. Catholic theology paradoxically has thereby become estranged from the world, because in the Middle Ages, in line with the then modern trends of Scholasticism, it adapted itself all too closely not only to the form but to the content of contemporary philosophy and lost contact with the biblical idea.

What was ominous, too, was the crowding out of the biblical essentials by much too great an adaptation, by a purely speculative point of view which disregarded the concrete historical working of God through history, as it is made known to us in the Bible. At this point one diverged from the biblical basis.

I should especially like to mention one declaration which, if all its consequences for the further development of the effort for renewal and for the facilitation of discussions are followed up, seemed to me perhaps one of the most promising of all the Council's texts, although curiously it promises so little. It is in the Decree on Ecumenism. There it is stated that there is "an order of precedence, a hierarchy" among the truths of Catholic doctrine, according to their relationship with the fundamentals of the Christian faith. Although similar statements may have been made here and there in earlier Catholicism, it has never before been so announced in an official Conciliar text. Indeed, an Encyclical of Pius XII states on the contrary that all dogmas are of equal worth. From the new text it follows naturally, without its being specifically stated, that, say, the dogma on the Assumption of the Virgin Mary, or the dogmas on the primacy of the Pope, do not have the same significance as, say, the dogmas on Christ dating from the 4th and 5th centuries, which were accepted also by the Reformers.

Here there appears also, besides the weakening of the old dogmas by the addition of an opposing theory, already alluded to, a wider and particularly promising possibility of renewal within the framework and with the survival of the old dogmas. The wording of these dogmas will not be affected, but from the principle of biblical renewal a certain shift within the nucleus may be accepted, without anything being lost from these essentials. From this there arise incalculable possibilities for the future, and of course for our discussions. The basis for it is in the Decree on Ecumenism.

And now, to sum up: What have we Protestants to learn from the Council?

First of all, we must be prepared to renew ourselves also. It is not enough to say with Pharisaic satisfaction: "Thank God things have at last become at least a little better with the Catholics." As if everything were all for the best with ourselves. As if, on the pretext that we have already had our Reformation, in the 16th century, we might say that we have been renewed once and for all. Certainly our renewal must have a different aspect from that of the Catholics. It must deliberately proceed from *our* foundations, thus from the Bible alone, not from the Bible combined with traditions. In this respect, it is easier for us. We are also doing our Catholic brethren a service if we make an effort towards a conscious Protestant renewal, in which we consider the positive, not the negative polemical side of our foundations. But our churches too stand in need of a renewal, in the sense of a purification and a deepening. The individual Protestant Churches—Lutheran, Reformed, Methodist, etc.—must each on its own account concern itself with that renewal. With us too ecumenism can only be the outcome of the renewal of the churches.

However, I might wish that our Protestant churches would strive in the same spirit of purification and sincerity as we observed in so many of our Catholic brethren at the Council. We share with Catholicism a concern to make the Gospel accessible to the modern world. But here we must learn from the positive weaknesses of the Council, and not, as recently happened in the American weekly *Newsweek,* try to outdo all their mistakes and so make the modern world our idol. For us it might well be a permanent order to go forth into the world. We must not lose sight of the questions, How are we preaching the Gospel to the modern world? How are we ensuring, so far as we are able, that the Gospel penetrates the world?

We must make ourselves understood by the world, adapt ourselves, but must not thereby betray the Gospel, but be mindful of Paul's words referring to the essential of our mission: "Do not be conformed to this world but be transformed by the renewal of your mind" (Rom. 12:2).

Many a time has the world expected us to say something different from what it has already said, perhaps better. In this connection we may also learn from the admitted weakness of many Conciliar texts. Too often we forget that we should first of all ask: What factors may and must change, and what is the enduring substance?

## Chapter X

# The Ecumenism of the Second Vatican Council

Ecumenism is the special subject of the *Decretum de Oecumenismo,* promulgated on November 21, 1964. This decree was in fact the subject of a special article in the series of Evangelical Lutheran opinions on the Council (*Dialogue on the Way,* 1965, pp. 186-230). That article welcomed in particular the recommendations in Chapter II of the decree on an ecumenical attitude, as being specially encouraging for a new relationship between the Roman Church and other churches. There still remains the question whether the ecumenism of the Council is limited to this decree or whether it really extends to other conclusions of the Council. In other words, is the Decree on Ecumenism isolated and unrelated to other Council conclusions, or do its ideas permeate other conclusions too? The Dogmatic Constitutions on the Church and on Divine Revelation must be considered in answering this question, since they form the basis of the Council's ecumenical program. And we must further consider how far the ecumenical recommendations formulated on this basis are taken into consideration in other decrees and declarations, such as the Pastoral Constitution on the Church in the Modern World.

In the Decree on the Instruments of Social Communication, which indeed was promulgated before the Decree on Ecumenism, it is not so much ecumenical cooperation that is dealt with as how the church is going to deal with these problems in the sphere of press, radio, and television. The Declaration on Christian Education does not indeed speak of any cooperation of the churches in school and educational problems, but welcomes ecumenical conversations. In many other conclusions, though, explicit reference is made to ecumenical responsibility, as in the decree on bishops, priests, and laity. The program of the Decree on Ecumenism adopts these allusions, even though it gives no concrete expression to what is said there. In the Pastoral Constitution on the Church in the Modern World we find this declaration: "In addition, the Catholic Church gladly holds in high esteem the things which other Christian Churches or ecclesial communities have done or are doing cooperatively by way of achieving the same goal" (40). But even though the subject matter and directives of this Constitution come very near to what has been discussed and worked out in World Conferences of Churches since Stockholm, it does not make any actual reference to them, even in footnotes. For the future, the Pastoral Constitution states: "Finally, this Council desires that by way of fulfilling their role properly in the international community, Catholics should seek to cooperate actively and in a positive manner both with their separated brothers, who together with them profess the gospel of love, and with all men thirsting for true peace" (90, cf. 92).

The most explicit and emphatic adoption and further development of the ideas of the Decree on Ecumenism are to be found in the decree on the church's missionary activities. There are in fact many parallels between the missionary and ecumenical programs, their ideas being very similar, since ecumenism might be regarded merely as a special case of missionary activity. "Elements" of truth and grace are recognized in both the non-Roman churches and the non-Christian religions. An opening is to be offered to both of them. The members of the Roman Church are to be encouraged in a new, amicable understanding with both of them, and in a dialogue with both in which the full Catholic doctrine is to be expounded. In both cases the goal is the unity which is already a reality in the Roman Church, whereby a development of its Catholicity in relation to the special assets possessed by the non-Roman Churches and the non-Christian religions is foreseen. But these analogies must not be misunderstood. The decree on missions clearly emphasizes the community in which all Christians stand together, in contrast to the non-Christian religions, and more than once issues a warning that missionary activities must not strive after such a community with the non-Christian religions. "Thus, missionary activity among the nations differs from pastoral activity exercised among the faithful, as well as from undertakings aimed at restoring unity among Christians" (6). Missions and ecumenism are indeed most closely linked together, insofar as any division between Christians brings missionary preaching into disrepute and makes it unlikely to be believed in. The missionary task renders urgent the ecumenical task of uniting all believers "in one flock" (6). But instruction must come before union: along with the Secretariat for the Promotion of Christian Unity, the Congregation for the Propagation of the Faith is seeking "ways and means for bringing about and directing fraternal cooperation as well as harmonious living with the missionary undertakings of other Christian communities. Thus, as far as possible, the scandal of division can be removed" (29). "This living testimony will more easily achieve its effect if it is given in unison with other Christian communities, according to the norms of the Decree on Ecumenism, 12" (36). Here indeed there is no question of dividing mission fields between the churches, but rather by the Decree on Missions the Roman Catholic mission is cutting away the ground from beneath the feet of the young churches of other denominations.

If we consider all the other conclusions of the Council, it is clear that the Council's ecumenical ideas have penetrated the most varied fields of the church's concerns. But indeed most of the ecumenical references are only formal, going no farther than the Decree on Ecumenism, and—apart from the Decree on Missions—falling short of the impressiveness of their admonitions. But it must be borne in mind that the Roman Church officially approved the ecumenical movement of our time for the first time at this Council, that the Decree on Ecumenism is a beginning, and that the ecumenical idea must first become integrated in the wide sphere of the Roman

Church. An ecumenical determination became apparent in the Council, however, not only in the Decree on Ecumenism. Wider implementation of the ecumenical program may be expected from the post-Conciliar "Ecumenical Directorate" that is announced, which is to carry into execution the Decree on Ecumenism.

In this chapter excerpts from the Constitutions and Decrees of the Ecumenical Council are taken from *The Documents of Vatican II,* published by Guild Press, America Press, and Association Press, and copyrighted 1966 by the America Press. Used by permission.

## Chapter XI

# The Reverse Side of the Council

*"All things have their reverse
side; Christ alone has none."*
(Hans Urs von Balthasar)

The Council is already long past. Between its announcement in January 1959 and its close in December 1965 an immense amount of concentrated work was done. The almost unbelievable spiritual potential of the Roman Catholic Church was confirmed in a truly sublime manner in these five or six years.

Now, scarcely a year after the close of the Council, the clue to the significance of this event is being sought on all sides. The post-Council commissions were established not only to implement the conclusions of the Council, but also, and above all, to give the correct interpretation of the Council, so as to avoid misunderstandings of any kind. The Council certainly has not only one but many meanings. It is important to give the right explanation. But who is to do this?

What the Council really means, both for Roman Catholics and for all other Christians, will become apparent only in the course of the next few decades. History is not always determined by our intentions, however genuine they may be. Thus the final judgment on this event must be left to the future—it is beyond our power. And so we can but do as we did before, state the question and try to answer

199

it: What was this Council? What is noteworthy is that even our answer to this question, our approval and our criticisms, are not wholly without effect on the further history of the Council. Opinions or ideas have historical weight—or at all events may have—in the sense that they have a formative influence that may have a decisive significance for history, whether on a large or a small scale.

Pope John XXIII was anxious that this Council should above all be a *pastoral* Council. This does not mean that the Council had or should have no *dogmatic* influence, for what would a Council be without any distinct dogmatic trend? Dogmatic thought and meditation appeared in the documents as in the Council itself. It is true that no new dogmas were defined, and this was intentional. The nearest we find to a dogmatic definition is perhaps the statement on the collegiality of the bishops and the sacramental nature of the bishop's ordination—but it is not quite that. In the dogmatically important Constitution on Divine Revelation the Council fathers even avoided adopting a dogmatic position with regard to the relation between the written word and tradition.

The purpose of the Council was not to produce dogmatic novelties, but rather to state dogmas in language that is comprehensible to men today. A French Dominican once said that the truth of dogmas "must be released from its crippling padding." The Lutheran observer understood this very well, and realized too how urgently necessary was the effort towards a new interpretation of dogma if Christianity is not to become increasingly unintelligible and therefore lacking in compelling force. The almost hidden tendency towards a "trans-dogmatization" of the old dogmas framed in a specialized language was at times perceptible, stimulating, and challenging, even to the Lutherans. So then we come back to the pastoral tendency of this Council. What does this mean? Fundamentally it means that the Council was to be a Council of renewal. The word *aggiornamento* often used by Pope John himself might seem to mean a pragmatic adaptation to the times, but in fact goes much deeper. It actually aims at a renewal of heart and mind, both in individuals and in the church as a whole. If this tendency was often very obscure, because many people were alarmed by that word "renewal," yet it was perceptible often in an astonishing form. It is not surprising that even the critics among the Council theologians, who really were not indulgent towards the Council, were still forced to admit that all in all it had surpassed their expectations.

All of this must make a strong impression on us Lutherans, and induces us to revise our impression of the Roman Catholic Church. Who among us expected that a church, noted and notorious for its "inflexibility," would be capable of such a transformation? Naturally it has remained the same, and will show itself to be so in the future. But it has also become different. If we can understand this paradox, we can understand the Council.

Without sacrificing its identity, the Roman Catholic Church has committed itself to a path that signifies a break with the Counter-Reforming post-Trent tradition. A new spirit of flexibility, frankness, and love has come to life through John XXIII and through the Council that he convened. Whatever may have gone on behind the scenes in the way of undesirable maneuvering, this new spirit was a very real thing that could be perceived by anyone who was able to follow the Council from outside.

The Council, thus understood, means for us on the one hand a challenge to do on our side and in our situation what it has accomplished for its part. On the other hand, it raises the difficult question of how far this is possible for us today. We also are familiar with the spirit of intransigence, self-satisfaction, and withdrawal within ourselves. The Second Vatican Council was for the Lutheran observer an admonition, an inspiration, and a challenge to critical self-examination.

The same thing happens here as always when something important occurs. Criticism is very soon forthcoming. Criticism is an inevitable part of the Council and its history. Human history is always open to question, because everything human has its reverse side, especially when it makes pretensions. And few things on earth have such high pretensions as a Roman Catholic Council. There *must* then be criticism, even for the Council's own sake. Criticism, though, is no agreeable thing, but rather something dangerous. Even when apparently most justified, it has its reverse side, and this must not be forgotten. Who is there that ventures to criticize?

In this connection I am not going to speak of the criticism that is now flourishing especially in the Roman Catholic Church, arising from the dissatisfaction of the "conservatives," who regard the renewal simply as innovation. They, and especially the Bishop of Rome, are being strongly urged, both publicly and privately, to interpret the Council and its documents as little and as traditionally as possible. Nor do I refer to the discontent of those who feel that the Council did not go nearly far enough, and that it can be regarded only as the modest beginning of a widespread renewal. No, there is a much more serious test of the Council: not whether it has said or done too much or too little, but whether essentially, or at any rate clearly and plainly enough, it said what had to be said.

Is this not after all a very improper and ungrateful question? In my view it is the only important and relevant question.

Recently (June 15, 1966) there appeared in the very stimulating and thoughtful periodical *Orientierung* an article, "Was it all worth the trouble?" Here all these main criticisms are expressed, not because the author accepts them without question, but because he thinks they ought to be heard. "Is the Council not avoiding the true problems, in the midst of so much reform, improvement, and modernization? Have the Council fathers rightly appreciated the church's situation? Have they told us the salutary and essential truth? Will historians in future centuries not be obliged to look back on the Second Vatican Council with some embarrassment? Has not the general trend proved a dangerous path to follow?" This criticism "is not inspired by secondary matters, but by the well-intentioned main trends of the Council, applauded by the people in general."

This criticism is almost startlingly expressed in some quotations from a book by Urs von Balthasar, in which he puts under the magnifying-glass a few of the main trends of contemporary Catholicism. ". . . There appears in fact to be a fatal aspect to all these enterprises, whereby the whole trend appears under the following slogans: Let us at all costs leave our splendid isolation, which is becoming unpleasant: hence rapprochements, fraternization, movements to abdicate from thrones and pedestals, collegial movements, democratization, simplification, leveling down . . . an attempt to visualize so far as possible what is up-to-date for today, tomorrow, and the day after tomorrow. . . . All of these enterprises that lie before us, just because they are apparently so clear in meaning, and urgently called for by the Christian crisis . . . are two-edged, ambiguous, and might generally become definitely dangerous, as they give the appearance of containing the 'one essential thing.' . . . *All things have their reverse side; Christ alone has none."* I leave these words to speak for themselves.

Has the Council really spoken of *God* to men today? Many Christian things were said, but did the Council let the word of God himself be heard?

The following questions were put in the article in *Orientierung:* "Were not the whole of the Council debates basically a flight from God, a fear of the scandal of the cross and thus—we use this expression to give point to the reproach—a human failure?" If we look back at the Council, it is true that the scandal of Jesus' person and words, as reported in the Gospels, and the "stumbling-block of the cross" which Paul speaks of, play a very subdued part. The Roman Catholic Church meets the world halfway in most friendly fashion, doing all it can to make itself comprehensible, to present its message attractively and sympathetically. Any truly biblical aspect is noticeably lacking here. Doubtless these criticisms will become stronger, from both Catholic and Protestant sides.

This shortcoming became evident also in the splendid closing ceremony on December 8, 1965, with the "messages" of the various groups to the world. Here one might quite well speak of failure, as a closing ceremony sums up the whole event. Was this finally a flight from God and a fear of the scandal of the cross? The Council has often been referred to as a "spectacle" before the world. A dangerous word, too popular, too smooth, too splendid. Yes, splendid it was in many ways. One cannot but think of Paul's words in 1 Cor. 4:9, where the apostle, too, is speaking of a spectacle, though in a somewhat different sense! Here we are touching on a weak side of the Council. This splendid event truly has its reverse side.

The criticisms also have *their* reverse side. It might well be that this openness to the world, this attempt to make the message attractive, and this effort to achieve a dialogue with the world may be understood otherwise. It might well be that the Roman Catholic Church, with its "world optimism," is doing penance: we have remained long enough withdrawn within ourselves—in hardness and indifference. We have presented a false image to the world. The attitude of our church towards the world, for example in the last third of last century, was surely, in its harsh antithesis to the world, just such a stumbling-block, far removed from the spirit of Jesus. Now things will be different. The world shall know that the church is there for its sake. It is not an isolated religious eminence, but shares the destiny of the world, of which it is itself a part. Thus it is said, in the introduction to the Constitution of the Church in the Modern World, that it shares everything with the world, its hopes and its fears, its sorrows and joys. Therefore it should also help the world with its manifold apparently insoluble problems. It might well be that these "enterprises" referred to by the critics as an endeavor to escape from self and be obedient to Christ's charge, "Go ye into all the world" might be comprehended as all arising from love.

All things have their reverse side. This is true of the Council, but also of the criticisms leveled against the Council. This is not entirely simple.

The Lutherans would address their critical inquiry to the Council thus: Has the Council proclaimed the Gospel? This question is a cogent one, but it is also dangerous, for who can be so sure that he is actually proclaiming the Gospel? No church can claim a monopoly in the Gospel, neither the Roman Catholic Church nor the Lutheran. The word Gospel is greater than the word church, since the church is but the servant of the Gospel. The same is true of the kingdom of God. The kingdom of God is greater than the church, since the church is there for its sake. The kingdom of God will come, and the church will disappear, when the time comes.

It can at any rate be said that the Council according to its own ideas was anxious for one thing only: to expound the Gospel truly and make it live. The Gospel must be the source of everything in the church, in both its doctrine and its morality. In this sense the Council and the Gospel are indissociable.

But what is meant by the Gospel? So far as I can understand, this term for the Council signifies all that is to be found in the Gospel. It is a comprehensive term, comprising many elements. It would be particularly interesting to seek out all the places in the Council documents where the word Gospel is used. We should certainly discover that the word is rich in meaning, covering a wide variety of equally important topics: forgiveness, grace, commandment, precept, aspiration toward perfection, consecration, doctrine, discipline, church order, church organization, etc. Thus understood, the Gospel is everything, and in this sense the Council is indeed an exposition of the Gospel. Highest among its diverse elements is perhaps consecration by grace, the perfecting of mankind. Each individual person is called by the Gospel to become a saint.

The Lutherans must be closely attentive when the Roman Catholic Church speaks thus of the Gospel, and act accordingly. I should like to stress one thing in particular. A quite distinctive trend became apparent in the Council when poverty was referred to in Council speeches or, in a milder way, in its documents at times. Naturally the Roman Catholic Church is aware of the power of Mammon, the curse of money. Much too often in its history, like most other churches, it has been on the side of the rich and powerful. And yet the Gospel says that Jesus was on the side of the poor and needy. Another idea radiated from the Council, sometimes secretly and sometimes quite noticeably: love for the poor, for those who have nothing and are nothing. The church must be a church for the poor. Bishops and priests must not be people with many possessions. High titles and honors are to be done away with.

Do not poverty and the Gospel go together? Have people not always spoken of "scriptural poverty"? Is there not some close link between poverty and the Gospel? What are we to think? The Council has here found something that is significant. How does it happen that the Lutheran churches in many lands draw their members mainly from the comparatively prosperous middle class? Certainly here too it is true that all things have their reverse side; Christ alone has none. Gospel and poverty do go together. Luther had a particularly keen eye for basic and absolute essentials. For him the word Gospel was no comprehensive word, no general concept, but a glowing, radiant central idea from which everything emanates: God's boundless, undeserved mercy and love for lost sinners, for those who have nothing and are nothing, no sanctity, no merit, no prerogative. *Everything* else comes from this central fount, this living spring. The Gospel is the resurrection to a new life. Therefore Luther could say that the Gospel—thus understood—was the church's only wealth and treasure.

I have the impression that this understanding of the Gospel for the Roman Catholic Church is something "specific," something peculiar to Luther, indeed that this interpretation is a very questionable

limitation of the word Gospel. And here we return to the hardest
spiritual struggles of Reformation times. Does this all belong only
to times past? Must not this struggle continue today too, and indeed
in *all* churches? Perhaps we have here reached the critical point, on
which everything else depends.

It is clear that the world today has need of better and stronger
Christian and human principles, that must be carefully thought out
and worked out. The Council forcefully drew attention to this, and
it is a good thing that this happened. And yet the question remains:
Has the Council proclaimed the Gospel? One thing the world can
in no circumstances preach to itself—the Gospel. If the church does
not do this, no one can do it, but then the church is no longer the
church, but has become something quite different. The question is
whether the church has not in the last instance had too much to say
of us and our goodness, of our duty and our ability (even if only
granted through grace) to sanctify the world, rather than of God.
The order of the facts is not always immaterial. Though the Council
might try to escape this question, it will not be possible. No church—
including the Lutheran—will be able to shirk this question. Here
basically we are at one. Have we the courage, we who call ourselves
Christians, to admit this, and to live according to the Gospel thus
understood? This would truly change the relation of the church to
the world. The forgiveness of sin changes all, and means a new life
with and for each other. It would mean a way out of ourselves.
Through this way out of ourselves into the world, the churches would
be able to meet together in a new way, as joyfully pardoned people,
without credit, without claim to any special consideration in one
way or another. The meaning that Luther gave to the word Gospel
cannot be forgotten. It must always shine out. The Council was a
great event for us all, not only for the Roman Catholic Church. But
serious questions were decided at that Council. "All things have
their reverse side; Christ alone has none." This "Christ alone," finally,
is the Gospel for all men and for all churches.

## Chapter XII

# Some Consequences of Conciliar Ecclesiology

The Council was a Roman Council. Thorough and conscientious work yielded an astonishing output which takes the form of greatly varied documents. Catholic theologians as well as those of other churches will have to deal with these for a long time. The reality of the Council is by no means limited to the texts. To its reality belong the phase of preparation and expectation, the occasionally exciting dialogue in the Council, the post-conciliar work, and not least of all the practical realization in the breadth of ecclesiastical and theological existence. To be sure, all of this has primary relevance for the Roman Catholic Church, for it was her Council.

At the same time, however, it was also a Council which assented to the world-wide ecumenical reality. The Council recognized the signs of the times and intended an ecumenical openness to the non-Roman churches and Christians. We on the Evangelical Lutheran side appreciate this fact. In this intention we see an attempt to take up the concerns of the ecclesiology of the Reformation and at the same time to gather together and to digest the hitherto existing output of the ecumenical movement. We on the evangelical side are addressed by the Council and called upon to give an answer. Relating ourselves to the conciliar tradition of the Reformation, we will, therefore, have to consider the possibility of an evangelical

207

Council and thereby seek to make a connection with the tradition of general councils. The experiences of the ecumenical movement in the last 40 years would especially have to be taken into consideration. Beyond this, however, every alert evangelical Christian is forced to reflect upon the basis of his faith.

In our opinion, the Council was one which could not overcome the divisions in the church, although it attained a considerably mild statement in the central theme of ecclesiology. A hazy enthusiasm for unity, therefore, would be false. Only sober testing is fitting to the realists. It is my personal conviction—and I can in this connection also call attention to the declaration of the synod of the Evangelical Church in Germany—that such testing demonstrates that the divisions in the church especially in regard to ecclesiology and in the understanding of divine revelation have not yet been overcome. Even with all readiness to let ourselves be put to the test, we will not by any means have to become uncertain of our evangelical basis.

The Council was open to dialogue and encouraged dialogue in a world-wide ecumenical dimension. The dynamic motif of the theology of the people of God in the Constitution on the Church should be regarded positively in this dialogue. It is, however, a theologically controversial problem how the concept of the people of God appears in the light of the concentric ecclesiology in the papal encyclical *Ecclesiam Suam*. A further theologically controversial problem lies in the broad thematic circle of the structure of the church (Chapter 3 of the Constitution on the Church). In the broadest sense of the word it is the problem of the ministry. It appears to us that a fixation of certain developments in church history occurs just in this chapter, even though progress beyond Vatican I is evident. It cannot be overlooked that just at that point where collegiality is urged the infallible primacy of the Pope is also constantly emphasized. The most important theologically controversial problem which relates to the Decree on Ecumenism lies in the question whether the ecclesiological reality existing outside the Roman Church can be assessed when the Roman Church is the point of orientation. We are not failing to recognize the positive beginnings in the Decree on Ecumenism, let us say the recognition of the baptism of the divided brothers and the stress upon their spiritual life in and with the Word. The assessment of the sacramental reality in regard to the Sacrament of the Altar, however, causes us distress. As Lutherans we do not feel ourselves understood at this point in the Decree on Ecumenism. We ask whether the statements on the Decree on Ecumenism about the other churches and their spiritual life do not become ambiguous when the thesis is pointedly presented that the Roman Church represents the perfect institutional realization of the church of Christ. Once more from this point the problem of the ministry arises as the decisive hindrance for a better understanding. From the Lutheran side we maintain firmly that the understanding of the church must be developed from Article VII of the *Confessio Augustana*. We shall have to advance even further to the roots of a Christo-centric *communio* theology. There is further concern that the beginnings of the joint ecumenical work, as they are emphasized in the Decree on Missions, should also emerge stronger in the questions of education and in the difficult question of mixed marriages. A positive point to emphasize is the astonishingly wide consensus which the Council attained in the questions about the church and the world and in the questions dealing with Christian sanctification (in order to summarize the thematic of different decrees in a general fashion). We can stress this fact approvingly. We would, however, like to suggest that the basis for this consensus would have to lie in a still deeper understanding of what Gospel really means. Does the Roman Catholic Church really know about the absolving power of the Gospel which grants justification or does she bind the Gospel too much with the *nova lex?* It is evident that this question would have to be raised especially in the discussion concerning the Constitution on Revelation. From this point then it would be in order to raise the critical questions regarding the relation between Scripture and tradition.

The Council places us before common tasks. First of all, it is a matter of deepening the spirit of ecumenism so that all Christians get to know one another and understand one another better. It is a question of strong considerations in the direction of a concrete working together in missions, in education, in action in the world. It appears to me that the problem does not lie in the question of joint action in accordance with natural law but in the task already raised in the Decree on Ecumenism, that of joint witness to Christ. In this regard it would be an especially important task soberly to examine the question of common worship services. Personally I view the matter in the following manner. According to the Roman Catholic understanding every service in which the Word is preached must lead to a service with the celebration of the sacrament. The service with the Word does not theologically play the central role as it does with us evangelical Christians. For this reason I stand opposed to a general propaganda for common worship services. It is a different matter when forms for such common worship services are worked out in responsible circles. In this regard it would be important that one would not too quickly return to models which have been used up to now but that something new would develop. There is no doubt that there is a very important task here. However, it has promise only if the Roman Catholic Church disregards the instruction on the question of mixed marriages and solves this problem in the spirit of the Decree on Ecumenism and the Declaration on Religious Liberty. The small amount of space which is at our disposal does not permit us at this point also to analyze concretely the possibilities of a reform of evangelical Christianity in an ecumenical spirit. We do not doubt the fact that the Council reminds the churches of the Reformation that Reformation is never something which is already behind us but implies an obligation which must daily be grasped anew: *ecclesia semper reformanda*. To be sure, we do not as yet understand the same thing with this phrase. In accordance with this slogan, however, we hope for further steps toward understanding on both sides.

Chapter XIII

# An Interpretation of the Council

Vatican II is now behind us as a historical fact. It will not cease, however, to influence and penetrate the course of history before us. No one outside of the Catholic Church with unbiased judgment can ever challenge the historic importance of this event as reaching beyond the borderlines of the Catholic world. The influence this Council will exert on the life of other churches will depend mainly on the interpretation given to this Council.

## 1. Harmony or Contradictions?

Protestant readers of conciliary documents will find that there are often different tendencies of theological tradition, different lines of thought, sometimes different emphases, or different methods employed in the same documents. Let us remember a few of them: side by side with the spiritual-mystical conception of the church as the body of Christ we will find a more juridical and canonical conception; beside acknowledgment of the authority of the Holy Scripture and emphasis on the proclamation of the Word we will find the subordination of Scripture to the tradition and of preaching to the sacramental (eucharistic) emphasis; the call of the people of God for the evangelization of the world and the priesthood of all believers as development of the grace of baptism will be balanced against the special call of the hierarchy and the responsibility of the special priesthood and its powers over against the laity. On the

211

one hand we find the acknowledgment of the validity of baptism
as the basic sacrament of the Christian existence and of the manifestation of the unity of the church, whereas on the other hand
we are faced with the refusal to accept the other churches as
"churches" and only recognize elements of the true church in them.
Some parts of the documents will have an astonishingly biblical
development of the subject, others will rely upon patristic arguments; whereas some documents, or at least parts of them, will
almost exclusively utilize references to papal encyclicals from the
last hundred years. Biblical and patristic thought-forms will often
alternate with scholastic terms or canonical definitions. All this
will have the effect of confusing the outsider. Is he faced with evident contradictions, forced attempts at harmonization, an eclectic
collection of documents, a somewhat lamentable effort at compromise, or is there a system after all and a higher harmony which dis-
solves the dissonant elements?

The answers can vary. If directed to Catholic theologians, the
question will often be acknowledged as justified. Catholic readers
will themselves admit this variety though many of them will regard
it as an advantage. They will express their satisfaction over the
wide range of Catholic thinking, which leaves space for many tendencies and does not limit the dogma to one specific straitjacket.
Especially theologians with biblical and patristic orientation will
claim that this diversity gives an opportunity for the development
of Catholic doctrine in new and unusual thought patterns in comparison with traditional theological treatises. The Council documents—so they will claim—are not theological dissertations of one
consequent line of thought but milestones on the way of doctrinal
thinking and helps for orientation. The task of the Council is not
to canonize any theological school or thought-form but to leave as
much openness as possible for the theological work within the limits
of orthodoxy.

Realistically speaking, this answer must give a preliminary satisfaction even to Protestant interpreters. They have to acknowledge
that a biblically oriented theology and a corresponding dogmatic
development in the Catholic Church actually have a better chance
in this manner. Only if biblical material can invade the Catholic
thinking will it be possible to question the foreign philosophical sys-

tem and prepare the way for new thought-forms. It may be that the present results cannot satisfy. Those who have worked in great assemblies and have responsibly attempted to formulate reports of *consensus* will nevertheless see with some compassion the products of the Council and even acknowledge the cleverness of those who had to tackle sensitive items of Catholic doctrine. We must at least recognize that doors were left open even where pressure was heavy to do the contrary.

The acknowledgment of the advantages and disadvantages of this nature of the conciliary documents will not be the only answer. There will be those who will claim that the documents are of a consummate totality, where each piece has its function within a given system of theological thought. Interestingly enough, we will find this interpretation among conservative Catholics as well as among critical Protestants. Whereas the Catholic will work out the context from the system of his scholastic mind, the Protestant will do the same in order to prove that nothing actually has changed and the elements pointing to biblical reconsiderations can fit into the scholastic system. It is nevertheless questionable that both are right. Moreover, such Protestant interpretation renders bad service to the tendencies of renewal in the Catholic world.

More dangerous than the interpretation according to one specific system is another tendency of Catholic interpreters. It is the claim of Catholic comprehensiveness. According to this interpretation, though the disparate elements do not belong to a perfect system of theological thought, they all find their place in the Catholic fullness, of which they show different aspects. A kind of Catholic broad-mindedness is gaining the field in some circles. Recent Reformation research has paved the way, for example, for an acknowledgment of the religious quality of both intentions and doctrines of the Reformation. Suddenly the doctrine of active participation in the liturgy or the priesthood of all believers no longer appears as foreign to Catholic tradition. Even justification by faith alone can be accepted in a right context of Catholic doctrine. The spiritual treasure of hymns and prayers and the concern for the Word of God and its preaching in the congregational devotions appear to this thinking of comprehensiveness as parts of the treasure of the Catholic tradition. The failure to have excluded them by mistake in previous times may willingly be accepted and regretted. Now it is time to present world Christianity with the possibility of Catholic fullness. Whereas in other churches some legitimate aspect of Christian doctrine has been emphasized and carefully guarded, although through historic circumstances separated from the RCC, now the time has come to integrate these gifts of the Holy Spirit into the all-comprehensive RCC.

Insofar as Reformation concerns find recognition in the RCC we should rejoice. Insofar as the challenge of these concerns is not seen and the optimistic dream of an integration of these concerns is cherished, we should be on our guard. It would certainly be unjust to accuse the Council of tendencies here outlined. We should only use adequate care if interpretation of the Council's decisions may weaken the concerns of the Reformation by combining them with elements foreign to the biblical renewal. It is from this point of view not mere advantage if the Council avoided the usual conciliar *"anathema."* The condemnation of heresies may be a somewhat delicate task, and no one should deny that it has been handled in an unfortunate way during the course of history. What is missing in present conciliar documents is not so much this concrete narrowing down of Catholic dogma, which may close doors irrevocably. What *is* missing is the clarification of certain limits, which are at hand and which were even evident presuppositions of the Council's dealings. The lack of interest in marking out the self-evident limits for Catholic thinking and instead paying more attention to general application of the dogma (*aggiornamento*) is a weakness which may have its repercussions in the interpretation of the Council. At the moment it demands extreme sharpness of intelligence besides thorough historic knowledge of Catholic as well as Reformation doctrine in order not to transgress the limits in either direction, i.e., not to suppose an interpretation of conciliar documents in terms of the Reformation, where adequate historic evidence prohibits it; or, vice versa, to fail to discover avenues of understanding where Catholic dogma has guarded its openness. Perhaps this difficulty is faced by any interpreter, Catholic or non-Catholic. And perhaps the creation of a dogmatic no-man's-land, undefined and unexplored, can in the end be an opportunity to leave the trenches and meet in this no-man's-land without prejudices.

## 2. Evangelical Affirmation, Scholastic Implementation

We have to push the problem of interpretation one step farther. If a dialogue is to start, we must find the normative method by which, out of the variety in the material accepted by the Council, we can find converging points of doctrinal affirmation. Is there any such hope, and, in case a positive answer can be given, where should we start our discussion? These questions seem to have primary importance for the future.

Earlier in this report we cited a number of statements showing the complexity of conciliar decisions. We asked whether we are faced with contradictions or with a harmonious system. Whatever the Catholic answer may be, Protestant evangelical interpreters will find many conflicting assertions which they cannot reconcile. They will recognize sentences in which the Gospel message is fully expressed. Thus in *de ecclesia* (chapters I-II) the description of the mission of Christ to the world and the people belonging to him as being collected by the Holy Spirit represent fresh New Testament material and fructify the dogmatic development of ecclesiology. So is also the basic statement about the unity of the Church in *de oecumenismo*, where the Holy Spirit is affirmed as the principle and fundament of unity (§2). Again the biblical affirmations of the one Spirit as the life-giving and unifying Spirit by which the body is held together and the new temple is edified can find an essential evangelical affirmation. No theologian seeking his doctrinal orientation in the *norma normans* of Holy Scripture should ever hesitate to accept such evangelical affirmations. The problem begins, however, when interpreters are faced with sentences which have stepped off the biblical ground and contradict the first affirmations, at least for Protestant judgment. Thus we discover that the fundamental biblical affirmations on ecclesiology are tied with an implementation, where the pneumatic body of Christ finds its concreteness in the canonically ordained ecclesiastical structure governed by the bishop of Rome as the principle and fundament of the unity of the church of Christ (de eccl. § 18). This is where the "protest of the Protestants" is raised in reference to the first principle. The scholastic implementation of the evangelical affirmations is the invasion of foreign powers, which must be counteracted. Here lies the passion of all evangelical Protestantism and the crux of all dialogue.

Let us remember that the "protest" is not simply raised on the formal principle of the authority of the Scripture. It is deepened to penetrate the essence of the Gospel. Christ alone rules over his church because he alone redeemed his people and now distributes salvation to all people. The critical hermeneutic principle of justification by faith alone has its function in this context. The affirmation of the first principle of Christ as the Lord may be reconciled with the sending of messengers as servants by whom the call goes to all nations. To bind salvation to any other than the Lord is against the liberating message of the Gospel.

In the Council documents—as in RC theology in general—we will find two conflicting sentences side by side. What should we then say? Like Luther in the Smalcald Articles: *"Also sind und bleiben wir ewiglich geschieden und widernander"* (We are and remain eternally divided and opposed the one to the other)? Luther formulated this resignation after decades of desperate attempts to get a hearing for his intention. Do we today—after the Council—stand at the same point or could we find a method which could enable us to open up the dialogue? Let us try a positive answer.

The unique lordship of Christ by his unique sacrifice on the cross and by his sole communion with man through faith does not tolerate any competition. In agreement with this we must look around to find the procedure by starting from this evangelical affirmation. The first principles of Catholic doctrine will have an understanding for this assertion. If Catholic doctrine adds a second sentence as an implementation of the first principle, it does not find it competing with the basic truth. The controversy is at this point of the secondary principle. Protestant interpreters have for a long time employed the method of starting with these secondary principles of Catholic dogma and interpreting the first principles in the light of Protestant understanding of the second affirmations. Thereby a common ground for developing a promising dialogue is definitely missed. This type of inter-confessional conversation is in its nature monological, necessarily also polemical or apologetical in consequence.

Unfortunately we can hear loud voices of Protestant interpreters after the Council pronouncing the unchanged dogmatic validity of doctrines like papal supremacy and infallibility, the doctrine of the sacrifice of the Mass, the ascension of the Virgin Mary, the sacra-

ment of orders and in addition the sacramental view of the episcopacy, the acceptance of tradition and of the subordination of Holy
Scripture to the magisterium of the church, etc., etc. Why is this
unfortunate? Because it is an easy method of escape from the painful
duty of study and the burden of engaging in the dialogue. Moreover, it is an easy way of self-assertion and of unchallenged and
unconcerned affirmation of the positions taken 400 years ago. This is
the type of attitude which lulls the congregations into the dream
of security instead of awakening them with the call of listening to
what the Spirit says to them today.

The demand of post-conciliary interpretation is to discover the
evangelical affirmations in Catholic doctrine where the Reformation churches can substantially agree. It will then be their duty
to declare the incompatibility of these affirmations with the scholastic implementation. What we primarily need today is a reaffirmation of the basic articles of the Christian faith. Luther has in the
Smalcald Articles referred to articles where no controversy existed.
(The same method was also employed by the Conf. Augustana.)
Bishop Dietzfelbinger has rightly pointed to this fact. The question
is whether we do not need a reaffirmation of these fundamental
truths of essential concord before we question the position of dogmatic definitions within the RCC.

Let us take an example of really hardboiled controversy, namely
mariology. We Protestants had our fears of a new mariological definition being presented with a schema on the Virgin Mary, which
tended to go farther than the present dogma. The Council had
finally decided to include it as a special chapter (ch. VIII) in *de
ecclesia*. The information is widespread about this fact and generally regretted. Special attention is being given to the title *"mediatrix"* which has been allotted to the Virgin Mary though in somewhat tempered form by naming other titles. Does it mean then that
discussion is once and for all closed on the matter? If we start
with the secondary principles, the answer is yes. A more thorough
study of the text must nevertheless leave open possibilities of a
methodologically right dialogue. In § 60 e.g. of *de ecclesia* we read
a straight affirmation of the unique Mediator Christ with reference
to 1 Tim. 2:5-6. The function of Mary, so it is stated, "makes for
no dimming or diminution of this unique mediation of Christ, but

rather demonstrates its power . . . . It is no impediment to the immediate union of believers and Christ, but an encouragement." What does this mean for the dialogue? Most likely this: We need to engage ourselves in the dialogue on the common affirmation of the unique mediation of Christ. We have to penetrate its nature, its exclusiveness, its all-embracing validity. It will probably lead us deep into basic christological principles. Is it possible that the common affirmation of the first principle will cast light upon the criticism of Protestant mariology as well as clarify the sense of compatibility with regard to Christ's and Mary's mediation? The Council has claimed such compatibility though it did not develop it. Is not our task to tackle the first affirmation and if possible reaffirm our unity in faith before the point of divergence is approached?

Prof. Cullmann has rightly pointed to the importance of the "hierarchy of truths" which is included in the decree of the Council on ecumenism (§ 11). We may request a somewhat more explicit statement as to what such hierarchy of truths may imply for Catholic ecumenical procedures. It is, however, hopeful to learn that the RCC may not ascribe the same doctrinal dignity to all definitions of Christian truth. If it means that the fundamental articles of the Trinity, of the saving acts of God in Jesus Christ, of his presence in Word and sacraments can be regarded as first principles of faith, whereas the structures of the church and its ministry as well as other developments of tradition could in comparison with them be placed second, we could have a convergence of method as suggested above.

The interpretation of the decisions of this Council is a basic theological task. To make distinctions between the primary and the secondary affirmations belongs to this area. Therefore, nothing seems to be more important at this historic juncture than thorough theological preparation for the task before us. Experience has shown that not only practicing pastors of our churches reveal a lack of adequate knowledge of facts concerning the decisions of the Council and its historic and dogmatic background. Even our theological schools often neglect the task and fail to understand their obligation. Nothing is therefore more desirable for the future than an organized concern for ecumenical research. Each church and each diocese needs persons responsible not only for the general observation of interchurch relations but also for primary research. Inspiration of the theological faculties for taking responsibility and refresher courses for pastors and laymen would soon appear as elementary demands if our churches would continue their historic vocation and not only preserve for themselves what they might believe is their privilege. The interpretation of the Council decisions is also an interpretation of our own existence as churches of the Reformation.

# Postscript

The Second Vatican Council is over. If I am not mistaken, at this moment it is more important than ever that the church of the Reformation should not lose sight of "the whole of Christendom on earth," of which Luther speaks in his commentary on the third section of the Creed. Rome's entry into the mainstream of the ecumenical movement—something which since the Council has been a fact, though the manner of it has, to be sure, been Roman Catholic —has given the whole movement a new impetus. The Roman view of this impetus was revealed at the end of the Council by Pope Paul VI himself in the ecumenical service he held with the non-Roman observers. It is an inevitable consequence of this step that all kinds of contacts should now be established between Rome and Geneva, between Rome and the Lutheran World Federation and probably between other confessions as well. Such attempts may be viewed in a variety of ways—positively and critically, enthusiastically or with disapproval. But it seems to me that the Reformation church has the least right of all to say, "The Council is over; Rome does not concern us." The Reformation and an ecumenical horizon go together. We shall lose the power of the Reformation to the precise degree that we wish to keep it to ourselves in a particularist or isolationist spirit. After all, Lutheran confessional writings are to some extent a forceful "decree on ecumenism" from the Reformation side. The Augsburg Confession, for instance, is conscious of its witness to and on behalf of the whole of Christendom. It seeks to show that "we are all enlisted under one Christ."

The Lutheran Foundation for Inter-Confessional Research has in recent years made a few contributions to the newly opened dialogue with Rome. The collection of articles *The Papal Council and the Gospel* appeared immediately before the Council. The theological investigations in the second book, *Dialogue on the Way*, reflected something of the critical situation at the end of the Council's third session. It is followed by a third volume *Challenge and Response*. In this work we hear what the Lutheran observers at the Council have to say.

It cannot be disputed that for the Reformation church this Roman Catholic Council represents an earnest inquiry and a challenge that cannot be ignored. As one observer noted, the Council has made the Roman Church more "evangelical." Many examples can be given: attention to and respect for Holy Scripture have increased; the new awareness of the relationship between human and divine freedom, between faith and works, the concern for an effective and up-to-date witness—all this and much more may justly be mentioned when the Catholic Professor Hans Küng suggests that the Council has to a very great extent, if not completely, achieved certain crucial aims of the Reformation. Decisive steps have also been taken in the renewal of divine services; and with the use of the vernacular, the much greater active participation by the congregation, even occasional Communion under both kinds, at least in certain services, the Roman Catholic Mass and the Reformed Communion Service may already resemble each other so closely that many a person not fully informed might have difficulty in detecting the differences, just as now it is often hard to distinguish between evangelical and Roman Catholic church buildings.

The question is therefore frequently asked: Can it be then that four hundred years after Luther the Reformation's protest has been met, and perhaps become superfluous? "What more do you want?" H. Küng seems to ask. Have not the essentials in the Reformation's just demands now been realized in the Roman Catholic Church? Even Luther has almost been rehabilitated. What is there now to prevent reunion or return to the church?

This question becomes even more challenging if we today compare, in rough outline, the movement toward renewal in the Roman Catholic Church with the situation inside the Reformation church.

No one who follows the Council's discussions can help recognizing plainly, through all the disputations, the great strength which was given to its common witness. Here the Church of Rome was faced with modern pluralism in all its forms, with the strongly marked variety of cultures, peoples, races, and languages. The very fact that this variety was accepted and assimilated increases the significance of the united message delivered by the Council. The "magnus consensus," or general agreement among congregations and churches, is claimed in the writings of the Lutheran Confession as vital evidence of the truth. But where, in the Reformed churches of today, is the *magnus consensus* on the doctrine of the church, the significance of Holy Scripture, the ministry, ordination, or the relation between faith and history? One of the characteristic features of the Council was "aggiornamento"—adaptation of the church to the modern situation. This adaptation has actually taken place in an astonishing degree, yet the Roman Catholic Church has not lost its internal structure or become untrue to itself; it has remained Roman Catholic. Among us, too, *aggiornamento* or adaptation is being brought about, but in many respects it is very different. It is frequently taken to excess, degenerating into assimilation to the age and its spirit. "Conversion to the world" often leads to absorption in the world, so that man becomes the measure of all things. *Nolumus ludere de doctrina*—"we will not trifle with doctrine"—said Luther. It is clear that in our relations with the Church of Rome we abide firmly by that principle. But where do we stand among ourselves with regard to trifling with doctrine? In the declaration of the Synod of the Evangelical Church in Germany dated March 1966 we read, "We readily admit the difficulties that our Roman Catholic brethren find in our own plight—the fact that crucial statements of our faith, which were originally common to the Roman Catholic Church and the churches of the Reformation, are not accepted by all Protestants." As Evangelical Lutheran Christians we may, indeed we must, entertain the strongest reservations with regard to Roman doctrine—the Papacy, the Marian dogmas, indulgences, and the new teaching on mixed marriages—and yet be tormented by agonizing questions about the situation of our own church. I agree with Edmund Schlink: "I am sure that the mission given by God to the Reformation churches has not been taken away from them by the Council. But I am not so certain that the evangelical church today is fulfilling that mission in the way God expects of it."

In this critical situation we may ask: What is the *mission* of the Reformation today? It is still valid, however often we disclaim it. It certainly seems to me that God has used this Roman Catholic Council to confirm it. It is not us he has confirmed, but the Reformation! I recall how on many occasions in the Council's discussions the central problems and themes of the Reformation reemerged and found, at least in outline, answers and solutions in which the voice of the Reformation was frequently to be heard. "It can only be described as delayed action by Luther among the Catholics. To that extent Luther was a secret participant at the Council" (P. Althaus, *M. Luther und die Einheit der Kirche Christi* in *Luther-Zeitschrift der Luthergesellschaft*, 1966, p. 7). The categories of faith as opposed to sight, grace as opposed to works and the *viva vox evangelii* as opposed to the written text may indeed have made a new appearance at the Council. Should we not now, in our gratitude for the Gospel, even though we ourselves only know it from a distance, hold fast to the Reformation's discovery of it for the whole of Christendom? It seems to me to be simply a question of *confidence* in the validity of the Reformation, or rather of the Gospel, through changing times.

Concentration on the problem of *salvation* is a characteristic of the Reformation. "How can I find a gracious God?" The question may have to undergo a variety of transformations down through the centuries, even as far as my relationship with my fellow man is concerned. But is it *the* question or is it not? Is it *the* question, even in the midst of all our human, social, political, and other preoccupations? Do we, as the Evangelical Lutheran Church in the year 1966, dare to abide by it—or do we want to leave it to the psychologists of the subconscious or the many judges and writers who probe still deeper, such as Albert Camus, who says, "The Last Judgment takes place every day"? Even amidst the grandiose attempts at self-justification that are being made, which today often seem to have not so much a moral as an intellectual basis, fundamentally all are waiting, unknown to themselves, for the message of the sinner's justification by grace alone through faith to be proclaimed with new tongues, perhaps even affecting the communal spheres of human activity.

The relationship between the *church* and the *world*, with all its individual aspects, stands today at the center of church work and thought. The Council's adoption of the Pastoral Constitution on the Church in the World of Today was nothing less than a breakthrough for the Roman Catholic Church. But a Catholic bishop who devotes much work to Luther asked me what I thought of the basic conception underlying the Constitution, and he practically anticipated the answer himself by saying that it was exceedingly wide-ranging but that much of it was too optimistic and superficial; solutions were offered and advice given, no doubt from a sense of Christian responsibility, but often in such a manner that people asked why one had to be a Christian and belong to the Christian church in order to give and follow this advice. How does it all look when compared with Luther's profound insight into the structure of the world under the wrath and grace of God, with his talk of sin, death and the devil, as for instance in his 1534 interpretation of the Ninetieth Psalm? (W.A. 40/III, pp. 484 ff.) Are we prepared to venture such a radical approach today, or do we prefer to mix it with an optimistic faith in progress, which a modern Swiss historian has called the only salvation left to the world? What if this enterprise progress comes to a standstill or fails? It is significant, when we lack the courage to take this radical view, how many areas of life are left out of consideration, brushed aside, or passed over in silence, perhaps even in the Constitution on the Church and the world. There is sin, guilt, suffering and sickness, temptation—when we no longer know whether it is of God or the devil—old age, dying, death, and judgment—and hope, hope in God as the light of the world! And let me add this: Recognition of the sorry state of the world most certainly does not mean abandonment of God's creation or neglect of manifold endeavors to secure and develop its gifts. Indeed, it may be that only in this abyss there will be unfolded all the sobriety, freedom, patience, and strength that are needed for the task today and tomorrow. It may after all be true, as Luther says, that man's humanity lies in the fact that he is both righteous and a sinner.

May we not keep this confidence in the message of the Reformation, with its heights and its depths, even when we approach the
problems which so agitate us today of the *church* and the *churches*,
of ecumenism and ecumenicity, and of church unity? The Roman
Catholic understanding of the church has itself become wider, indeed astonishingly wide, embracing even the non-Christian religions. Many passages in the Council documents do not draw a perfectly clear line between Christians and men of good will throughout
the world. The Roman Catholic theologian Karl Rahner has noted
this. In an article, *Die Sünde in der Kirche* ("Sin in the Church"),
which appeared recently in G. Barauna's compilation *De Ecclesia*,
he says of the Constitution on the Church, "The parenetic duct of
the phrases is almost always from the virtuous to the more virtuous, not from sin and the realization of it to a constantly renewed
apprehension of forgiving grace. Yet this would be possible even
if one presupposes inner justification, for he who is justified is still
a sinner in permanent need of fresh divine forgiveness." Here a
perceptive Catholic asks that the very church itself should be
understood, taught, and experienced in terms of the message of
the Reformation! We Reformed Christians should hold fast to this
understanding of the church. Here she too becomes a novice in God's
new creation, but the battle between church and anti-church, between Christ and Antichrist, is fought within her as well as outside.
Secularism is to be found not only outside her but inside as well,
indeed the church herself is the greatest sinner, according to Luther,
for it is in her that sin is first recognized as sin. But at the same time
she is holy, through the forgiveness of sins! If, just for a start, we
understand the Reformation in this way, then it is not only a program of church reform, but repentance and return, in which God
is given his due and, according to Calvin, the resurrection of the
dead is awaited—even for the church in times of lassitude and ener-
vation, for the whole of her history is a series of such resurrections.

This might even have repercussions on the whole ecumenical
movement. Embracing as it does such wide extremes as the Pente-
costals and the Orthodox, the movement cannot do without the
Reformation note which, moreover, is assuredly not only critical
or negative. For the Reformation, despite all its divisions, has its
own peculiar conviction of a single church, because it believes in

the one church in Jesus Christ as a fact, something which does not first have to be established by man. But even in our approach one to another, in our longing for unity, we shall not be able to evade the question of truth, the truth before God, his judgment and his grace.

Christian ecumenicity today is growing together with, and in the midst of, a non-Christian, secularized ecumenicity. As a result, we are faced on every side with questions and problems which frequently offer challenges to the Christian world in a domain in which historic divisions are tending to recede. This is affecting our confrontations on the mission field as well as our cooperation in social work. What is at issue in such a situation? Any renewal of the church must consist essentially in a growth of fidelity to her own mission, says the Decree on Ecumenism. With that we would agree. "The secret of true ecumenical work lies in the tension between separateness and brotherhood" (H. Sasse). Arguments will still be required. But they need not necessarily be such that we fight one another. They will avoid falsely irenical tendencies and may, after all, occur in a dialogue in which we examine the Scriptures, either in opposition or in partnership, in order to ascertain "if those things were so" (Acts 17:11). They may also take the form of competition in presenting the truth of the Gospel to each other and the world in the right way, as well and as authentically as we can. In this sense, it seems to me, the church of the Reformation will continue to owe the whole of Christendom, including the Roman Catholic Church, the parrhesia of the Gospel witness.